NIST Special Publication 800-53
Revision 3

NIST

**National Institute of
Standards and Technology**

U.S. Department of Commerce

Recommended Security Controls
for Federal Information Systems
and Organizations

**JOINT TASK FORCE
TRANSFORMATION INITIATIVE**

INFORMATION   SECURITY

Computer Security Division
Information Technology Laboratory
National Institute of Standards and Technology
Gaithersburg, MD 20899-8930

August 2009
INCLUDES UPDATES AS OF 09-14-2009 (ERRATA PAGE XI)

U.S. Department of Commerce
Gary Locke, Secretary

National Institute of Standards and Technology
Patrick D. Gallagher, Deputy Director

Reports on Computer Systems Technology

The Information Technology Laboratory (ITL) at the National Institute of Standards and Technology (NIST) promotes the U.S. economy and public welfare by providing technical leadership for the nation's measurement and standards infrastructure. ITL develops tests, test methods, reference data, proof of concept implementations, and technical analyses to advance the development and productive use of information technology. ITL's responsibilities include the development of management, administrative, technical, and physical standards and guidelines for the cost-effective security and privacy of other than national security-related information in federal information systems. The Special Publication 800-series reports on ITL's research, guidelines, and outreach efforts in information system security, and its collaborative activities with industry, government, and academic organizations.

Authority

This publication has been developed by NIST to further its statutory responsibilities under the Federal Information Security Management Act (FISMA), Public Law (P.L.) 107-347. NIST is responsible for developing information security standards and guidelines, including minimum requirements for federal information systems, but such standards and guidelines shall not apply to national security systems without the express approval of appropriate federal officials exercising policy authority over such systems. This guideline is consistent with the requirements of the Office of Management and Budget (OMB) Circular A-130, Section 8b(3), Securing Agency Information Systems, as analyzed in Circular A-130, Appendix IV: Analysis of Key Sections. Supplemental information is provided in Circular A-130, Appendix III.

Nothing in this publication should be taken to contradict the standards and guidelines made mandatory and binding on federal agencies by the Secretary of Commerce under statutory authority. Nor should these guidelines be interpreted as altering or superseding the existing authorities of the Secretary of Commerce, Director of the OMB, or any other federal official. This publication may be used by nongovernmental organizations on a voluntary basis and is not subject to copyright in the United States. Attribution would, however, be appreciated by NIST.

NIST Special Publication 800-53, Revision 3, 237 pages

(August 2009)

Comments on this publication may be submitted to:

National Institute of Standards and Technology
Attn: Computer Security Division, Information Technology Laboratory
100 Bureau Drive (Mail Stop 8930) Gaithersburg, MD 20899-8930
Electronic mail: sec-cert@nist.gov

Compliance with NIST Standards and Guidelines

In accordance with the provisions of FISMA,[1] the Secretary of Commerce shall, on the basis of standards and guidelines developed by NIST, prescribe standards and guidelines pertaining to federal information systems. The Secretary shall make standards compulsory and binding to the extent determined necessary by the Secretary to improve the efficiency of operation or security of federal information systems. Standards prescribed shall include information security standards that provide minimum information security requirements and are otherwise necessary to improve the security of federal information and information systems.

- Federal Information Processing Standards (FIPS) are approved by the Secretary of Commerce and issued by NIST in accordance with FISMA. FIPS are compulsory and binding for federal agencies.[2] FISMA requires that federal agencies comply with these standards, and therefore, agencies may not waive their use.

- Special Publications (SPs) are developed and issued by NIST as recommendations and guidance documents. For other than national security programs and systems, federal agencies must follow those NIST Special Publications mandated in a Federal Information Processing Standard. FIPS 200 mandates the use of Special Publication 800-53, as amended. In addition, OMB policies (including OMB Reporting Instructions for FISMA and Agency Privacy Management), state that for other than national security programs and systems, federal agencies must follow certain specific NIST Special Publications.[3]

- Other security-related publications, including interagency reports (NISTIRs) and ITL Bulletins, provide technical and other information about NIST's activities. These publications are mandatory only when specified by OMB.

- Compliance schedules for NIST security standards and guidelines are established by OMB.

---

[1] The E-Government Act (P.L. 107-347) recognizes the importance of information security to the economic and national security interests of the United States. Title III of the E-Government Act, entitled the Federal Information Security Management Act (FISMA), emphasizes the need for organizations to develop, document, and implement an organization-wide program to provide security for the information systems that support its operations and assets.

[2] The term *agency* is used in this publication in lieu of the more general term *organization* only in those circumstances where its usage is directly related to other source documents such as federal legislation or policy.

[3] While federal agencies are required to follow certain specific NIST Special Publications in accordance with OMB policy, there is flexibility in how agencies apply the guidance. Federal agencies should apply the security concepts and principles articulated in the NIST Special Publications in accordance with and in the context of the agency's missions, business functions, and environment of operation. Consequently, the application of NIST guidance by federal agencies can result in different security solutions that are equally acceptable, compliant with the guidance, and meet the OMB definition of *adequate security* for federal information systems. When assessing federal agency compliance with NIST Special Publications, Inspectors General, evaluators, auditors, and assessors, should consider the intent of the security concepts and principles articulated within the specific guidance document and how the agency applied the guidance in the context of its mission/business responsibilities, operational environment, and unique organizational conditions.

Acknowledgements

This publication was developed by the *Joint Task Force Transformation Initiative* Interagency Working Group with representatives from the Civil, Defense, and Intelligence Communities in an ongoing effort to produce a unified information security framework for the federal government—including a consistent process for selecting and specifying safeguards and countermeasures (i.e., security controls) for federal information systems. The Project Leader, Ron Ross, from the National Institute of Standards and Technology, wishes to acknowledge and thank the senior leadership team from the U.S. Departments of Commerce and Defense, the Office of the Director of National Intelligence, the Committee on National Security Systems, and the members of the interagency working group whose dedicated efforts contributed significantly to the publication. The senior leadership team, working group members, and their organizational affiliations include:

U.S. Department of Defense

Cheryl J. Roby
Assistant Secretary of Defense
DOD Chief Information Officer (Acting)

Robert Lentz
Deputy Assistant Secretary of Defense
for Cyber, Identity, and Information Assurance

Gus Guissanie
Principal Director, ODASD (CIIA)

Don Jones
Senior Policy Advisor, ODASD (CIIA)

National Institute of Standards and Technology

Cita M. Furlani
Director, Information Technology Laboratory

William C. Barker
Chief, Computer Security Division

Ron Ross
FISMA Implementation Project Leader

Office of the Director of National Intelligence

Honorable Priscilla Guthrie
Associate Director of National Intelligence
and Chief Information Officer

Sherrill Nicely
Deputy Intelligence Community Chief
Information Officer

Mark J. Morrison
Deputy Associate Director of National
Intelligence for IC Information Assurance

Roger Caslow
Lead, C&A Transformation

Committee on National Security Systems

Cheryl J. Roby
Chairman, Committee on National Security
Systems (Acting)

Eustace D. King
CNSS Subcommittee Co-Chairman (DOD)

William Hunteman
CNSS Subcommittee Co-Chairman (DOE)

Joint Task Force Transformation Initiative Interagency Working Group

Ron Ross *NIST, JTF Leader*	Gary Stoneburner *Johns Hopkins APL*	Esten Porter *MITRE Corporation*	George Rogers *BAE Systems, Inc.*
Marianne Swanson *NIST*	Richard Graubart *MITRE Corporation*	Bennett Hodge *Booz Allen Hamilton*	Arnold Johnson *NIST*
Stuart Katzke *NIST*	Glenda Turner *MITRE Corporation*	Kelley Dempsey *NIST*	Christian Enloe *NIST*

In addition to the above acknowledgments, a special note of thanks goes to Peggy Himes and Elizabeth Lennon for their superb technical editing and administrative support; to Donna Dodson, Pat Toth, Matt Scholl, Sharon Keller, Randy Easter, Tim Polk, Murugiah Souppaya, Kevin Stine, Matt Barrett, Steve Quinn, Bill MacGregor, Karen Scarfone, Bill Burr, Doug Montgomery, Scott Rose, Mark Wilson, Annabelle Lee, Ed Roback, and Erika McCallister for their review of the security controls and insightful recommendations. The authors also wish to recognize Marshall Abrams, Jennifer Fabius Greene, Harriett Goldman, John Woodward, Karen Quigg, Joe Weiss, Peter Gouldmann, Roger Johnson, Sarbari Gupta, Dennis Bailey, Richard Wilsher, Nadya Bartol,

Mike Rubin, Tom Madden, Denise Farrar, Paul Bicknell, Robert Niemeyer, and Brett Burley for their exceptional contributions in helping to improve the content of the publication. And finally, the authors gratefully acknowledge and appreciate the significant contributions from individuals and organizations in the public and private sectors, both nationally and internationally, whose thoughtful and constructive comments improved the overall quality and usefulness of this publication.

A special acknowledgment is given to the participants in the *Industrial Control System (ICS) Security Project* who have put forth significant effort in helping to augment the security controls in NIST Special Publication 800-53 for industrial control systems. These participants include: Keith Stouffer, Stu Katzke, and Marshall Abrams from the ICS Security Project Development Team; federal agencies participating in the ICS workshops; and individuals and organizations in the public and private sector ICS community providing insightful comments on the proposed augmentations.

Postscript

Making any significant changes to the publication without public review is not in keeping with the obligation we have to the public and private sector organizations employing the NIST standards and guidelines. Some thoughtful and insightful recommendations received during the final public comment period suggesting changes to the publication have been retained and deferred until the next major revision to Special Publication 800-53. We continue to balance the need for stability in the NIST publications to ensure cost-effective implementation with the need to keep the publications current.

FIPS 200 AND SP 800-53

IMPLEMENTING INFORMATION SECURITY STANDARDS AND GUIDELINES

FIPS 200, *Minimum Security Requirements for Federal Information and Information Systems*, is a mandatory federal standard developed by NIST in response to FISMA. To comply with the federal standard, organizations must first determine the security category of their information system in accordance with FIPS 199, *Standards for Security Categorization of Federal Information and Information Systems*, derive the information system impact level from the security category in accordance with FIPS 200, and then apply the appropriately tailored set of baseline security controls in NIST Special Publication 800-53, *Security Controls for Federal Information Systems and Organizations*. Organizations have flexibility in applying the baseline security controls in accordance with the guidance provided in Special Publication 800-53. This allows organizations to tailor the relevant security control baseline so that it more closely aligns with their mission and business requirements and environments of operation.

FIPS 200 and NIST Special Publication 800-53, in combination, help ensure that appropriate security requirements and security controls are applied to all federal information and information systems. An organizational assessment of risk validates the initial security control selection and determines if any additional controls are needed to protect organizational operations (including mission, functions, image, or reputation), organizational assets, individuals, other organizations, or the Nation. The resulting set of security controls establishes a level of security due diligence for the organization.

DEVELOPING COMMON INFORMATION SECURITY FOUNDATIONS

COLLABORATION AMONG PUBLIC AND PRIVATE SECTOR ENTITIES

In developing standards and guidelines required by FISMA, NIST consults with other federal agencies and offices as well as the private sector to improve information security, avoid unnecessary and costly duplication of effort, and ensure that NIST publications are complementary with the standards and guidelines employed for the protection of national security systems. In addition to its comprehensive public review and vetting process, NIST is collaborating with the Office of the Director of National Intelligence (ODNI), the Department of Defense (DOD), and the Committee on National Security Systems (CNSS) to establish a common foundation for information security across the federal government. A common foundation for information security will provide the Intelligence, Defense, and Civil sectors of the federal government and their support contractors, more uniform and consistent ways to manage the risk to organizational operations and assets, individuals, other organizations, and the Nation that results from the operation and use of information systems. A common foundation for information security will also provide a strong basis for reciprocal acceptance of security authorization decisions and facilitate information sharing. NIST is also working with public and private sector entities to establish specific mappings and relationships between the security standards and guidelines developed by NIST and the International Organization for Standardization and International Electrotechnical Commission (ISO/IEC) 27001, Information Security Management System (ISMS).

Table of Contents

Prologue

"...Through the process of risk management, leaders must consider risk to US interests from adversaries using cyberspace to their advantage and from our own efforts to employ the global nature of cyberspace to achieve objectives in military, intelligence, and business operations... "

"...For operational plans development, the combination of threats, vulnerabilities, and impacts must be evaluated in order to identify important trends and decide where effort should be applied to eliminate or reduce threat capabilities; eliminate or reduce vulnerabilities; and assess, coordinate, and deconflict all cyberspace operations... "

"...Leaders at all levels are accountable for ensuring readiness and security to the same degree as in any other domain..."

-- THE NATIONAL STRATEGY FOR CYBERSPACE OPERATIONS
   OFFICE OF THE CHAIRMAN, JOINT CHIEFS OF STAFF, U.S. DEPARTMENT OF DEFENSE

Errata

The following changes have been incorporated into Special Publication 800-53, Revision 3, as of date indicated in table.

DATE	TYPE	CHANGE	PAGE NO.
08-12-2009	Editorial	Concatenate AC-19 d. and AC-19 e.	Page F-17
08-12-2009	Editorial	Change AC-19 f. to AC-19 e.	Page F-17
08-12-2009	Editorial	Change AC-19 g. to AC-19 f.	Page F-17
08-12-2009	Editorial	Change AC-19 h. to AC-19 g.	Page F-17
09-14-2009	Editorial	Change SC-32 Priority Code from P0 to P1.	Page D-7
09-14-2009	Editorial	Change AC-16 (3) from Enhanced to Enhancement	Page F-14
09-14-2009	Editorial	Change AC-16 (4) from Enhanced to Enhancement	Page F-14
09-14-2009	Editorial	Change SC-32 Priority Code from P0 to P1.	Page F-122

CHAPTER ONE

INTRODUCTION

THE NEED FOR SECURITY CONTROLS TO PROTECT INFORMATION AND INFORMATION SYSTEMS

The selection and implementation of appropriate *security controls* for an information system[4] or a system-of-systems[5] are important tasks that can have major implications on the operations[6] and assets of an organization[7] as well as the welfare of individuals and the Nation. Security controls are the management, operational, and technical safeguards or countermeasures employed within an organizational information system to protect the confidentiality, integrity, and availability of the system and its information. There are several important questions that should be answered by organizational officials when addressing the security considerations for their information systems:

- What security controls are needed to adequately mitigate the risk incurred by the use of information and information systems in the execution of organizational missions and business functions?

- Have the selected security controls been implemented or is there a realistic plan for their implementation?

- What is the desired or required level of assurance (i.e., grounds for confidence) that the selected security controls, as implemented, are effective[8] in their application?

The answers to these questions are not given in isolation but rather in the context of an effective *information security program* for the organization that identifies, mitigates as deemed necessary, and monitors on an ongoing basis, risks[9] arising from its information and information systems. The security controls defined in this publication and recommended for use by organizations in protecting their information systems should be employed in conjunction with and as part of a well-defined and documented information security program. The program management controls (Appendix G), complement the security controls for an information system (Appendix F) by focusing on the organization-wide information security requirements that are independent of any particular information system and are essential for managing information security programs.

---

[4] An information system is a discrete set of *information resources* organized expressly for the collection, processing, maintenance, use, sharing, dissemination, or disposition of information. Information systems also include specialized systems such as industrial/process controls systems, telephone switching/private branch exchange (PBX) systems, and environmental control systems.

[5] In certain situations within an organization, an information system can be viewed from both a logical and physical perspective as a complex *system-of-systems* (e.g., Federal Aviation Administration National Air Space System) when there are multiple information systems involved with a high degree of connectivity and interaction among the systems.

[6] Organizational operations include mission, functions, image, and reputation.

[7] The term *organization* describes an entity of any size, complexity, or positioning within an organizational structure (e.g., a federal agency or, as appropriate, any of its operational elements).

[8] Security control effectiveness addresses the extent to which the controls are implemented correctly, operating as intended, and producing the desired outcome with respect to meeting the security requirements for the information system in its operational environment.

[9] Risk is a measure of the extent to which an entity is threatened by a potential circumstance or event, and typically a function of: (i) the adverse impacts that would arise if the circumstance or event occurs; and (ii) the likelihood of occurrence. Information system-related security risks are those risks that arise from the loss of confidentiality, integrity, or availability of information or information systems and consider the adverse impacts to organizational operations and assets, individuals, other organizations, and the Nation.

It is of paramount importance that responsible officials understand the risks and other factors that could adversely affect organizational operations and assets, individuals, other organizations, and the Nation.[10] These officials must also understand the current status of their security programs and the security controls planned or in place to protect their information and information systems in order to make informed judgments and investments that mitigate risks to an acceptable level. The ultimate objective is to conduct the day-to-day operations of the organization and to accomplish the organization's stated missions and business functions with what the OMB Circular A-130 defines as *adequate security*, or security commensurate with risk resulting from the unauthorized access, use, disclosure, disruption, modification, or destruction of information.

1.1 PURPOSE AND APPLICABILITY

The purpose of this publication is to provide guidelines for selecting and specifying security controls for information systems supporting the executive agencies of the federal government to meet the requirements of FIPS 200, *Minimum Security Requirements for Federal Information and Information Systems*. The guidelines apply to all components[11] of an information system that process, store, or transmit federal information. The guidelines have been developed to help achieve more secure information systems and effective risk management within the federal government by:

- Facilitating a more consistent, comparable, and repeatable approach for selecting and specifying security controls for information systems and organizations;

- Providing a recommendation for minimum security controls for information systems categorized in accordance with FIPS 199, *Standards for Security Categorization of Federal Information and Information Systems*;

- Providing a stable, yet flexible catalog of security controls for information systems and organizations to meet current organizational protection needs and the demands of future protection needs based on changing requirements and technologies;

- Creating a foundation for the development of assessment methods and procedures for determining security control effectiveness; and

- Improving communication among organizations by providing a common lexicon that supports discussion of risk management concepts.

The guidelines in this special publication are applicable to all federal information systems[12] other than those systems designated as national security systems as defined in 44 U.S.C., Section 3542. The guidelines have been broadly developed from a technical perspective to complement similar guidelines for national security systems and may be used for such systems with the approval of appropriate federal officials exercising policy authority over such systems.[13] State, local, and tribal governments, as well as private sector organizations are encouraged to consider using these guidelines, as appropriate.

---

[10] Includes risk to U.S. critical infrastructure/key resources as described in Homeland Security Presidential Directive 7.

[11] Information system components include, for example, mainframes, workstations, servers (e.g., database, electronic mail, authentication, web, proxy, file, domain name), network components (e.g., firewalls, routers, gateways, voice and data switches, wireless access points, network appliances, sensors), operating systems, middleware, and applications.

[12] A federal information system is an information system used or operated by an executive agency, by a contractor of an executive agency, or by another organization on behalf of an executive agency.

[13] CNSS Instruction 1253 provides implementing guidance for NIST Special Publication 800-53 for *national security systems*.

1.2 TARGET AUDIENCE

This publication is intended to serve a diverse audience of information system and information security professionals including:

- Individuals with information system or security management and oversight responsibilities (e.g., authorizing officials, chief information officers, senior information security officers,[14] information system managers, information security managers);

- Individuals with information system development responsibilities (e.g., program and project managers, information technology product developers, information system designers and developers, systems integrators);

- Individuals with information security implementation and operational responsibilities (e.g., mission/business owners, information system owners, common control providers, information owners/stewards, information system security engineers, information system administrators, information system security officers); and

- Individuals with information system and information security assessment and monitoring responsibilities (e.g., auditors, Inspectors General, system evaluators, assessors/assessment teams, independent verification and validation assessors, information system owners).

Commercial companies producing information technology products and systems, creating information security-related technologies, and providing information security services can also benefit from the information in this publication.

1.3 RELATIONSHIP TO OTHER SECURITY CONTROL PUBLICATIONS

To create a technically sound and broadly applicable set of security controls for information systems and organizations, a variety of sources were considered during the development of this special publication. The sources included security controls from the defense, audit, financial, healthcare, and intelligence communities as well as controls defined by national and international standards organizations. The objective of NIST Special Publication 800-53 is to provide a set of security controls that can satisfy the breadth and depth of security requirements[15] levied on information systems and organizations and that is consistent with and complementary to other established information security standards.

The catalog of security controls provided in Special Publication 800-53 can be effectively used to demonstrate compliance with a variety of governmental, organizational, or institutional security requirements. It is the responsibility of organizations to select the appropriate security controls, to implement the controls correctly, and to demonstrate the effectiveness of the controls in satisfying their stated security requirements. The security controls in the catalog facilitate the development of assessment methods and procedures that can be used to demonstrate control effectiveness in a consistent and repeatable manner—thus contributing to the organization's confidence that there is ongoing compliance with its stated security requirements.[16]

---

[14] At the *agency* level, this position is known as the Senior Agency Information Security Officer. Organizations may also refer to this position as the *Senior Information Security Officer* or the *Chief Information Security Officer*.

[15] Security requirements are those requirements levied on an information system that are derived from laws, Executive Orders, directives, policies, instructions, regulations, standards, guidelines, or organizational (mission) needs to ensure the confidentiality, integrity, and availability of the information being processed, stored, or transmitted.

[16] NIST Special Publication 800-53A provides guidance on assessing the effectiveness of security controls defined in this publication.

1.4 ORGANIZATIONAL RESPONSIBILITIES

Organizations[17] use FIPS 199 to categorize their information and information systems. Security categorization is accomplished as an organization-wide activity[18] with the involvement of senior-level organizational officials including, for example, authorizing officials, chief information officers, senior information security officers, information owners/stewards, information system owners, and risk executive (function). As required by FIPS 200, organizations use the security categorization results to designate information systems as low-impact, moderate-impact, or high-impact systems. For each information system, the recommendation for minimum security controls from Special Publication 800-53 (i.e., the *baseline* security controls defined in Appendix D, adjusted in accordance with the *tailoring* guidance in Section 3.3) is intended to be used as a starting point for and as input to the organization's security control *supplementation* process.[19]

While the FIPS 199 security categorization associates the operation of the information system with the potential adverse impact on organizational operations and assets, individuals, other organizations, and the Nation,[20] the incorporation of refined threat and vulnerability information during the risk assessment facilitates the selection of additional security controls *supplementing* the tailored baseline to address specific organizational needs and tolerance for risk. The final, agreed-upon[21] set of security controls is documented with appropriate rationale in the security plan for the information system. The use of security controls from Special Publication 800-53 and the incorporation of tailored baseline controls as a starting point in the control selection process, facilitate a more consistent level of security across federal information systems and organizations. It also offers the needed flexibility to appropriately modify the controls based on specific organizational policies and requirements, particular conditions and circumstances, known threat and vulnerability information, and tolerance for risk.

Building more secure information systems is a multifaceted undertaking that requires:

- Well-defined security requirements and security specifications;

- Well-designed and well-built information technology products;

- Sound systems/security engineering principles and practices to effectively integrate information technology products into information systems;

- State-of-the-art techniques and methods for information technology product/information system assessment; and

- Comprehensive system security planning and life cycle management.[22]

---

[17] An organization typically exercises managerial, operational, and/or financial control over its information systems and the security provided to those systems, including the authority and capability to implement or require the security controls deemed necessary by the organization to protect organizational operations and assets, individuals, other organizations, and the Nation.

[18] See FIPS Publication 200, footnote 7.

[19] Risk assessments can be accomplished in a variety of ways depending on the specific needs of an organization. NIST Special Publication 800-30 provides guidance on the assessment of risk as part of an overall risk management process.

[20] Considerations for potential national-level impacts and impacts to other organizations in categorizing organizational information systems derive from the USA PATRIOT Act and Homeland Security Presidential Directives.

[21] The authorizing official or designated representative, by accepting the security plan, agrees to the set of security controls proposed to meet the security requirements for the information system.

[22] NIST Special Publication 800-64 provides guidance on security considerations in life cycle management.

From a systems engineering viewpoint, security is just one of many required operational capabilities for an information system supporting organizational mission/business processes— capabilities that must be funded by the organization throughout the life cycle of the system in order to achieve mission/business success. It is important that the organization *realistically* assesses the risk to organizational operations and assets, individuals, other organizations, and the Nation that arises by placing the information system into operation or continuing its operation.

In addition, information security requirements for organizational information systems must be satisfied with full consideration of the risk management strategy[23] of the organization, in light of the potential cost, schedule, and performance issues associated with the acquisition, deployment, and operation of the information system.

1.5 ORGANIZATION OF THIS SPECIAL PUBLICATION

The remainder of this special publication is organized as follows:

- **Chapter Two** describes the fundamental concepts associated with security control selection and specification including: (i) the structural components of security controls and how the controls are organized into families; (ii) security control baselines; (iii) the use of common security controls in support of organization-wide information security programs; (iv) security controls in external environments; (v) assurance in the effectiveness of security controls; and (vi) the commitment to maintain currency of the individual security controls and the control baselines.

- **Chapter Three** describes the process of selecting and specifying security controls for an information system including: (i) applying the organization's overall approach to managing risk; (ii) categorizing the information system and determining the system impact level in accordance with FIPS 199 and FIPS 200, respectively; (iii) selecting the initial set of baseline security controls, tailoring the baseline controls, and supplementing the tailored baseline, as necessary, in accordance with an organizational assessment of risk; and (iv) assessing the security controls as part of a comprehensive continuous monitoring process.

- **Supporting appendices** provide essential security control selection and specification-related information including: (i) general references; (ii) definitions and terms; (iii) acronyms; (iv) baseline security controls for low-impact, moderate-impact, and high-impact information systems; (v) minimum assurance requirements; (vi) a master catalog of security controls; (vii) information security program management controls; (viii) international information security standards; and (ix) the application of security controls to industrial control systems.

---

[23] NIST Special Publication 800-39 provides guidance on organization-wide risk management.

CHAPTER TWO

THE FUNDAMENTALS

SECURITY CONTROL STRUCTURE, ORGANIZATION, BASELINES, AND ASSURANCE

This chapter presents the fundamental concepts associated with security control selection and specification including: (i) the structure of security controls and the organization of the controls in the control catalog; (ii) security control baselines; (iii) the identification and use of common security controls; (iv) security controls in external environments; (v) security control assurance; and (vi) future revisions to the security controls, the control catalog, and baseline controls.

2.1 SECURITY CONTROL ORGANIZATION AND STRUCTURE

Security controls described in this publication have a well-defined organization and structure. For ease of use in the security control selection and specification process, controls are organized into seventeen *families*.[24] Each security control family contains security controls related to the security functionality of the family. A two-character identifier is assigned to uniquely identify each security control family. In addition, there are three general classes of security controls: management, operational, and technical.[25] Table 1-1 summarizes the classes and families in the security control catalog and the associated security control family identifiers.

TABLE 1-1: SECURITY CONTROL CLASSES, FAMILIES, AND IDENTIFIERS

IDENTIFIER	FAMILY	CLASS
AC	Access Control	Technical
AT	Awareness and Training	Operational
AU	Audit and Accountability	Technical
CA	Security Assessment and Authorization	Management
CM	Configuration Management	Operational
CP	Contingency Planning	Operational
IA	Identification and Authentication	Technical
IR	Incident Response	Operational
MA	Maintenance	Operational
MP	Media Protection	Operational
PE	Physical and Environmental Protection	Operational
PL	Planning	Management
PS	Personnel Security	Operational
RA	Risk Assessment	Management
SA	System and Services Acquisition	Management
SC	System and Communications Protection	Technical
SI	System and Information Integrity	Operational
PM	Program Management	Management

---

[24] Of the eighteen security control families in NIST Special Publication 800-53, seventeen families are described in the security control catalog in Appendix F, and are closely aligned with the seventeen minimum security requirements for federal information and information systems in FIPS 200. One additional family (Program Management [PM] family) in Appendix G provides controls for information security programs. This family, while not referenced in FIPS 200, provides security controls at the organizational rather than the information-system level.

[25] A control *family* is associated with a given *class* based on the dominant characteristics of the controls in that family.

To identify each security control, a numeric identifier is appended to the family identifier to indicate the number of the control within the family. For example, CP-9 is the ninth control in the Contingency Planning family and AC-2 is the second control in the Access Control family.

The security control structure consists of the following components: (i) a *control* section; (ii) a *supplemental guidance* section; (iii) a *control enhancements* section; (iv) a *references* section; and (v) a *priority* and *baseline allocation* section. The following example from the Auditing and Accountability family illustrates the structure of a typical security control.

AU-5   RESPONSE TO AUDIT PROCESSING FAILURES

Control: The information system:

a. Alerts designated organizational officials in the event of an audit processing failure; and

b. Takes the following additional actions: [*Assignment: organization-defined actions to be taken (e.g., shut down information system, overwrite oldest audit records, stop generating audit records)*].

Supplemental Guidance: Audit processing failures include, for example, software/hardware errors, failures in the audit capturing mechanisms, and audit storage capacity being reached or exceeded. Related control: AU-4.

Control Enhancements:

(1) The information system provides a warning when allocated audit record storage volume reaches [*Assign*ment: organiz*ation-defined percentage of maximum audit record storage capacity*].

(2) The information system provides a real-time alert when the following audit failure events occur: [*Assignment: organization-defined audit failure events requiring real-time alerts*].

(3) The information system enforces configurable traffic volume thresholds representing auditing capacity for network traffic and [*Selection: rejects; delays*] network traffic above those thresholds.

(4) The information system invokes a system shutdown in the event of an audit failure, unless an alternative audit capability exists.

References: None.

Priority and Baseline Allocation:

P1	LOW AU-5	MOD AU-5	HIGH AU-5 (1) (2)

The control section provides a concise statement of the specific security capabilities needed to protect a particular aspect of an information system.[26] The control statement describes specific security-related activities or actions to be carried out by the organization or by the information system. For some security controls in the control catalog, a degree of flexibility is provided by allowing organizations to selectively define input values for certain parameters associated with the controls. This flexibility is achieved through the use of *assignment* and *selection* operations within the control (see Section 3.3). Assignment and selection operations provide an opportunity for an organization to tailor the security controls to support specific mission, business, or operational needs. For example, an organization can specify the actions to be taken by the information system in the event of an audit processing failure (see AU-5 example above), the specific events to be audited within the system, the frequency of conducting system backups, restrictions on password use, or the distribution list for organizational policies and procedures.[27]

---

[26] Security controls are generally designed to be *technology* and *implementation* independent and therefore, do not contain specific requirements in these areas. Organizations provide such requirements as deemed necessary in the security plan for the information system.

[27] The organization determines whether a specific assignment or selection operation is completed at the organizational level, information system level, or a combination of the two.

Once specified, the organization-defined values become part of the control, and the control implementation is assessed against the completed control statement. Selection statements narrow the potential input values by providing a specific list of items from which the organization must choose.

The supplemental guidance[28] section provides additional information related to a specific security control, but contains no requirements. Organizations are expected to apply the supplemental guidance as appropriate, when defining, developing, and implementing security controls. The supplemental guidance provides important considerations for implementing security controls in the context of an organization's operational environment, mission requirements, or assessment of risk. Security control enhancements may also contain supplemental guidance. Enhancement supplemental guidance is used in situations where the guidance is not generally applicable to the entire control but instead focused on the particular control enhancement.

The security control enhancements section provides statements of security capability to: (i) build in additional functionality to a control; and/or (ii) increase the strength of a control. In both cases, the control enhancements are used in an information system requiring greater protection due to the potential impact of loss or when organizations seek additions to the basic control functionality based on the results of a risk assessment. Control enhancements are numbered sequentially within each control so that the enhancements can be easily identified when selected to supplement the basic control. In the previous example for AU-5, if the first three control enhancements are selected, the control designation becomes AU-5 (1) (2) (3).[29] The numerical designation of a security control enhancement is used only to identify a particular enhancement within the control structure. The designation is neither indicative of the relative strength of the control enhancement nor assumes any hierarchical relationship among the enhancements.

The references section[30] includes a list of applicable federal laws, Executive Orders, directives, policies, standards, and guidelines (e.g., OMB Circulars, FIPS, and NIST Special Publications), that are relevant to a particular security control or control enhancement.[31] The references provide appropriate federal legislative and policy mandates as well as supporting information for the implementation of specific management, operational, or technical controls/enhancements. The references section also contains pertinent websites for organizations to use in obtaining additional information with regard to security control implementation and assessment.

The priority and baseline allocation section provides: (i) the recommended priority codes used for sequencing decisions during security control implementation (see Appendix D); and (ii) the initial allocation of security controls and control enhancements for low-impact, moderate-impact, and high-impact information systems (see Appendix F).

---

[28] The supplemental guidance section may contain information on *related controls* (i.e., security controls that either directly impact or support the control). For example, AC-6 (Least Privilege) is a related control to AC-3 (Access Control Enforcement) because AC-6 is a source for some of the authorizations to be enforced by AC-3.

[29] AU-5 Enhancement (3) is an example of a requirement in the security control catalog (Appendix F) that is *not* in any of the control baselines (Appendix D). Such requirements can be used by organizations in *supplementing* the tailored baselines as described in Section 3.3 in order to achieve what the organization deems to be adequate risk mitigation.

[30] Publications listed in the *References* section of security controls refer to the most recent versions of the publications. Organizations confirm from the respective official sources of the publications (e.g., OMB, NIST, NARA), that the most recent versions are being used for organizational application.

[31] The references listed in the security control *references section* are provided to assist organizations in applying the controls and are not intended to be inclusive or complete.

2.2 SECURITY CONTROL BASELINES

Organizations are required to adequately mitigate the risk arising from use of information and information systems in the execution of missions and business functions. A significant challenge for organizations is to determine the appropriate set of security controls, which if implemented and determined to be effective, would most cost-effectively mitigate risk while complying with the security requirements defined by applicable federal laws, Executive Orders, directives, policies, standards, or regulations (e.g., FISMA, OMB Circular A-130). Selecting the appropriate set of security controls to adequately mitigate risk by meeting the specific, and sometimes unique, security requirements of an organization is an important task—a task that clearly demonstrates the organization's commitment to security and the due diligence exercised in protecting the confidentiality, integrity, and availability of organizational information and information systems.

To assist organizations in making the appropriate selection of security controls for an information system, the concept of *baseline* controls is introduced. Baseline controls are the starting point for the security control selection process described in this document and are chosen based on the security category and associated impact level of the information system determined in accordance with FIPS 199 and FIPS 200, respectively. The tailored security control baseline (i.e., the appropriate control baseline from Appendix D adjusted in accordance with the guidance in Section 3.3) is the minimum set of security controls for the information system. Because the baseline is intended to be a broadly applicable starting point, supplements to the tailored baseline (see Section 3.3) will likely be necessary in order to achieve adequate risk mitigation. The tailored security control baseline is supplemented based on an organizational assessment of risk and the resulting controls documented in the security plan for the information system.

Appendix D provides a listing of baseline security controls. Three sets of baseline controls have been identified corresponding to the low-impact, moderate-impact, and high-impact information-system levels defined in FIPS 200 and used in Section 3.2 of this document to provide an initial set of security controls for each impact level.[32] Appendix F provides a detailed catalog of security controls for information systems, arranged by control families. Chapter Three provides additional information on how to use FIPS 199 security categories and FIPS 200 impact levels in applying the tailoring guidance to the baseline security controls and supplementing the tailored baseline in order to achieve adequate risk mitigation.

Implementation Tip

There are additional security controls and control enhancements that appear in the security control catalog (Appendix F) that are found in only higher-impact baselines or not used in any of the baselines. These additional security controls and control enhancements for the information system are available to organizations and can be used in supplementing the tailored baselines to achieve the needed level of protection in accordance with an organizational assessment of risk. Moreover, security controls and control enhancements contained in higher-level baselines can also be used to strengthen the level of protection provided in lower-level baselines, if deemed appropriate. At the end of the security control selection process, the agreed-upon set of controls in the security plan must be sufficient to adequately mitigate risks to organizational operations and assets, individuals, other organizations, and the Nation.

---

[32] The baseline security controls contained in Appendix D are not necessarily absolutes in that the tailoring guidance described in Section 3.3 provides organizations with the ability to eliminate certain controls or specify compensating controls in accordance with the terms and conditions established by authorizing officials.

2.3 COMMON CONTROLS

Common controls are security controls that are *inheritable* by one or more organizational information systems.[33] The organization assigns responsibility for common controls to appropriate organizational officials and coordinates the development, implementation, assessment, authorization, and monitoring of the controls.[34] The identification of common controls is most effectively accomplished as an organization-wide exercise with the active involvement of the chief information officer, senior information security officer, risk executive (function), authorizing officials, information system owners, information owners/stewards, and information system security officers. The organization-wide exercise considers the security categories and associated impact levels of the information systems within the organization in accordance with FIPS 199 and FIPS 200, as well as the security controls necessary to adequately mitigate the risks arising from the use of those systems (see *baseline* security controls in Section 2.2).[35] For example, common controls can be identified for all low-impact information systems by considering the associated baseline security controls in Appendix D. Similar exercises can be conducted for moderate-impact and high-impact information systems as well. When common controls protect multiple organizational information systems of differing impact levels, the controls are implemented with regard to the highest impact level among the systems.

Many of the security controls needed to protect organizational information systems (e.g., contingency planning controls, incident response controls, security training and awareness controls, personnel security controls, physical and environmental protection controls, and intrusion detection controls) are excellent candidates for common control status. Information security program management controls (see Appendix G, PM family) may also be deemed common controls by the organization since the controls are employed at the organization level and typically serve multiple information systems. By centrally managing and documenting the development, implementation, assessment, authorization, and monitoring of common controls, security costs can be amortized across multiple information systems.

Common controls are generally documented in the organization-wide *information security program plan* unless implemented as part of a specific information system, in which case the controls are documented in the security plan for that system.[36] Organizations have the flexibility to describe common controls in a single document or in multiple documents. In the case of multiple documents, the documents describing the common controls are included as attachments to the information security program plan. If the information security program plan contains multiple documents, the organization specifies in each document the organizational official or officials responsible for the development, implementation, assessment, authorization, and monitoring of the respective common controls. For example, the organization may require that

---

[33] A security control is *inheritable* by an information system or application when that system or application receives protection from the security control (or portions of the security control) and the control is developed, implemented, assessed, authorized, and monitored by entities other than those responsible for the system or application—entities either internal or external to the organization where the system or application resides.

[34] The Chief Information Officer, Senior Information Security Officer, or other designated organizational officials at the senior leadership level assign responsibility for the development, implementation, assessment, authorization, and monitoring of common controls to appropriate entities (either internal or external to the organization). Organizational entities assigned responsibility for common controls use the Risk Management Framework described in Chapter Three to help ensure appropriate security capabilities are provided.

[35] Each common control identified by the organization is reviewed for applicability to each specific organizational information system.

[36] Information security program plans are described in Appendix G.

the Facilities Management Office develop, implement, assess, authorize, and continuously monitor physical and environmental protection controls from the PE family when such controls are not associated with a particular information system but instead, support multiple systems. When common controls are included in a separate security plan for an information system (e.g., security controls employed as part of an intrusion detection system providing boundary protection inherited by one or more organizational information systems), the information security program plan indicates which separate security plan contains a description of the common controls.

Security controls not designated as common controls are considered *system-specific controls* or *hybrid controls*. System-specific controls are the primary responsibility of information system owners and their respective authorizing officials. Organizations assign a *hybrid* status to a security control when one part of the control is deemed to be common and another part of the control is deemed to be system-specific. For example, an organization may implement the Incident Response Policy and Procedures security control (IR-1) as a hybrid control with the policy portion of the control deemed to be common and the procedures portion of the control deemed to be system-specific. Hybrid controls may also serve as templates for further control refinement. An organization may choose, for example, to implement the Contingency Planning security control (CP-2) as a template for a generalized contingency plan for all organizational information systems with individual information system owners tailoring the plan, where appropriate, for system-specific uses. Partitioning security controls into common, hybrid, and system-specific controls can result in significant savings to the organization in implementation and assessment costs as well as a more consistent application of the security controls across the organization. While the concept of security control partitioning into common, hybrid, and system-specific controls is straightforward and intuitive, the application within an organization takes significant planning and coordination.

Security plans for individual information systems identify which security controls required for those systems have been designated by the organization as common controls and which controls have been designated as system-specific or hybrid controls. Information system owners are responsible for any system-specific implementation details associated with an organization's common controls. These implementation details are identified and described in the security plans for the individual information systems. The senior information security officer for the organization coordinates with *common control providers* (e.g., facilities/site manager, human resources manager, intrusion detection system owner) to ensure that the required controls are developed, implemented, and assessed for effectiveness. The security plans for individual information systems and the organization-wide information security program plan together, provide complete coverage for all security controls employed within the organization.

Common controls, whether employed in an information system or in the environment of operation, are authorized by a senior organizational official[37] with at least the same level of authority and responsibility for managing risk as the authorization officials for information systems inheriting the controls.[38] Authorization results relating to common controls are shared with the appropriate information system owners. A plan of action and milestones is developed and maintained for the common controls that are deemed through assessment to be less than effective. Common controls are subject to the same continuous monitoring requirements as system-specific security controls employed in individual organizational information systems.

---

[37] The authorizing official role, whether applied to information systems or common controls, has inherent U.S. Government authority and is assigned to government personnel only.

[38] When common controls are inherited from external environments, organizations should consult Section 2.4.

> **Implementation Tip**
>
> The selection of common controls is most effectively accomplished on an organization-wide basis with the involvement of the organization's senior leadership (i.e., authorizing officials, chief information officer, senior information security officer, information system owners, mission/business owners, information owners/stewards, risk executive [function]). These individuals have the collective corporate knowledge to understand the organization's priorities, the importance of the organization's operations and assets, and the relative importance of the organizational information systems that support those operations and assets. The organization's senior leaders are also in the best position to select the common controls for each security control baseline and assign organizational responsibilities for developing, implementing, assessing, authorizing, and monitoring those controls.

2.4 SECURITY CONTROLS IN EXTERNAL ENVIRONMENTS

Organizations are becoming increasingly reliant on information system services provided by external providers to carry out important missions and business functions. External information system services are services implemented outside of the authorization boundaries established by the organization for its information systems. These external services may be used by, but are not part of, organizational information systems. In some situations, external information system services may completely replace the functionality of internal information systems. Organizations are responsible and accountable for the *risk* incurred by use of services provided by external providers and address this risk by implementing compensating controls when the risk is greater than the authorizing official or the organization is willing to accept.

Relationships with external service providers are established in a variety of ways, for example, through joint ventures, business partnerships, outsourcing arrangements (i.e., through contracts, interagency agreements, lines of business arrangements), licensing agreements, and/or supply chain exchanges. The growing dependence on external service providers and new relationships being forged with those providers present new and difficult challenges for the organization, especially in the area of information system security. These challenges include:

- Defining the types of external services provided to the organization;

- Describing how the external services are protected in accordance with the security requirements of the organization; and

- Obtaining the necessary assurances that the risk to organizational operations and assets, individuals, other organizations, and the Nation arising from the use of the external services is acceptable.

FISMA and OMB policy require external providers handling federal information or operating information systems on behalf of the federal government to meet the same security requirements as federal agencies. Security requirements for external providers including the security controls for information systems processing, storing, or transmitting federal information are expressed in appropriate contracts or other formal agreements using the Risk Management Framework and associated NIST security standards and guidelines described in Chapter Three. Organizations can require external providers to implement all steps in the Risk Management Framework described in Chapter Three with the exception of the security authorization step, which remains an inherent federal responsibility that is directly linked to the management of risk related to the use of external information system services.[39]

---

[39] See Implementation Tip in Section 3.3 for applying the Risk management Framework to external service providers.

The assurance or confidence that the risk from using external services is at an acceptable level depends on the trust[40] that the organization places in the external service provider. In some cases, the level of trust is based on the amount of direct control the organization is able to exert on the external service provider with regard to employment of security controls necessary for the protection of the service and the evidence brought forth as to the effectiveness of those controls. The level of control is usually established by the terms and conditions of the contract or service-level agreement with the external service provider and can range from extensive (e.g., negotiating a contract or agreement that specifies detailed security control requirements for the provider) to very limited (e.g., using a contract or service-level agreement to obtain commodity services[41] such as commercial telecommunications services). In other cases, the level of trust is based on factors that convince the organization that the requisite security controls have been employed and that a credible determination of control effectiveness exists. For example, a separately authorized external information system service provided to an organization through a well-established line of business relationship may provide a degree of trust in the external service within the tolerable risk range of the authorizing official.

The provision of services by external providers may result in some services without explicit agreements between the organization and the external entities responsible for the services. Whenever explicit agreements are feasible and practical (e.g., through contracts, service-level agreements, etc.), the organization develops such agreements and requires the use of the security controls in Special Publication 800-53. When the organization is not in a position to require explicit agreements with external providers (e.g., the service is imposed on the organization or the service is commodity service), the organization establishes explicit assumptions about the service capabilities with regard to security.[42] Contracts between the organization and external providers may also require the active participation of the organization. For example, the organization may be required by the contract to install public key encryption-enabled client software recommended by the service provider.

Ultimately, the responsibility for adequately mitigating unacceptable risks arising from the use of external information system services remains with the authorizing official. Organizations require that an appropriate *chain of trust* be established with external service providers when dealing with the many issues associated with information system security. A chain of trust requires that the

---

[40] The level of trust that an organization places in an external service provider can vary widely, ranging from those who are highly trusted (e.g., business partners in a joint venture that share a common business model and common goals) to those who are less trusted and represent greater sources of risk (e.g., business partners in one endeavor who are also competitors in another market sector).

[41] Commercial providers of commodity-type services typically organize their business models and services around the concept of shared resources and devices for a broad and diverse customer base. Therefore, unless organizations obtain fully dedicated services from commercial service providers, there may be a need for greater reliance on compensating security controls to provide the necessary protections for the information system that relies on those external services. The organization's risk assessment and risk mitigation activities reflect this situation.

[42] In situations where an organization is procuring information system services or technologies through a centralized acquisition vehicle (e.g., governmentwide contract by the General Services Administration or other preferred and/or mandatory acquisition organization), it may be more efficient and cost-effective for the originator of the contract to establish and maintain a stated level of trust with the external provider (including the definition of required security controls and level of assurance with regard to the provision of such controls). Organizations subsequently acquiring information system services or technologies from the centralized contract can take advantage of the negotiated trust level established by the procurement originator and thus avoid costly repetition of the activities necessary to establish such trust. For example, a procurement originator could authorize an information system providing external services to the federal government under specific terms and conditions of the contract. A federal agency requesting information system services under the terms of the contract would not be required to reauthorize the information system when acquiring such services (unless the request included services outside the scope of the original contract).

organization establish and retain a level of confidence that each participating service provider in the potentially complex consumer-provider relationship provides adequate protection for the services rendered to the organization. The chain of trust can be complicated due to the number of entities participating in the consumer-provider relationship and the type of relationship between the parties. External service providers may also in turn outsource the services to other external entities, making the chain of trust even more complicated and difficult to manage. Depending on the nature of the service, it may simply be unwise for the organization to place significant trust in the provider—not due to any inherent untrustworthiness on the provider's part, but due to the intrinsic level of risk in the service. Where a sufficient level of trust cannot be established in the external services and/or service providers, the organization employs compensating controls or accepts a greater degree of risk.

2.5 SECURITY CONTROL ASSURANCE

Assurance is the grounds for confidence that the security controls implemented within an information system are effective in their application. Assurance can be obtained in a variety of ways including:

- Actions taken by developers, implementers, and operators in the specification, design, development, implementation, operation, and maintenance of security controls;[43] and

- Actions taken by security control assessors to determine the extent to which the controls are implemented correctly, operating as intended, and producing the desired outcome with respect to meeting the security requirements for the system.

Appendix E describes the minimum assurance requirements[44] for security controls in low-impact, moderate-impact, and high-impact information systems. For security controls in low-impact systems, the emphasis is on the control being in place with the expectation that no obvious errors exist and that as flaws are discovered, they are addressed in a timely manner. For security controls in moderate-impact systems, in addition to the assurance requirements for low-impact systems, the emphasis is on increasing the grounds for confidence in control correctness. While flaws are still likely to be uncovered (and addressed expeditiously), the control developer or control implementer incorporates, as part of the control, specific capabilities to increase grounds for confidence that the control meets its function or purpose. For security controls in high-impact systems, in addition to the assurance requirements for moderate-impact systems, the emphasis is on requiring within the control, the capabilities that are needed to support ongoing, consistent operation of the control and to support continuous improvement in the control's effectiveness. There are additional assurance requirements available to developers/implementers of security controls supplementing the minimum assurance requirements for the moderate-impact and high-impact information systems in order to protect against threats from highly skilled, highly motivated, and well-resourced threat agents. This level of protection is necessary for those information systems where the organization is not willing to accept the risks associated with the type of threat agents cited above.

---

[43] In this context, a developer/implementer is an individual or group of individuals responsible for the development or implementation of security controls. This may include in addition to organizational personnel, for example, hardware and software vendors providing the security controls and contractors implementing the controls.

[44] Assurance requirements imposed upon developers and implementers of security controls are addressed in this special publication. Assurance gained from the assessment of security controls (e.g., by testers, evaluators, auditors, Inspectors General, information system owners) is addressed in NIST Special Publication 800-53A.

2.6 REVISIONS AND EXTENSIONS

The set of security controls listed in this publication represents the current state-of-the-practice safeguards and countermeasures for federal information systems and organizations. The security controls will be carefully reviewed and revised periodically to reflect:

- Experience gained from using the controls;

- Changing security requirements;

- Emerging threats, vulnerabilities, and attack methods; and

- Availability of new technologies.[45]

The security controls in the security control catalog are expected to change over time, as controls are withdrawn, revised, and added. The security controls defined in the low, moderate, and high baselines are also expected to change over time as the level of security and due diligence for mitigating risks within organizations changes. In addition to the need for change, the need for stability will be addressed by requiring that proposed additions, deletions, or modifications to the catalog of security controls go through a rigorous public review process to obtain government and private sector feedback and to build consensus for the changes. A stable, yet flexible and technically rigorous set of security controls will be maintained in the security control catalog.

---

[45] The security control catalog in Appendix F will be updated as needed with new controls developed from national-level threat databases containing information on known cyber attacks. The proposed modifications to security controls and security control baselines will be carefully weighed with each revision cycle, considering the desire for stability on one hand, and the need to respond to changing threats and vulnerabilities, new attack methods, new technologies, and the important objective of raising the foundational level of security over time. Organizations may develop new controls when appropriate controls are not available in Appendix F.

CHAPTER THREE

THE PROCESS

SELECTION AND SPECIFICATION OF SECURITY CONTROLS

This chapter describes the process of selecting and specifying security controls for an organizational information system to include: (i) applying the organization's approach to managing risk; (ii) categorizing the information system and determining the system impact level in accordance with FIPS 199 and FIPS 200, respectively; (iii) selecting security controls, including tailoring the initial set of baseline security controls and supplementing the tailored baseline as necessary based on an organizational assessment of risk; and (iv) assessing the security controls as part of a comprehensive continuous monitoring process.

3.1 MANAGING RISK

The selection and specification of security controls for an information system is accomplished as part of an organization-wide information security program for the management of risk—that is, the risk to organizational operations and assets, individuals, other organizations, and the Nation associated with the operation of an information system. The management of risk is a key element in the organization's information security program and provides an effective framework for selecting the appropriate security controls for an information system—the security controls necessary to protect individuals and the operations and assets of the organization. The risk-based approach to security control selection and specification considers effectiveness, efficiency, and constraints due to applicable federal laws, Executive Orders, directives, policies, regulations, standards, or guidelines. The following activities related to managing risk, included as part of the *Risk Management Framework*, are paramount to an effective information security program and can be applied to both new and legacy information systems within the context of the Federal Enterprise Architecture and system development life cycle—

- *Categorize* the information system and the information processed, stored, and transmitted by that system based on a FIPS 199 impact analysis.

- *Select* an initial set of baseline security controls for the information system based on the system impact level and minimum security requirements defined in FIPS 200; apply tailoring guidance;[46] supplement the tailored baseline security controls based on an organizational assessment of risk[47] and local conditions including environment of operation, organization-specific security requirements, specific threat information, cost-benefit analyses, or special circumstances; and specify assurance requirements.

- *Implement* the security controls and describe how the controls are employed within the information system and its environment of operation.[48]

- *Assess* the security controls using appropriate assessment procedures to determine the extent to which the controls are implemented correctly, operating as intended, and producing the desired outcome with respect to meeting the security requirements for the system.[49]

---

[46] Tailoring guidance provides organizations with specific considerations on the applicability and implementation of individual security controls in the control baselines (see Section 3.3).

[47] NIST Special Publication 800-30 provides guidance on the assessment of risk.

[48] For legacy systems, some or all of the security controls selected may already be implemented.

[49] NIST Special Publication 800-53A provides guidance on assessing the effectiveness of security controls.

- *Authorize* information system operation based on a determination of the risk to organizational operations and assets, individuals, other organizations, and the Nation resulting from the operation of the information system and the decision that this risk is acceptable.[50]

- *Monitor* the security controls in the information system on an ongoing basis including assessing control effectiveness, documenting changes to the system or its environment of operation, conducting security impact analyses of the associated changes, and reporting the security state of the system to designated organizational officials.

Figure 3-1 illustrates the specific activities in the Risk Management Framework and the information security standards and guidance documents associated with each activity.[51] The remainder of this chapter focuses on several key activities in the Risk Management Framework associated with security control selection and specification.

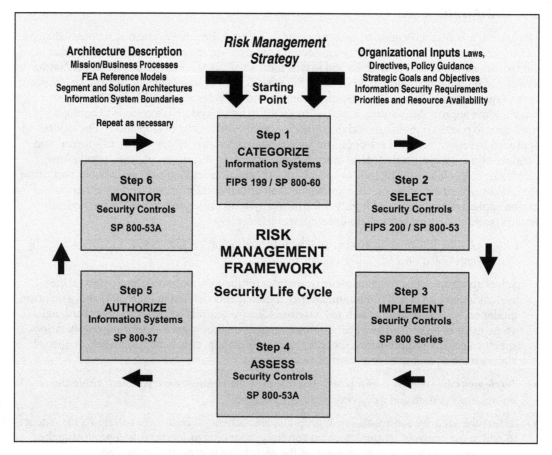

FIGURE 3-1: RISK MANAGEMENT FRAMEWORK

---

[50] NIST Special Publication 800-37 provides guidance on the security authorization of information systems.

[51] NIST Special Publication 800-39 provides guidance on organization-wide risk management including the development of risk management strategies, risk-related governance issues, defining protection requirements and associated risks for organizational mission/business processes, integration of security and privacy requirements into enterprise architectures, and managing risk within the system development life cycle.

3.2 CATEGORIZING THE INFORMATION SYSTEM

FIPS 199, the mandatory security categorization standard, is predicated on a simple and well-established concept—determining appropriate security priorities for organizational information systems and subsequently applying appropriate measures to adequately protect those systems. The security controls applied to a particular information system are commensurate with the potential adverse impact on organizational operations, organizational assets, individuals, other organizations, and the Nation should there be a loss of confidentiality, integrity, or availability. FIPS 199 requires organizations to categorize their information systems as low-impact, moderate-impact, or high-impact for the security objectives of confidentiality, integrity, and availability (**RMF Step 1**). The potential impact values assigned to the respective security objectives are the highest values (i.e., high water mark) from among the security categories that have been determined for each type of information processed, stored, or transmitted by those information systems.[52] The generalized format for expressing the security category (SC) of an information system is:

$$SC_{\text{information system}} = \{(\textbf{confidentiality}, \textit{impact}), (\textbf{integrity}, \textit{impact}), (\textbf{availability}, \textit{impact})\},$$

where the acceptable values for potential impact are low, moderate, or high.

Since the potential impact values for confidentiality, integrity, and availability may not always be the same for a particular information system, the high water mark concept is introduced in FIPS 200 to determine the impact level of the information system for the express purpose of selecting an initial set of security controls from one of the three security control baselines.[53] Thus, a *low-impact* system is defined as an information system in which all three of the security objectives are low. A *moderate-impact* system is an information system in which at least one of the security objectives is moderate and no security objective is greater than moderate. And finally, a *high-impact* system is an information system in which at least one security objective is high.

Implementation Tip

To determine the overall impact level of the information system:

- First, determine the different types of information that are processed, stored, or transmitted by the information system (e.g., financial sector oversight, inspections and auditing, official information dissemination, etc.). NIST Special Publication 800-60 provides guidance on a variety of information types commonly used by organizations.

- Second, using the impact levels in FIPS 199 and the recommendations of NIST Special Publication 800-60, categorize the confidentiality, integrity, and availability of each information type.

- Third, determine the information system security categorization, that is, the highest impact level for each security objective (confidentiality, integrity, availability) from among the categorizations for the information types associated with the information system.

- Fourth, determine the overall impact level of the information system from the highest impact level among the three security objectives in the system security categorization.

---

[52] NIST Special Publication 800-60, *Guide for Mapping Types of Information and Information Systems to Security Categories*, provides guidance on the assignment of security categories to information systems.

[53] The high water mark concept is employed because there are significant dependencies among the security objectives of confidentiality, integrity, and availability. In most cases, a compromise in one security objective ultimately affects the other security objectives as well. Accordingly, the security controls in the control catalog are not categorized by security objective—rather, they are grouped into baselines to provide a general protection capability for classes of information systems based on impact level. The application of scoping guidance may allow selective security control baseline tailoring based on the individual impact levels for confidentiality, integrity, and availability (see Section 3.3).

3.3 SELECTING SECURITY CONTROLS

Once the impact level of the information system is determined, the organization begins the security control selection process (**RMF Step 2**). There are three steps in the control selection process carried out sequentially: (i) *selecting* the initial set of baseline security controls; (ii) *tailoring* the baseline security controls; and (iii) *supplementing* the tailored baseline. The following sections describe each of these steps in greater detail.[54]

Selecting the Initial Baseline Security Controls

The first step in selecting security controls for the information system is to choose the appropriate set of baseline controls. The selection of the initial set of baseline security controls is based on the impact level of the information system as determined by the security categorization process described in Section 3.2. The organization selects one of three sets of baseline security controls from Appendix D corresponding to the low-impact, moderate-impact, or high-impact rating of the information system. Note that not all security controls are assigned to baselines, as indicated by the phrase *not selected*. Similarly, not all control enhancements are assigned to baselines, as indicated by the security control being *not selected* or the enhancement number enclosed in parenthesis, not appearing in any baseline.

Tailoring the Baseline Security Controls

After selecting the initial set of baseline security controls from Appendix D, the organization initiates the tailoring process to appropriately modify and more closely align the controls with the specific conditions within the organization (i.e., conditions specific to the information system or its environment of operation). The tailoring process includes:

- Applying *scoping guidance* to the initial baseline security controls to obtain a preliminary set of applicable controls for the tailored baseline;

- Selecting (or specifying) *compensating security controls*, if needed, to adjust the preliminary set of controls to obtain an equivalent set deemed to be more feasible to implement; and

- Specifying *organization-defined parameters* in the security controls via explicit assignment and selection statements to complete the definition of the tailored baseline.

To achieve a cost-effective, risk-based approach to providing adequate information security organization-wide, the baseline tailoring activities are coordinated with and approved by appropriate organizational officials (e.g., authorizing officials, authorizing official designated representatives, risk executive (function), chief information officers, or senior information security officers) prior to implementing the security controls. Organizations have the flexibility to perform the tailoring process at the organization level for all information systems (either as the required tailored baseline or as the starting point for system-specific tailoring), at the individual information system level, or using a combination of organization-level and system-specific approaches. Tailoring decisions for all affected security controls in the selected baseline, including the specific rationale for those decisions, are documented in the security plan for the information system and approved by appropriate organizational officials as part of the security plan approval process.[55]

---

[54] The general security control selection process may be augmented or further detailed by additional sector-specific guidance such as that provided for industrial control systems in Appendix I.

[55] The level of detail required in documenting tailoring decisions in the security control selection process is strictly at the discretion of the organization and is consistent with the impact level of the information system.

Scoping Guidance

Scoping guidance provides organizations with specific terms and conditions on the applicability and implementation of individual security controls in the security control baselines. Application of scoping guidance helps to ensure that organizations implement *only* those controls that are essential to providing the appropriate level of protection for the information system based on specific mission/business requirements and particular environments of operation. There are several scoping considerations described below, that can potentially affect how the baseline security controls are applied and implemented by organizations:

- COMMON CONTROL-RELATED CONSIDERATIONS—

  Security controls designated by the organization as common controls are, in most cases, managed by an organizational entity other than the information system owner. Organizational decisions on which security controls are viewed as common controls may greatly affect the responsibilities of individual information system owners with regard to the implementation of controls in a particular baseline. Every security control in the tailored and supplemented set of controls for an information system is identified in the security plan as a common, system-specific, or hybrid control (see Section 2.3).

- SECURITY OBJECTIVE-RELATED CONSIDERATIONS—

  Security controls that support only one or two of the confidentiality, integrity, or availability security objectives may be downgraded to the corresponding control in a lower baseline (or modified or eliminated if not defined in a lower baseline) if, and only if, the downgrading action: (i) is consistent with the FIPS 199 security category for the supported security objective(s) before moving to the FIPS 200 impact level (i.e., high water mark);[56] (ii) is supported by an organizational assessment of risk; and (iii) does not adversely affect the level of protection for the security-relevant information within the information system.[57] The following security controls are recommended candidates for downgrading: (i) confidentiality [MA-3 (3), MP-2 (1), MP-3, MP-4, MP-5 (1) (2) (3), MP-6, PE-5, SC-4, SC-9]; (ii) integrity [SC-8]; and (iii) availability [CP-2, CP-3, CP-4, CP-6, CP-7, CP-8, MA-6, PE-9, PE-10, PE-11, PE-13, PE-15, SC-6].[58]

---

[56] When applying the "high water mark" process in Section 3.2, some of the original FIPS 199 confidentiality, integrity, or availability security objectives may have been upgraded to a higher baseline of security controls. As part of this process, security controls that uniquely support the confidentiality, integrity, or availability security objectives may have been upgraded unnecessarily. Consequently, it is recommended that organizations consider appropriate and allowable downgrading actions to ensure cost-effective, risk-based application of security controls.

[57] Information that is security-relevant at the system level (e.g., password files, network routing tables, cryptographic key management information) is distinguished from user-level information within an information system. Certain security controls within an information system are used to support the security objectives of confidentiality and integrity for both user-level and system-level information. Caution should be exercised in downgrading confidentiality or integrity-related security controls to ensure that the downgrading action does not result in insufficient protection for the security-relevant information within the information system. Security-relevant information must be protected at the high water mark in order to achieve that level of protection for any of the security objectives related to user-level information.

[58] Downgrading actions apply only to the moderate and high baselines. Certain security controls that are uniquely attributable to confidentiality, integrity, or availability that would ordinarily be considered as potential candidates for downgrading (e.g., AC-16, AU-10, IA-7, PE-12, PE-14, PL-5, SC-5, SC-13, SC-14, SC-16) are eliminated from consideration because the controls are either selected for use in all baselines and have no enhancements that could be downgraded, or the controls are optional and not selected for use in any baseline. Organizations should exercise caution when considering downgrading security controls that do not appear in the list in Section 3.3 to ensure that the downgrading action does not affect security objectives other than the objectives targeted for downgrading.

- SYSTEM COMPONENT ALLOCATION-RELATED CONSIDERATIONS—

Security controls in the baseline represent an information system-wide set of controls that may not be necessary for or applicable to every component in the system. Security controls are applicable only to the components of the information system that provide or support the security capability addressed by the control and are sources of potential risk being mitigated by the control. For example, auditing controls are typically allocated to components of an information system that provide auditing capability (e.g., servers, etc.) and are not necessarily applied to every user-level workstation within the organization; or when information system components are single-user, not networked, or part of a physically isolated network, one or more of these characteristics may provide appropriate rationale for not allocating selected controls to that component. Organizations assess the inventory of information system components to determine which security controls are applicable to the various components and subsequently make explicit decisions regarding where to allocate the controls in order to satisfy organizational security requirements.[59]

- TECHNOLOGY-RELATED CONSIDERATIONS—

Security controls that refer to specific technologies (e.g., wireless, cryptography, public key infrastructure) are applicable only if those technologies are employed or are required to be employed within the information system. Security controls that can be supported by automated mechanisms do not require the development of such mechanisms if the mechanisms do not already exist or are not readily available in commercial or government off-the-shelf products. For example, automated mechanisms may be used to maintain up-to-date, complete, accurate, and readily available baseline configurations of organizational information systems. If automated mechanisms are not readily available, cost-effective, or technically feasible, compensating security controls, implemented through nonautomated mechanisms or procedures, are used to satisfy specified security control requirements (see terms and conditions for selecting and applying compensating controls below).

- PHYSICAL INFRASTRUCTURE-RELATED CONSIDERATIONS—

Security controls that refer to organizational facilities (e.g., physical controls such as locks and guards, environmental controls for temperature, humidity, lighting, fire, and power) are applicable only to those sections of the facilities that directly provide protection to, support for, or are related to the information system (including its information technology assets such as electronic mail or web servers, server farms, data centers, networking nodes, workstations, boundary protection devices, and communications equipment).

- POLICY/REGULATORY-RELATED CONSIDERATIONS—

Security controls that address matters governed by applicable federal laws, Executive Orders, directives, policies, standards, or regulations (e.g., privacy impact assessments) are required only if the employment of those controls is consistent with the types of information and information systems covered by the applicable laws, Executive Orders, directives, policies, standards, or regulations.

---

[59] As technology advances, more powerful and diverse functionality can be found in such devices as personal digital assistants and cellular telephones. These devices may require the application of security controls in accordance with an organizational assessment of risk. While the scoping guidance may support not allocating a particular security control to a specific component, any residual risk associated with the absence of that control must be addressed to adequately protect organizational operations and assets, individuals, other organizations, and the Nation.

- OPERATIONAL/ENVIRONMENTAL-RELATED CONSIDERATIONS—

    Security controls that are based on specific assumptions about the operational environment are applicable only if the information system is employed in the assumed environment. For example, certain physical security controls may not be applicable to space-based information systems, and temperature and humidity controls may not be applicable to remote sensors that exist outside of the indoor facilities that contain information systems.

- SCALABILITY-RELATED CONSIDERATIONS—

    Security controls are scalable with regard to the extent and rigor of the implementation. Scalability is guided by the FIPS 199 security categorization and associated FIPS 200 impact level of the information system being protected. For example, a contingency plan for a high-impact information system may be quite lengthy and contain a significant amount of implementation detail. In contrast, a contingency plan for a low-impact information system may be considerably shorter and contain much less implementation detail. Organizations use discretion in applying the security controls to information systems, giving consideration to the scalability factors in particular environments. This approach facilitates a cost-effective, risk-based approach to security control implementation that expends no more resources than necessary, yet achieves sufficient risk mitigation and adequate security.

- PUBLIC ACCESS-RELATED CONSIDERATIONS—

    When public access to organizational information systems is allowed, security controls are applied with discretion since some security controls from the specified control baselines (e.g., identification and authentication, personnel security controls) may not be applicable to public access. For example, while the baseline controls require identification and authentication of organizational personnel that maintain and support information systems providing the public access services, the same controls might not be required for access to those information systems through public interfaces to obtain publicly available information. On the other hand, identification and authentication would be required for users accessing information systems through public interfaces in some instances, for example, to access/change their personal information.

Compensating Security Controls

Organizations may find it necessary on occasion, to employ compensating security controls. This may occur, for example, when an organization is unable to implement a security control in the baseline or when, due to the specific nature of an information system or its environment of operation, the control in the baseline is not a cost-effective means of obtaining the needed risk mitigation. A compensating security control is a management, operational, or technical control (i.e., safeguard or countermeasure) employed by an organization in lieu of a recommended security control in the low, moderate, or high baselines described in Appendix D, that provides an equivalent or comparable level of protection for an information system and the information processed, stored, or transmitted by that system.[60] Compensating controls are typically selected after applying the scoping considerations in the tailoring guidance to the initial set of baseline security controls. For example, compensating controls may be needed by the organization when

---

[60] More than one compensating control may be required to provide the equivalent or comparable protection for a particular security control in NIST Special Publication 800-53. For example, an organization with significant staff limitations may compensate for the separation of duty security control by strengthening the audit, accountability, and personnel security controls within the information system. Acceptable compensating controls do not necessarily require the development of new security controls.

applying technology-based considerations addressing the lack of capability to support automated mechanisms as part of a security control or control enhancement requirement. A compensating control for an information system may be employed only under the following conditions:

- The organization selects the compensating control from NIST Special Publication 800-53, or if an appropriate compensating control is not available, the organization adopts a suitable compensating control from another source;[61]

- The organization provides supporting rationale for how the compensating control delivers an equivalent security capability for the information system and why the related baseline security control could not be employed; and

- The organization assesses and formally accepts the risk associated with employing the compensating control in the information system.

Organization-Defined Security Control Parameters

Security controls containing organization-defined parameters (i.e., assignment and/or selection operations) give organizations the flexibility to define certain portions of the controls to support specific organizational requirements or objectives (see AU-5 example in Section 2.1). After the application of scoping guidance and selection of compensating security controls, organizations review the list of security controls for assignment and selection operations and determine the appropriate organization-defined values for the identified parameters. Values for organization-defined parameters are adhered to unless more restrictive values are prescribed by applicable federal laws, Executive Orders, directives, policies, standards, guidelines, or regulations. Organizations may choose to specify values for security control parameters before selecting compensating controls since the specification of those parameters completes the definition of the security control and may affect the compensating control requirements.

Supplementing the Tailored Baseline

The tailored security control baseline is the foundation or starting point for determining the needed set of security controls for an information system. As described in Section 3.1, the final determination of the appropriate set of security controls necessary to provide adequate security for an information system is a function of the organization's assessment of risk and what is required to sufficiently mitigate the risks to organizational operations and assets, individuals, other organizations, and the Nation.[62]   In many cases, additional security controls or control enhancements will be needed to address specific threats to and vulnerabilities in an information system and to satisfy the requirements of applicable federal laws, Executive Orders, directives, policies, standards, or regulations. The risk assessment at this stage in the security control selection process provides important inputs to determine the sufficiency of the security controls in the tailored baseline. Organizations are encouraged to make maximum use of the security control catalog in Appendix F to facilitate the process of enhancing security controls and/or adding controls to the tailored baseline.[63]

---

[61] Organizations should make every attempt to select compensating controls from the security control catalog in NIST Special Publication 800-53. Organization-defined compensating controls are employed only as a last resort when the organization deems that the security control catalog does not contain suitable compensating controls.

[62] Considerations for potential national-level impacts and impacts to other organizations in categorizing organizational information systems derive from the USA PATRIOT Act and Homeland Security Presidential Directives.

[63] Security controls and control enhancements selected to supplement tailored baselines are allocated to appropriate information system components in the same manner as the control allocations carried out by the organization in the initial baselines. See Section 3.3, *Scoping Guidance,* for security control allocation.

In selecting the security controls and control enhancements to supplement the tailored baseline, an organization can employ a *requirements definition* approach or a *gap analysis* approach. In the requirements definition approach, the organization acquires specific and credible threat[64] information (or makes a reasonable assumption) about the activities of adversaries with certain capabilities or attack potential (e.g., skill levels, expertise, available resources). To effectively withstand cyber attacks from adversaries with the stated capabilities or attack potential, the organization strives to achieve a certain level of security capability or cyber preparedness. Organizations can choose additional security controls and control enhancements from Appendix F to obtain such security capability or level of preparedness. In contrast to the requirements definition approach, the gap analysis approach begins with an organizational assessment of its current security capability or level of cyber preparedness. From that initial security capability assessment, the organization determines the types of threats it can reasonably expect to address. If the organization's current security capability or level of cyber preparedness is insufficient, the gap analysis determines the required capability and level of preparedness. The organization subsequently defines the security controls and control enhancements from Appendix F needed to achieve the desired capability or cyber preparedness level.[65]

There may be situations in which an organization is employing information technology beyond its ability to adequately protect essential missions and business functions (e.g., certain web-based, social networking, and collaborative computing-based technologies). That is, the organization cannot apply sufficient security controls within an information system to adequately reduce or mitigate risk. In those situations, an alternative strategy is needed to prevent the mission and business functions from being adversely affected; a strategy that considers the mission/business risks that result from an aggressive use of information technology. Restrictions on the types of technologies used and how the information system is employed provide an alternative method to reduce or mitigate risk when security controls cannot be implemented within technology/resource constraints, or when controls lack reasonable expectation of effectiveness against identified threat sources. Restrictions on the use of information systems and specific information technologies are in many situations, the only practical or reasonable course of action an organization can take in order to have the ability to carry out its assigned missions and business functions in the face of determined adversaries. Examples of use restrictions include:

- Limiting the information an information system can process, store, or transmit or the manner in which an organizational mission or business function is automated;

- Prohibiting external access to organizational information by removing selected information system components from the network (i.e., air gapping); and

- Prohibiting public access to moderate-impact or high-impact information systems, unless an explicit determination is made authorizing such access.

Organizations document the decisions taken during the security control selection process, providing a sound rationale for those decisions. This documentation is essential when examining the security considerations for information systems with respect to potential mission/business impact. The resulting set of security controls along with the supporting rationale for selection decisions and any information system use restrictions are documented in the security plan for the information system. Documenting in the security plan any significant risk management decisions

---

[64] While this example focuses on threats to information systems from purposeful attacks, the scope of concern to most organizations also includes environmental disruptions and human errors.

[65] NIST Special Publication 800-30 provides guidance on conducting risk assessments. Future updates to Special Publication 800-30 will include additional information on threat taxonomies and security capabilities.

in the security control selection process is imperative in order for authorizing officials to have the necessary information to make credible, risk-based decisions regarding the authorization of organizational information systems. In addition, without such information, the understanding, assumptions, and rationale supporting those important risk decisions will, in all likelihood, not be available when the state of the information systems or environments of operation change, and the original risk decisions are revisited.

Figure 3-2 summarizes the security control selection process,[66] including tailoring of the initial security control baseline and any additional modifications to the baseline required based on an organizational assessment of risk.[67]

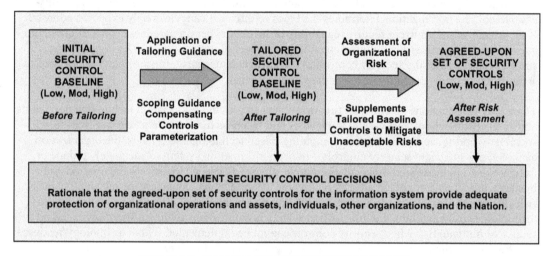

FIGURE 3-2: SECURITY CONTROL SELECTION PROCESS

---

[66] Some of the steps in the Risk Management Framework are represented by actual security controls (e.g., RA-2, *Security Categorization*, CA-2, *Security Assessment*, CA-6, *Security Authorization*, and CA-7, *Continuous Monitoring*) in Appendix F. A few other selected security controls must be implemented initially to complete the first two steps in the Risk Management Framework. For example, RA-3, Risk Assessment, is implemented to conduct an organizational assessment of risk to support selecting, tailoring, and supplementing the security control baseline. Security control PL-2, Security Plan, is implemented to document the agreed-upon security controls upon completion of the control selection process. Organizations select and implement security controls in the appropriate sequence to fully execute the steps in the Risk Management Framework.

[67] An information system can employ security controls at different layers within the system. An operating system, for example, typically provides an access control capability that includes the identification and authentication of users. An application, hosted by that operating system, may also provide its own access control capability requiring users to go through a second level of identification and authentication, thus rendering an additional level of protection for the information system. Organizations carrying out the security control selection process consider components at all layers within the information system as part of effective organizational security architecture implementing a defense-in-depth security strategy.

> **Implementation Tip**
>
> Many organizations own and operate large and complex information systems, sometimes referred to as a system-of-systems. System architecture plays a key part in the security control selection process for these types of information systems. Organizations can address a large and complex system by dividing the system into two or more subsystems and applying the FIPS 199 security categorization and FIPS 200 impact level determination to each subsystem. Applying separate impact levels to each subsystem does not change the overall impact level of the information system; rather, it allows the constituent subsystems to receive a separate allocation of security controls instead of deploying higher impact controls across every subsystem. It is not valid to treat the subsystems as entirely independent entities, however, since the subsystems are interdependent and interconnected. The organization develops a security architecture to allocate security controls among the subsystems including monitoring and controlling communications at key internal boundaries within the large and complex system (or system-of-systems) and provides system-wide controls that meet or exceed the highest information system impact level of the constituent subsystems inheriting the security capability from those system-wide controls.
>
> The organization considers that replicated subsystems within a large and complex information system may exhibit common vulnerabilities that can be exploited by a common threat source; thereby negating the redundancy that might be relied upon as a risk mitigation measure. The impact due to a security incident against one constituent subsystem might cascade and impact many subsystems at the same time. Risk levels can be adjusted upward or downward based on the actual deployment of security controls, the effectiveness of the controls, the environment in which the information system is operating, and how the organization is using its information technology.

New Development and Legacy Systems

The security control selection process described in this section can be applied to organizational information systems from two different perspectives: (i) new development; and (ii) legacy. For a new development system, the security control selection process is applied from a *requirements definition* perspective since the information system does not yet exist and the organization is conducting an initial security categorization. The security controls included in the security plan for the information system serve as a security specification for the organization and are expected to be incorporated into the system during the development and implementation phases of the system development life cycle. In contrast, for a legacy information system, the security control selection process is applied from a *gap analysis* perspective when the organization is anticipating significant changes to the system (e.g., during major upgrades, modifications, or outsourcing). Since the information system already exists, the organization in all likelihood has completed the security categorization and security control selection processes resulting in the documentation of a previously agreed-upon set of security controls in the security plan and the implementation of those controls within the information system. Therefore, the gap analysis can be applied in the following manner:

- First, reconfirm or update as necessary, the FIPS 199 security category and FIPS 200 impact level for the information system based on the different types of information that are *currently* being processed, stored, or transmitted by the system.

- Second, review the existing security plan that describes the security controls that are currently employed considering any updates to the security category and information system impact level as well as any changes to the organization, the system, or the operational environment. Reassess the risk and revise the security plan as necessary, including documenting any additional security controls that *would* be needed by the system to ensure that the risk to organizational operations, organizational assets, individuals, other organizations, and the Nation, remains at an acceptable level.

- Third, *implement* the security controls described in the updated security plan, document in the plan of action and milestones any controls not implemented, and continue with the remaining steps in the Risk Management Framework in the same manner as a new development system.

Applying Gap Analyses to External Service Providers

The gap analysis perspective is also applied when interacting with external service providers. As described in Section 2.4, organizations are becoming increasingly reliant on external providers for critical information system services. Using the steps in the gap analysis described above, the organization can effectively use the acquisition process and appropriate contractual vehicles to require external providers to carry out, in collaboration with the organization, the security categorization and security control selection steps in the RMF. The resulting information can help determine what security controls the external provider either has in place or intends to implement for the information system services that are to be provided to the organization. If a security control deficit exists, the responsibility for adequately mitigating unacceptable risks arising from the use of external information system services remains with the authorizing official. In such situations, the organization can reduce the organizational risk to an acceptable level by:

- Using the existing contractual vehicle to require the external provider to meet the additional security control requirements established by the organization;

- Negotiating with the provider for additional security controls (including compensating controls) if the existing contractual vehicle does not provide for such added requirements; or

- Employing alternative risk mitigation measures[68] within the organizational information system when a contract either does not exist or the contract does not provide the necessary leverage for the organization to obtain needed security controls.

3.4 MONITORING SECURITY CONTROLS

After the security controls are implemented and assessed for effectiveness, the information system is authorized for operation in accordance with the organization's risk management strategy (**RMF Steps 3, 4, and 5**). The organization subsequently initiates specific follow-on actions as part of a comprehensive continuous monitoring program. The continuous monitoring program includes an ongoing assessment of security control effectiveness to determine if there is a need to modify or update the current deployed set of security controls based on changes in the information system or its environment of operation (**RMF Step 6**). In particular, the organization revisits on a regular basis, the risk management activities described in the Risk Management Framework. In addition to the ongoing activities associated with the implementation of the Risk Management Framework, there are certain events which can trigger the immediate need to assess the security state of the information system and if required, modify or update the current security controls. These events include, for example:

- An incident results in a breach to the information system, producing a loss of confidence by the organization in the confidentiality, integrity, or availability of information processed, stored, or transmitted by the system;

- A newly identified, credible, information system-related threat to organizational operations and assets, individuals, other organizations, or the Nation is identified based on intelligence information, law enforcement information, or other credible sources of information;

---

[68] For example, local policies, procedures, and/or compensating controls could be established on the organization side to serve as alternative mitigation measures for risks identified in a gap analysis.

- Significant changes to the configuration of the information system through the removal or addition of new or upgraded hardware, software, or firmware or changes in the operational environment[69] potentially degrade the security state of the system; or

- Significant changes to the organizational risk management strategy, information security policy, supported missions and/or business functions, or information being processed, stored, or transmitted by the information system.

When such events occur, organizations, at a minimum, take the following actions:[70]

- *Reconfirm the security category and impact level of the information system.*

  The organization reexamines the FIPS 199 security category and FIPS 200 impact level of the information system to confirm that the security category and system impact level previously established and approved by the authorizing official are still valid. The resulting analysis may provide new insights as to the overall importance of the information system in allowing the organization to fulfill its mission/business responsibilities.

- *Assess the current security state of the information system and the risk to organizational operations and assets, individuals, other organizations, and the Nation.*

  The organization investigates the information system vulnerability (or vulnerabilities) exploited by the threat source (or potentially exploitable by a threat source) and the security controls currently implemented within the system as described in the security plan. The exploitation of information system vulnerabilities by a threat source may be traced to one or more factors including but not limited to: (i) the failure of currently implemented security controls; (ii) missing security controls; (iii) insufficient strength of security controls; and/or (iv) an increase in the capability of the threat source. Using the results from the assessment of the current security state, the organization reassesses the risks arising from use of the information system.

- *Plan for and initiate any necessary corrective actions.*

  Based on the results of an updated risk assessment, the organization determines what additional security controls and/or control enhancements or corrective actions for existing controls are necessary to adequately mitigate risk. The security plan for the information system is updated to reflect any initial changes to the original plan. A plan of action and milestones is developed for any noted weaknesses or deficiencies that are not immediately corrected and for the implementation of any security control upgrades or additional controls. After the security controls and/or control upgrades have been implemented and any other weaknesses or deficiencies corrected, the controls are assessed for effectiveness to determine if the controls are implemented correctly, operating as intended, and producing the desired outcome with respect to meeting the security requirements for the information system. If necessary, the security plan is updated to reflect any additional corrective actions taken by the organization to mitigate risk.

---

[69] Examples of significant changes in the operational environment are interconnection of external information systems and large increases or decreases in the size of the community of users accessing the information system.

[70] Organizations determine the specific types of events that would trigger changes to the security controls within the information system or its environment of operation and a resulting modification to the security plan. The decision to commit resources in light of such events is guided by an organizational assessment of risk.

- *Consider reauthorizing the information system.*

  Depending on the severity of the event, the adverse impact on organizational operations and assets, individuals, other organizations, and the Nation, and the extent of the corrective actions required to fix the identified weaknesses or deficiencies in the information system, the organization may need to consider reauthorizing the information system in accordance with the provisions of NIST Special Publication 800-37. The authorizing official makes the final determination on the need to reauthorize the information system in consultation with the risk executive (function), system and mission/business owners, the senior information security officer, and the chief information officer. The authorizing official may choose to conduct a limited reauthorization focusing *only* on the affected components of the information system and the associated security controls and/or control enhancements which have been changed during the update. Authorizing officials have sufficient information available from security control assessments to initiate, with an appropriate degree of confidence, necessary corrective actions.

APPENDIX A

REFERENCES

LAWS, POLICIES, DIRECTIVES, REGULATIONS, MEMORANDA, STANDARDS, AND GUIDELINES

LEGISLATION

1. E-Government Act [includes FISMA] (P.L. 107-347), December 2002.

2. Federal Information Security Management Act (P.L. 107-347, Title III), December 2002.

3. Paperwork Reduction Act (P.L. 104-13), May 1995.

4. USA PATRIOT Act (P.L. 107-56), October 2001.

5. Privacy Act of 1974 (P.L. 93-579), December 1974.

6. Freedom of Information Act (FOIA), 5 U.S.C. § 552, As Amended By Public Law No. 104-231, 110 Stat. 3048, *Electronic Freedom of Information Act Amendments of 1996.*

7. Health Insurance Portability and Accountability Act (P.L. 104-191), August 1996.

8. The Atomic Energy Act of 1954 (P.L. 83-703), August 1954.

POLICIES, DIRECTIVES, REGULATIONS, AND MEMORANDA

1. Code of Federal Regulations, Title 5, *Administrative Personnel*, Section 731.106, *Designation of Public Trust Positions and Investigative Requirements* (5 C.F.R. 731.106).

2. Code of Federal Regulations, Part 5 Administrative Personnel, Subpart C—Employees Responsible for the Management or Use of Federal Computer Systems, Section 930.301 through 930.305 (5 C.F.R 930.301-305).

3. Director of Central Intelligence Directive 6/9, *Physical Security Standards For Sensitive Compartmented Information Facilities*, November 2002.

4. Federal Continuity Directive 1 (FCD 1), *Federal Executive Branch National Continuity Program and Requirements*, February 2008.

5. Homeland Security Presidential Directive 7, *Critical Infrastructure Identification, Prioritization, and Protection*, December 2003.

6. Homeland Security Presidential Directive 12, *Policy for a Common Identification Standard for Federal Employees and Contractors*, August 2004.

7. Intelligence Community Directive Number 704, *Personnel Security Standards and Procedures Governing Eligibility For Access To Sensitive Compartmented Information And Other Controlled Access Program Information*, October 2008.

8. Office of Management and Budget, Circular A-130, Appendix III, Transmittal Memorandum #4, *Management of Federal Information Resources*, November 2000.

9. Office of Management and Budget, Federal Enterprise Architecture Program Management Office, *FEA Consolidated Reference Model Document*, Version 2.3, October 2007.

10. Office of Management and Budget, *Federal Segment Architecture Methodology (FSAM)*, January 2009.

11. Office of Management and Budget Memorandum M-01-05, *Guidance on Inter-Agency Sharing of Personal Data - Protecting Personal Privacy*, December 2000.

12. Office of Management and Budget Memorandum M-02-01, *Guidance for Preparing and Submitting Security Plans of Action and Milestones*, October 2001.

13. Office of Management and Budget Memorandum M-03-19, *Reporting Instructions for the Federal Information Security Management Act and Updated Guidance on Quarterly IT Security Reporting,* August 2003.

14. Office of Management and Budget Memorandum M-03-22, *OMB Guidance for Implementing the Privacy Provisions of the E-Government Act of 2002*, September 2003.

15. Office of Management and Budget Memorandum M-04-04, *E-Authentication Guidance for Federal Agencies*, December 2003.

16. Office of Management and Budget Memorandum M-04-26, *Personal Use Policies and File Sharing Technology*, September 2004.

17. Office of Management and Budget Memorandum M-05-08, *Designation of Senior Agency Officials for Privacy,* February 2005.

18. Office of Management and Budget Memorandum M-05-24, *Implementation of Homeland Security Presidential Directive (HSPD) 12—Policy for a Common Identification Standard for Federal Employees and Contractors*, August 2005.

19. Office of Management and Budget Memorandum M-06-15, *Safeguarding Personally Identifiable Information*, May 2006.

20. Office of Management and Budget Memorandum M-06-16, *Protection of Sensitive Information*, June 2006.

21. Office of Management and Budget Memorandum M-06-19, *Reporting Incidents Involving Personally Identifiable Information and Incorporating the Cost for Security in Agency Information Technology Investments*, July 2006.

22. Office of Management and Budget Memorandum, *Recommendations for Identity Theft Related Data Breach Notification Guidance*, September 2006.

23. Office of Management and Budget Memorandum M-07-11, *Implementation of Commonly Accepted Security Configurations for Windows Operating Systems*, March 2007.

24. Office of Management and Budget Memorandum M-07-16, *Safeguarding Against and Responding to the Breach of Personally Identifiable Information*, May 2007.

25. Office of Management and Budget Memorandum M-07-18, *Ensuring New Acquisitions Include Common Security Configurations*, June 2007.

26. Office of Management and Budget Memorandum M-08-09, *New FISMA Privacy Reporting Requirements for FY 2008*, January 2008.

27. Office of Management and Budget Memorandum M-08-21, *FY08 Reporting Instructions for the Federal Information Security Management Act and Agency Privacy Management*, July 2008.

28. Office of Management and Budget Memorandum M-08-22, *Guidance on the Federal Desktop Core Configuration (FDCC)*, August 2008.

29. Office of Management and Budget Memorandum M-08-23, *Securing the Federal Government's Domain Name System Infrastructure*, August 2008.

30. The White House, Office of the Press Secretary, *Designation and Sharing of Controlled Unclassified Information (CUI)*, May 2008.

31. The White House, Office of the Press Secretary, *Classified Information and Controlled Unclassified Information*, May 2009.

STANDARDS

1. International Organization for Standardization/International Electrotechnical Commission 27001, *Information Security Management System Requirements*, October 2005.

2. International Organization for Standardization/International Electrotechnical Commission 15408-1, *Information technology -- Security techniques -- Evaluation criteria for IT security -- Part 1: Introduction and general model*, October 2005.

3. International Organization for Standardization/International Electrotechnical Commission 15408-2, *Information technology -- Security techniques -- Evaluation criteria for IT security -- Part 2: Security functional requirements*, October 2005.

4. International Organization for Standardization/International Electrotechnical Commission 15408-3, *Information technology -- Security techniques -- Evaluation criteria for IT security -- Part 3: Security assurance requirements*, October 2005.

5. National Institute of Standards and Technology Federal Information Processing Standards Publication 140-2, *Security Requirements for Cryptographic Modules*, May 2001.

   National Institute of Standards and Technology Federal Information Processing Standards Publication 140-3 (Draft), *Security Requirements for Cryptographic Modules*, July 2007.

6. National Institute of Standards and Technology Federal Information Processing Standards Publication 180-3, *Secure Hash Standard (SHS)*, October 2008.

7. National Institute of Standards and Technology Federal Information Processing Standards Publication 186-3, *Digital Signature Standard (DSS)*, June 2009.

8. National Institute of Standards and Technology Federal Information Processing Standards Publication 188, *Standard Security Labels for Information Transfer*, September 1994.

9. National Institute of Standards and Technology Federal Information Processing Standards Publication 190, *Guideline for the Use of Advanced Authentication Technology Alternatives*, September 1994.

10. National Institute of Standards and Technology Federal Information Processing Standards Publication 197, *Advanced Encryption Standard (AES)*, November 2001.

11. National Institute of Standards and Technology Federal Information Processing Standards Publication 198-1, *The Keyed-Hash Message Authentication Code (HMAC)*, July 2008.

12. National Institute of Standards and Technology Federal Information Processing Standards Publication 199, *Standards for Security Categorization of Federal Information and Information Systems*, February 2004.

13. National Institute of Standards and Technology Federal Information Processing Standards Publication 200, *Minimum Security Requirements for Federal Information and Information Systems*, March 2006.

14. National Institute of Standards and Technology Federal Information Processing Standards Publication 201-1, *Personal Identity Verification (PIV) of Federal Employees and Contractors*, March 2006.

15. Committee for National Security Systems (CNSS) Instruction 4009, *National Information Assurance Glossary*, June 2006.

16. National Security Telecommunications and Information Systems Security Instruction (NSTISSI) 7003, *Protective Distribution Systems (PDS)*, December 1996.

GUIDELINES

1. National Institute of Standards and Technology Special Publication 800-12, *An Introduction to Computer Security: The NIST Handbook*, October 1995.

2. National Institute of Standards and Technology Special Publication 800-13, *Telecommunications Security Guidelines for Telecommunications Management Network*, October 1995.

3. National Institute of Standards and Technology Special Publication 800-14, *Generally Accepted Principles and Practices for Securing Information Technology Systems*, September 1996.

4. National Institute of Standards and Technology Special Publication 800-15, *Minimum Interoperability Specification for PKI Components (MISPC)*, Version 1, September 1997.

5. National Institute of Standards and Technology Special Publication 800-16, *Information Technology Security Training Requirements: A Role- and Performance-Based Model*, April 1998.

6. National Institute of Standards and Technology Special Publication 800-17, *Modes of Operation Validation System (MOVS): Requirements and Procedures*, February 1998.

7. National Institute of Standards and Technology Special Publication 800-18, Revision 1, *Guide for Developing Security Plans for Federal Information Systems*, February 2006.

8. National Institute of Standards and Technology Special Publication 800-19, *Mobile Agent Security*, October 1999.

9. National Institute of Standards and Technology Special Publication 800-20, *Modes of Operation Validation System for the Triple Data Encryption Algorithm (TMOVS): Requirements and Procedures*, April 2000.

10. National Institute of Standards and Technology Special Publication 800-21-1, *Second Edition, Guideline for Implementing Cryptography in the Federal Government*, December 2005.

11. National Institute of Standards and Technology Special Publication 800-22, *A Statistical Test Suite for Random and Pseudorandom Number Generators for Cryptographic Applications*, May 2001.

12. National Institute of Standards and Technology Special Publication 800-23, *Guideline to Federal Organizations on Security Assurance and Acquisition/Use of Tested/Evaluated Products*, August 2000.

13. National Institute of Standards and Technology Special Publication 800-24, *PBX Vulnerability Analysis: Finding Holes in Your PBX Before Someone Else Does,* August 2000.

14. National Institute of Standards and Technology Special Publication 800-25, *Federal Agency Use of Public Key Technology for Digital Signatures and Authentication*, October 2000.

15. National Institute of Standards and Technology Special Publication 800-27, Revision A, *Engineering Principles for Information Technology Security (A Baseline for Achieving Security)*, June 2004.

16. National Institute of Standards and Technology Special Publication 800-28, Version 2, *Guidelines on Active Content and Mobile Code*, March 2008.

17. National Institute of Standards and Technology Special Publication 800-29, *A Comparison of the Security Requirements for Cryptographic Modules in FIPS 140-1 and FIPS 140-2*, June 2001.

18. National Institute of Standards and Technology Special Publication 800-30, *Risk Management Guide for Information Technology Systems*, July 2002.

19. National Institute of Standards and Technology Special Publication 800-32, *Introduction to Public Key Technology and the Federal PKI Infrastructure*, February 2001.

20. National Institute of Standards and Technology Special Publication 800-33, *Underlying Technical Models for Information Technology Security*, December 2001.

21. National Institute of Standards and Technology Special Publication 800-34, *Contingency Planning Guide for Information Technology Systems*, June 2002.

22. National Institute of Standards and Technology Special Publication 800-35, *Guide to Information Technology Security Services*, October 2003.

23. National Institute of Standards and Technology Special Publication 800-36, *Guide to Selecting Information Security Products*, October 2003.

24. National Institute of Standards and Technology Special Publication 800-37, *Guide for the Security Certification and Accreditation of Federal Information Systems*, May 2004.

25. National Institute of Standards and Technology Special Publication 800-38A, *Recommendation for Block Cipher Modes of Operation - Methods and Techniques*, December 2001.

26. National Institute of Standards and Technology Special Publication 800-38B, *Recommendation for Block Cipher Modes of Operation: The CMAC Mode for Authentication*, May 2005.

27. National Institute of Standards and Technology Special Publication 800-38C, *Recommendation for Block Cipher Modes of Operation: the CCM Mode for Authentication and Confidentiality*, May 2004.

28. National Institute of Standards and Technology Special Publication 800-38D, *Recommendation for Block Cipher Modes of Operation: Galois/Counter Mode (GCM) for Confidentiality and Authentication*, November 2007.

29. National Institute of Standards and Technology Special Publication 800-39 (Second Public Draft), *Managing Risk from Information Systems: An Organizational Perspective*, April 2008.

30. National Institute of Standards and Technology Special Publication 800-40, Version 2, *Creating a Patch and Vulnerability Management Program*, November 2005.

31. National Institute of Standards and Technology Special Publication 800-41, Revision 1 (Draft), *Guidelines on Firewalls and Firewall Policy*, July 2008.

32. National Institute of Standards and Technology Special Publication 800-43, *Systems Administration Guidance for Windows 2000 Professional*, November 2002.

33. National Institute of Standards and Technology Special Publication 800-44, Version 2, *Guidelines on Securing Public Web Servers*, September 2007.

34. National Institute of Standards and Technology Special Publication 800-45, Version 2, *Guidelines on Electronic Mail Security*, February 2007.

35. National Institute of Standards and Technology Special Publication 800-46, Revision 1, *Guide to Enterprise Telework and Remote Access Security*, June 2009.

36. National Institute of Standards and Technology Special Publication 800-47, *Security Guide for Interconnecting Information Technology Systems*, August 2002.

37. National Institute of Standards and Technology Special Publication 800-48, Revision 1, *Guide to Securing Legacy IEEE 802.11 Wireless Networks*, July 2008.

38. National Institute of Standards and Technology Special Publication 800-49, *Federal S/MIME V3 Client Profile*, November 2002.

39. National Institute of Standards and Technology Special Publication 800-50, *Building an Information Technology Security Awareness and Training Program*, October 2003.

40. National Institute of Standards and Technology Special Publication 800-51, *Use of the Common Vulnerabilities and Exposures (CVE) Vulnerability Naming Scheme*, September 2002.

41. National Institute of Standards and Technology Special Publication 800-52, *Guidelines for the Selection and Use of Transport Layer Security (TLS) Implementations*, June 2005.

42. National Institute of Standards and Technology Special Publication 800-53A, *Guide for Assessing the Security Controls in Federal Information Systems: Building Effective Security Assessment Plans*, July 2008.

43. National Institute of Standards and Technology Special Publication 800-54, *Border Gateway Protocol Security*, July 2007.

44. National Institute of Standards and Technology Special Publication 800-55, Revision 1, *Performance Measurement Guide for Information Security*, July 2008.

45. National Institute of Standards and Technology Special Publication 800-56A (Revised), *Recommendation for Pair-Wise Key Establishment Schemes Using Discrete Logarithm Cryptography*, March 2007.

46. National Institute of Standards and Technology Special Publication 800-57 (Revised), *Recommendation for Key Management*, March 2007.

47. National Institute of Standards and Technology Special Publication 800-58, *Security Considerations for Voice Over IP Systems*, January 2005.

48. National Institute of Standards and Technology Special Publication 800-59, *Guideline for Identifying an Information System as a National Security System*, August 2003.

49. National Institute of Standards and Technology Special Publication 800-60, Revision 1, *Guide for Mapping Types of Information and Information Systems to Security Categories*, August 2008.

50. National Institute of Standards and Technology Special Publication 800-61, Revision 1, *Computer Security Incident Handling Guide*, March 2008.

51. National Institute of Standards and Technology Special Publication 800-63-1 (Draft), *Electronic Authentication Guideline*, December 2008.

52. National Institute of Standards and Technology Special Publication 800-64, Revision 2, *Security Considerations in the System Development Life Cycle*, October 2008.

53. National Institute of Standards and Technology Special Publication 800-65, *Integrating Security into the Capital Planning and Investment Control Process*, January 2005.

54. National Institute of Standards and Technology Special Publication 800-66, Revision 1, *An Introductory Resource Guide for Implementing the Health Insurance Portability and Accountability Act (HIPAA) Security Rule*, October 2008.

55. National Institute of Standards and Technology Special Publication 800-67, Version 1.1, *Recommendation for the Triple Data Encryption Algorithm (TDEA) Block Cipher*, May 2008.

56. National Institute of Standards and Technology Special Publication 800-68, Revision 1, *Guide to Securing Microsoft Windows XP Systems for IT Professionals: A NIST Security Configuration Checklist*, October 2008.

57. National Institute of Standards and Technology Special Publication 800-69, *Guidance for Securing Microsoft Windows XP Home Edition: A NIST Security Configuration Checklist*, September 2006.

58. National Institute of Standards and Technology Special Publication 800-70, Revision 1 (Draft), *National Checklist Program for IT Products--Guidelines for Checklist Users and Developers*, September 2008.

59. National Institute of Standards and Technology Special Publication 800-72, *Guidelines on PDA Forensics*, November 2004.

60. National Institute of Standards and Technology Special Publication 800-73-2, *Interfaces for Personal Identity Verification*, September 2008.

61. National Institute of Standards and Technology Special Publication 800-76-1, *Biometric Data Specification for Personal Identity Verification*, January 2007.

62. National Institute of Standards and Technology Special Publication 800-77, *Guide to IPsec VPNs*, December 2005.

63. National Institute of Standards and Technology Special Publication 800-78-1, *Cryptographic Algorithms and Key Sizes for Personal Identity Verification*, August 2007.

64. National Institute of Standards and Technology Special Publication 800-79-1, *Guidelines for the Accreditation of Personal Identity Verification Card Issuers*, June 2008.

65. National Institute of Standards and Technology Special Publication 800-81, *Secure Domain Name System (DNS) Deployment Guide*, May 2006.

66. National Institute of Standards and Technology Special Publication 800-82 (Final Public Draft), *Guide to Industrial Control Systems (ICS) Security*, September 2008.

67. National Institute of Standards and Technology Special Publication 800-83, *Guide to Malware Incident Prevention and Handling*, November 2005.

68. National Institute of Standards and Technology Special Publication 800-84, *Guide to Test, Training, and Exercise Programs for IT Plans and Capabilities*, September 2006.

69. National Institute of Standards and Technology Special Publication 800-85A-1, *PIV Card Application and Middleware Interface Test Guidelines (SP 800-73 Compliance)*, March 2009.

70. National Institute of Standards and Technology Special Publication 800-85B, *PIV Data Model Test Guidelines*, July 2006.

71. National Institute of Standards and Technology Special Publication 800-86, *Guide to Integrating Forensic Techniques into Incident Response*, August 2006.

72. National Institute of Standards and Technology Special Publication 800-87, Revision 1, *Codes for the Identification of Federal and Federally-Assisted Organizations*, April 2008.

73. National Institute of Standards and Technology Special Publication 800-88, *Guidelines for Media Sanitization*, September 2006.

74. National Institute of Standards and Technology Special Publication 800-89, *Recommendation for Obtaining Assurances for Digital Signature Applications*, November 2006.

75. National Institute of Standards and Technology Special Publication 800-90 (Revised), *Recommendation for Random Number Generation Using Deterministic Random Bit Generators*, March 2007.

76. National Institute of Standards and Technology Special Publication 800-92, *Guide to Computer Security Log Management*, September 2006.

77. National Institute of Standards and Technology Special Publication 800-94, *Guide to Intrusion Detection and Prevention Systems (IDPS)*, February 2007.

78. National Institute of Standards and Technology Special Publication 800-95, *Guide to Secure Web Services*, August 2007.

79. National Institute of Standards and Technology Special Publication 800-96, *PIV Card / Reader Interoperability Guidelines*, September 2006.

80. National Institute of Standards and Technology Special Publication 800-97, *Establishing Robust Security Networks: A Guide to IEEE 802.11i*, February 2007.

81. National Institute of Standards and Technology Special Publication 800-98, *Guidance for Securing Radio Frequency Identification (RFID) Systems*, April 2007.

82. National Institute of Standards and Technology Special Publication 800-100, *Information Security Handbook: A Guide for Managers*, October 2006.

83. National Institute of Standards and Technology Special Publication 800-101, *Guidelines on Cell Phone Forensics*, May 2007.

84. National Institute of Standards and Technology Special Publication 800-103 (Draft), *An Ontology of Identity Credentials, Part I: Background and Formulation*, October 2006.

85. National Institute of Standards and Technology Special Publication 800-104, *A Scheme for PIV Visual Card Topography*, June 2007.

86. National Institute of Standards and Technology Special Publication 800-106, *Randomized Hashing Digital Signatures*, February 2009.

87. National Institute of Standards and Technology Special Publication 800-107, *Recommendation for Using Approved Hash Algorithms*, February 2009.

88. National Institute of Standards and Technology Special Publication 800-108, *Recommendation for Key Derivation Using Pseudorandom Functions*, November 2008.

89. National Institute of Standards and Technology Special Publication 800-111, *Guide to Storage Encryption Technologies for End User Devices*, November 2007.

90. National Institute of Standards and Technology Special Publication 800-113, *Guide to SSL VPNs*, July 2008.

91. National Institute of Standards and Technology Special Publication 800-114, *User's Guide to Securing External Devices for Telework and Remote Access*, November 2007.

92. National Institute of Standards and Technology Special Publication 800-115, *Technical Guide to Information Security Testing and Assessment*, September 2008.

93. National Institute of Standards and Technology Special Publication 800-116, *A Recommendation for the Use of PIV Credentials in Physical Access Control Systems (PACS)*, November 2008.

94. National Institute of Standards and Technology Special Publication 800-117 (Draft), *Guide to Adopting and Using the Security Content Automation Protocol (SCAP)*, May 2009.

95. National Institute of Standards and Technology Special Publication 800-118 (Draft), *Guide to Enterprise Password Management*, April 2009.

96. National Institute of Standards and Technology Special Publication 800-121, *Guide to Bluetooth Security*, September 2008.

97. National Institute of Standards and Technology Special Publication 800-122 (Draft), *Guide to Protecting the Confidentiality of Personally Identifiable Information (PII)*, January 2009.

98. National Institute of Standards and Technology Special Publication 800-123, *Guide to General Server Security*, July 2008.

99. National Institute of Standards and Technology Special Publication 800-124, *Guidelines on Cell Phone and PDA Security*, October 2008.

100. National Institute of Standards and Technology Special Publication 800-128 (Draft), *Guide for Security Configuration Management of Information Systems*, August 2009.

APPENDIX B

GLOSSARY
COMMON TERMS AND DEFINITIONS

Appendix B provides definitions for security terminology used within Special Publication 800-53. Unless specifically defined in this glossary, all terms used in this publication are consistent with the definitions contained in CNSS Instruction 4009, *National Information Assurance Glossary*.

Adequate Security [OMB Circular A-130, Appendix III]	Security commensurate with the risk and the magnitude of harm resulting from the loss, misuse, or unauthorized access to or modification of information.
Agency	See *Executive Agency*.
Attribute-Based Access Control	Access control based on attributes associated with and about subjects, objects, targets, initiators, resources, or the environment. An access control rule set defines the combination of attributes under which an access may take place.
Authentication [FIPS 200]	Verifying the identity of a user, process, or device, often as a prerequisite to allowing access to resources in an information system.
Authenticator	The means used to confirm the identity of a user, processor, or device (e.g., user password or token).
Authenticity	The property of being genuine and being able to be verified and trusted; confidence in the validity of a transmission, a message, or message originator. See *Authentication*.
Authorization (to operate)	The official management decision given by a senior organizational official to authorize operation of an information system and to explicitly accept the risk to organizational operations (including mission, functions, image, or reputation), organizational assets, individuals, other organizations, and the Nation based on the implementation of an agreed-upon set of security controls.
Authorization Boundary	All components of an information system to be authorized for operation by an authorizing official and excludes separately authorized systems, to which the information system is connected.
Authorize Processing	See *Authorization*.
Authorizing Official	A senior (federal) official or executive with the authority to formally assume responsibility for operating an information system at an acceptable level of risk to organizational operations (including mission, functions, image, or reputation), organizational assets, individuals, other organizations, and the Nation.

Availability [44 U.S.C., Sec. 3542]	Ensuring timely and reliable access to and use of information.
Boundary Protection	Monitoring and control of communications at the external boundary of an information system to prevent and detect malicious and other unauthorized communications, through the use of boundary protection devices (e.g., proxies, gateways, routers, firewalls, guards, encrypted tunnels).
Boundary Protection Device	A device with appropriate mechanisms that: (i) facilitates the adjudication of different interconnected system security policies (e.g., controlling the flow of information into or out of an interconnected system); and/or (ii) provides information system boundary protection.
Chief Information Officer [PL 104-106, Sec. 5125(b)]	Agency official responsible for:

(i) Providing advice and other assistance to the head of the executive agency and other senior management personnel of the agency to ensure that information technology is acquired and information resources are managed in a manner that is consistent with laws, Executive Orders, directives, policies, regulations, and priorities established by the head of the agency;

(ii) Developing, maintaining, and facilitating the implementation of a sound and integrated information technology architecture for the agency; and

(iii) Promoting the effective and efficient design and operation of all major information resources management processes for the agency, including improvements to work processes of the agency.

Note: Organizations subordinate to federal agencies may use the term *Chief Information Officer* to denote individuals filling positions with similar security responsibilities to agency-level Chief Information Officers.

Chief Information Security Officer	See *Senior Agency Information Security Officer*.
Classified Information	Information that has been determined: (i) pursuant to Executive Order 12958 as amended by Executive Order 13292, or any predecessor Order, to be classified national security information; or (ii) pursuant to the Atomic Energy Act of 1954, as amended, to be Restricted Data (RD).
Commodity Service	An information system service (e.g., telecommunications service) provided by a commercial service provider typically to a large and diverse set of consumers. The organization acquiring and/or receiving the commodity service possesses limited visibility into the management structure and operations of the provider, and while the organization may be able to negotiate service-level agreements, the organization is typically not in a position to require that the provider implement specific security controls.

Common Carrier	In a telecommunications context, a telecommunications company that holds itself out to the public for hire to provide communications transmission services. Note: In the United States, such companies are usually subject to regulation by federal and state regulatory commissions.
Common Control	A security control that is inherited by one or more organizational information systems. See *Security Control Inheritance*.
Compensating Security Controls	The management, operational, and technical controls (i.e., safeguards or countermeasures) employed by an organization in lieu of the recommended controls in the low, moderate, or high baselines described in NIST Special Publication 800-53, that provide equivalent or comparable protection for an information system.
Confidentiality [44 U.S.C., Sec. 3542]	Preserving authorized restrictions on information access and disclosure, including means for protecting personal privacy and proprietary information.
Configuration Control [CNSSI 4009]	Process for controlling modifications to hardware, firmware, software, and documentation to protect the information system against improper modifications before, during, and after system implementation.
Controlled Area	Any area or space for which the organization has confidence that the physical and procedural protections provided are sufficient to meet the requirements established for protecting the information and/or information system.
Controlled Unclassified Information	A categorical designation that refers to unclassified information that does not meet the standards for National Security Classification under Executive Order 12958, as amended, but is (i) pertinent to the national interests of the United States or to the important interests of entities outside the federal government, and (ii) under law or policy requires protection from unauthorized disclosure, special handling safeguards, or prescribed limits on exchange or dissemination. Henceforth, the designation CUI replaces *Sensitive But Unclassified (SBU)*.
Countermeasures [CNSSI 4009]	Actions, devices, procedures, techniques, or other measures that reduce the vulnerability of an information system. Synonymous with security controls and safeguards.
Defense-in-depth	Information security strategy integrating people, technology, and operations capabilities to establish variable barriers across multiple layers and missions of the organization.
Domain [CNSSI 4009]	An environment or context that includes a set of system resources and a set of system entities that have the right to access the resources as defined by a common security policy, security model, or security architecture. See *Security Domain*.

Executive Agency [41 U.S.C., Sec. 403]	An executive department specified in 5 U.S.C., Sec. 101; a military department specified in 5 U.S.C., Sec. 102; an independent establishment as defined in 5 U.S.C., Sec. 104(1); and a wholly owned Government corporation fully subject to the provisions of 31 U.S.C., Chapter 91.
External Information System (or Component)	An information system or component of an information system that is outside of the authorization boundary established by the organization and for which the organization typically has no direct control over the application of required security controls or the assessment of security control effectiveness.
External Information System Service	An information system service that is implemented outside of the authorization boundary of the organizational information system (i.e., a service that is used by, but not a part of, the organizational information system) and for which the organization typically has no direct control over the application of required security controls or the assessment of security control effectiveness.
External Information System Service Provider	A provider of external information system services to an organization through a variety of consumer-producer relationships including but not limited to: joint ventures; business partnerships; outsourcing arrangements (i.e., through contracts, interagency agreements, lines of business arrangements); licensing agreements; and/or supply chain exchanges.
External Network	A network not controlled by the organization.
Failover	The capability to switch over automatically (typically without human intervention or warning) to a redundant or standby information system upon the failure or abnormal termination of the previously active system.
Federal Agency	See *Executive Agency*.
Federal Enterprise Architecture [FEA Program Management Office]	A business-based framework for governmentwide improvement developed by the Office of Management and Budget that is intended to facilitate efforts to transform the federal government to one that is citizen-centered, results-oriented, and market-based.
Federal Information System [40 U.S.C., Sec. 11331]	An information system used or operated by an executive agency, by a contractor of an executive agency, or by another organization on behalf of an executive agency.
FIPS-Validated Cryptography	A cryptographic module validated by the Cryptographic Module Validation Program (CMVP) to meet requirements specified in FIPS 140-2 (as amended). As a prerequisite to CMVP validation, the cryptographic module is required to employ a cryptographic algorithm implementation that has successfully passed validation testing by the Cryptographic Algorithm Validation Program (CAVP). See *NSA-Approved Cryptography*.
Guard (System) [CNSSI 4009, Adapted]	A mechanism limiting the exchange of information between information systems or subsystems.

High-Impact System [FIPS 200]	An information system in which at least one security objective (i.e., confidentiality, integrity, or availability) is assigned a FIPS 199 potential impact value of high.
Hybrid Security Control	A security control that is implemented in an information system in part as a common control and in part as a system-specific control. See *Common Control* and *System-Specific Security Control*.
Identity-Based Access Control	Access control based on the identity of the user (typically relayed as a characteristic of the process acting on behalf of that user) where access authorizations to specific objects are assigned based on user identity.
Incident [FIPS 200]	An occurrence that actually or potentially jeopardizes the confidentiality, integrity, or availability of an information system or the information the system processes, stores, or transmits or that constitutes a violation or imminent threat of violation of security policies, security procedures, or acceptable use policies.
Industrial Control System	An information system used to control industrial processes such as manufacturing, product handling, production, and distribution. Industrial control systems include supervisory control and data acquisition (SCADA) systems used to control geographically dispersed assets, as well as distributed control systems (DCSs) and smaller control systems using programmable logic controllers to control localized processes.
Information [FIPS 199]	An instance of an information type.
Information Owner [CNSSI 4009]	Official with statutory or operational authority for specified information and responsibility for establishing the controls for its generation, collection, processing, dissemination, and disposal.
Information Resources [44 U.S.C., Sec. 3502]	Information and related resources, such as personnel, equipment, funds, and information technology.
Information Security [44 U.S.C., Sec. 3542]	The protection of information and information systems from unauthorized access, use, disclosure, disruption, modification, or destruction in order to provide confidentiality, integrity, and availability.
Information Security Policy [CNSSI 4009]	Aggregate of directives, regulations, rules, and practices that prescribes how an organization manages, protects, and distributes information.
Information Security Program Plan	Formal document that provides an overview of the security requirements for an organization-wide information security program and describes the program management controls and common controls in place or planned for meeting those requirements.

Information System [44 U.S.C., Sec. 3502]	A discrete set of information resources organized for the collection, processing, maintenance, use, sharing, dissemination, or disposition of information. [Note: Information systems also include specialized systems such as industrial/process controls systems, telephone switching and private branch exchange (PBX) systems, and environmental control systems.]
Information System Owner (or Program Manager)	Official responsible for the overall procurement, development, integration, modification, or operation and maintenance of an information system.
Information System Security Officer [CNSSI 4009]	Individual with assigned responsibility for maintaining the appropriate operational security posture for an information system or program.
Information Technology [40 U.S.C., Sec. 1401]	Any equipment or interconnected system or subsystem of equipment that is used in the automatic acquisition, storage, manipulation, management, movement, control, display, switching, interchange, transmission, or reception of data or information by the executive agency. For purposes of the preceding sentence, equipment is used by an executive agency if the equipment is used by the executive agency directly or is used by a contractor under a contract with the executive agency which: (i) requires the use of such equipment; or (ii) requires the use, to a significant extent, of such equipment in the performance of a service or the furnishing of a product. The term information technology includes computers, ancillary equipment, software, firmware, and similar procedures, services (including support services), and related resources.
Information Type [FIPS 199]	A specific category of information (e.g., privacy, medical, proprietary, financial, investigative, contractor sensitive, security management) defined by an organization or in some instances, by a specific law, Executive Order, directive, policy, or regulation.
Integrity [44 U.S.C., Sec. 3542]	Guarding against improper information modification or destruction, and includes ensuring information non-repudiation and authenticity.
Internal Network	A network where: (i) the establishment, maintenance, and provisioning of security controls are under the direct control of organizational employees or contractors; or (ii) cryptographic encapsulation or similar security technology implemented between organization-controlled endpoints, provides the same effect (at least with regard to confidentiality and integrity). An internal network is typically organization-owned, yet may be organization-controlled while not being organization-owned.
Label	See *Security Label*.

Line of Business	The following OMB-defined process areas common to virtually all federal agencies: Case Management, Financial Management, Grants Management, Human Resources Management, Federal Health Architecture, Information Systems Security, Budget Formulation and Execution, Geospatial, and IT Infrastructure.
Local Access	Access to an organizational information system by a user (or process acting on behalf of a user) communicating through a direct connection without the use of a network.
Low-Impact System [FIPS 200]	An information system in which all three security objectives (i.e., confidentiality, integrity, and availability) are assigned a FIPS 199 potential impact value of low.
Malicious Code	Software or firmware intended to perform an unauthorized process that will have adverse impact on the confidentiality, integrity, or availability of an information system. A virus, worm, Trojan horse, or other code-based entity that infects a host. Spyware and some forms of adware are also examples of malicious code.
Malware	See *Malicious Code*.
Management Controls [FIPS 200]	The security controls (i.e., safeguards or countermeasures) for an information system that focus on the management of risk and the management of information system security.
Marking	See *Security Marking*.
Media [FIPS 200]	Physical devices or writing surfaces including, but not limited to, magnetic tapes, optical disks, magnetic disks, Large-Scale Integration (LSI) memory chips, and printouts (but not including display media) onto which information is recorded, stored, or printed within an information system.
Mobile Code	Software programs or parts of programs obtained from remote information systems, transmitted across a network, and executed on a local information system without explicit installation or execution by the recipient.
Mobile Code Technologies	Software technologies that provide the mechanisms for the production and use of mobile code (e.g., Java, JavaScript, ActiveX, VBScript).
Mobile Device	Portable cartridge/disk-based, removable storage media (e.g., floppy disks, compact disks, USB flash drives, external hard drives, and other flash memory cards/drives that contain non-volatile memory). Portable computing and communications device with information storage capability (e.g., notebook/laptop computers, personal digital assistants, cellular telephones, digital cameras, and audio recording devices).

Moderate-Impact System [FIPS 200]	An information system in which at least one security objective (i.e., confidentiality, integrity, or availability) is assigned a FIPS 199 potential impact value of moderate and no security objective is assigned a FIPS 199 potential impact value of high.
Multifactor Authentication	Authentication using two or more factors to achieve authentication. Factors include: (i) something you know (e.g. password/PIN); (ii) something you have (e.g., cryptographic identification device, token); or (iii) something you are (e.g., biometric). See *Authenticator*.
National Security Emergency Preparedness Telecommunications Services [47 C.F.R., Part 64, App A]	Telecommunications services that are used to maintain a state of readiness or to respond to and manage any event or crisis (local, national, or international) that causes or could cause injury or harm to the population, damage to or loss of property, or degrade or threaten the national security or emergency preparedness posture of the United States.
National Security System [44 U.S.C., Sec. 3542]	Any information system (including any telecommunications system) used or operated by an agency or by a contractor of an agency, or other organization on behalf of an agency—(i) the function, operation, or use of which involves intelligence activities; involves cryptologic activities related to national security; involves command and control of military forces; involves equipment that is an integral part of a weapon or weapons system; or is critical to the direct fulfillment of military or intelligence missions (excluding a system that is to be used for routine administrative and business applications, for example, payroll, finance, logistics, and personnel management applications); or (ii) is protected at all times by procedures established for information that have been specifically authorized under criteria established by an Executive Order or an Act of Congress to be kept classified in the interest of national defense or foreign policy.
Network [CNSSI 4009]	Information system(s) implemented with a collection of interconnected components. Such components may include routers, hubs, cabling, telecommunications controllers, key distribution centers, and technical control devices.
Network Access	Access to an information system by a user (or a process acting on behalf of a user) communicating through a network (e.g., local area network, wide area network, Internet).
Non-Local Maintenance	Maintenance activities conducted by individuals communicating through a network; either an external network (e.g., the Internet) or an internal network.
Non-Organizational User	A user who is not an organizational user (including public users).

Non-repudiation	Protection against an individual falsely denying having performed a particular action. Provides the capability to determine whether a given individual took a particular action such as creating information, sending a message, approving information, and receiving a message.
NSA-Approved Cryptography	Cryptography that consists of: (i) an approved algorithm; (ii) an implementation that has been approved for the protection of classified information in a particular environment; and (iii) a supporting key management infrastructure.
Object	Passive information system-related entity (e.g., devices, files, records, tables, processes, programs, domains) containing or receiving information. Access to an object (by a subject) implies access to the information it contains. See *Subject*.
Operational Controls [FIPS 200]	The security controls (i.e., safeguards or countermeasures) for an information system that are primarily implemented and executed by people (as opposed to systems).
Organization [FIPS 200, Adapted]	An entity of any size, complexity, or positioning within an organizational structure (e.g., a federal agency or, as appropriate, any of its operational elements).
Organizational User	An organizational employee or an individual the organization deems to have equivalent status of an employee (e.g., contractor, guest researcher, individual detailed from another organization, individual from allied nation).
Penetration Testing	A test methodology in which assessors, typically working under specific constraints, attempt to circumvent or defeat the security features of an information system.
Plan of Action and Milestones [OMB Memorandum 02-01]	A document that identifies tasks needing to be accomplished. It details resources required to accomplish the elements of the plan, any milestones in meeting the tasks, and scheduled completion dates for the milestones.
Potential Impact [FIPS 199]	The loss of confidentiality, integrity, or availability could be expected to have: (i) a *limited* adverse effect (FIPS 199 low); (ii) a *serious* adverse effect (FIPS 199 moderate); or (iii) a *severe* or *catastrophic* adverse effect (FIPS 199 high) on organizational operations, organizational assets, or individuals.
Privacy Impact Assessment [OMB Memorandum 03-22]	An analysis of how information is handled: (i) to ensure handling conforms to applicable legal, regulatory, and policy requirements regarding privacy; (ii) to determine the risks and effects of collecting, maintaining, and disseminating information in identifiable form in an electronic information system; and (iii) to examine and evaluate protections and alternative processes for handling information to mitigate potential privacy risks.
Privileged Account	An information system account with authorizations of a privileged user.

Privileged Command	A human-initiated command executed on an information system involving the control, monitoring, or administration of the system including security functions and associated security-relevant information.
Privileged User [CNSSI 4009]	A user that is authorized (and therefore, trusted) to perform security-relevant functions that ordinary users are not authorized to perform.
Protective Distribution System	Wire line or fiber optic system that includes adequate safeguards and/or countermeasures (e.g., acoustic, electric, electromagnetic, and physical) to permit its use for the transmission of unencrypted information.
Reciprocity	Mutual agreement among participating enterprises to accept each other's security assessments in order to reuse information system resources and/or to accept each other's assessed security posture in order to share information.
Records	The recordings (automated and/or manual) of evidence of activities performed or results achieved (e.g., forms, reports, test results), which serve as a basis for verifying that the organization and the information system are performing as intended. Also used to refer to units of related data fields (i.e., groups of data fields that can be accessed by a program and that contain the complete set of information on particular items).
Red Team Exercise	An exercise, reflecting real-world conditions, that is conducted as a simulated adversarial attempt to compromise organizational missions and/or business processes to provide a comprehensive assessment of the security capability of the information system and organization.
Remote Access	Access to an organizational information system by a user (or a process acting on behalf of a user) communicating through an external network (e.g., the Internet).
Remote Maintenance	Maintenance activities conducted by individuals communicating through an external network (e.g., the Internet).
Removable Media	Portable electronic storage media such as magnetic, optical, and solid state devices, which can be inserted into and removed from a computing device, and that is used to store text, video, audio, and image information. Examples include hard disks, floppy disks, zip drives, compact disks, thumb drives, pen drives, and similar USB storage devices.
Restricted Data [Atomic Energy Act of 1954]	All data concerning (i) design, manufacture, or utilization of atomic weapons; (ii) the production of special nuclear material; or (iii) the use of special nuclear material in the production of energy, but shall not include data declassified or removed from the Restricted Data category pursuant to Section 142 [of the Atomic Energy Act of 1954].

Risk [FIPS 200, Adapted]	A measure of the extent to which an entity is threatened by a potential circumstance or event, and typically a function of: (i) the adverse impacts that would arise if the circumstance or event occurs; and (ii) the likelihood of occurrence. Information system-related security risks are those risks that arise from the loss of confidentiality, integrity, or availability of information or information systems and reflect the potential adverse impacts to organizational operations (including mission, functions, image, or reputation), organizational assets, individuals, other organizations, and the Nation.
Risk Assessment	The process of identifying risks to organizational operations (including mission, functions, image, reputation), organizational assets, individuals, other organizations, and the Nation, resulting from the operation of an information system. Part of risk management, incorporates threat and vulnerability analyses, and considers mitigations provided by security controls planned or in place. Synonymous with risk analysis.
Risk Management [FIPS 200, Adapted]	The process of managing risks to organizational operations (including mission, functions, image, reputation), organizational assets, individuals, other organizations, and the Nation, resulting from the operation of an information system, and includes: (i) the conduct of a risk assessment; (ii) the implementation of a risk mitigation strategy; and (iii) employment of techniques and procedures for the continuous monitoring of the security state of the information system.
Role-Based Access Control	Access control based on user roles (i.e., a collection of access authorizations a user receives based on an explicit or implicit assumption of a given role). Role permissions may be inherited through a role hierarchy and typically reflect the permissions needed to perform defined functions within an organization. A given role may apply to a single individual or to several individuals.
Safeguards [CNSSI 4009]	Protective measures prescribed to meet the security requirements (i.e., confidentiality, integrity, and availability) specified for an information system. Safeguards may include security features, management constraints, personnel security, and security of physical structures, areas, and devices. Synonymous with security controls and countermeasures.
Sanitization	A general term referring to the actions taken to render data written on media unrecoverable by both ordinary and, for some forms of sanitization, extraordinary means.

Scoping Guidance	A part of tailoring guidance providing organizations with specific policy/regulatory-related, technology-related, system component allocation-related, operational/environmental-related, physical infrastructure-related, public access-related, scalability-related, common control-related, and security objective-related considerations on the applicability and implementation of individual security controls in the security control baseline.
Security Attribute	An abstraction representing the basic properties or characteristics of an entity with respect to safeguarding information; typically associated with internal data structures (e.g., records, buffers, files) within the information system and used to enable the implementation of access control and flow control policies, reflect special dissemination, handling or distribution instructions, or support other aspects of the information security policy.
Security Authorization	See *Authorization*.
Security Authorization Boundary	See *Authorization Boundary*.
Security Categorization	The process of determining the security category for information or an information system. See *Security Category*.
Security Category [FIPS 199, Adapted]	The characterization of information or an information system based on an assessment of the potential impact that a loss of confidentiality, integrity, or availability of such information or information system would have on organizational operations, organizational assets, individuals, other organizations, and the Nation.
Security Control Assessment	The testing and/or evaluation of the management, operational, and technical security controls in an information system to determine the extent to which the controls are implemented correctly, operating as intended, and producing the desired outcome with respect to meeting the security requirements for the system.
Security Control Baseline [FIPS 200]	The set of minimum security controls defined for a low-impact, moderate-impact, or high-impact information system.
Security Control Enhancements	Statements of security capability to: (i) build in additional, but related, functionality to a security control; and/or (ii) increase the strength of the control.
Security Control Inheritance	A situation in which an information system or application receives protection from security controls (or portions of security controls) that are developed, implemented, assessed, authorized, and monitored by entities other than those responsible for the system or application; entities either internal or external to the organization where the system or application resides. See *Common Control*.

Security Controls [FIPS 199]	The management, operational, and technical controls (i.e., safeguards or countermeasures) prescribed for an information system to protect the confidentiality, integrity, and availability of the system and its information.
Security Domain [CNSSI 4009]	A domain that implements a security policy and is administered by a single authority.
Security Functions	The hardware, software, and/or firmware of the information system responsible for enforcing the system security policy and supporting the isolation of code and data on which the protection is based.
Security Impact Analysis	The analysis conducted by an organizational official to determine the extent to which changes to the information system have affected the security state of the system.
Security Incident	See *Incident*.
Security Label	The means used to associate a set of security attributes with a specific information object as part of the data structure for that object.
Security Marking	Human-readable information affixed to information system components, removable media, or output indicating the distribution limitations, handling caveats and applicable security markings.
Security Objective [FIPS 199]	Confidentiality, integrity, or availability.
Security Plan	Formal document that provides an overview of the security requirements for an information system or an information security program and describes the security controls in place or planned for meeting those requirements. See *System Security Plan* or *Information Security Program Plan*.
Security Policy [CNSSI 4009]	A set of criteria for the provision of security services.
Security Requirements [FIPS 200]	Requirements levied on an information system that are derived from applicable laws, Executive Orders, directives, policies, standards, instructions, regulations, procedures, or organizational mission/business case needs to ensure the confidentiality, integrity, and availability of the information being processed, stored, or transmitted.
Security-Relevant Information	Any information within the information system that can potentially impact the operation of security functions in a manner that could result in failure to enforce the system security policy or maintain isolation of code and data.

Senior (Agency) Information Security Officer [44 U.S.C., Sec. 3544]	Official responsible for carrying out the Chief Information Officer responsibilities under FISMA and serving as the Chief Information Officer's primary liaison to the agency's authorizing officials, information system owners, and information system security officers. Note: Organizations subordinate to federal agencies may use the term *Senior Information Security Officer* or *Chief Information Security Officer* to denote individuals filling positions with similar responsibilities to Senior Agency Information Security Officers.
Senior Information Security Officer	See *Senior Agency Information Security Officer*.
Sensitive Information [CNSSI 4009]	Information, the loss, misuse, or unauthorized access to or modification of, that could adversely affect the national interest or the conduct of federal programs, or the privacy to which individuals are entitled under 5 U.S.C. Section 552a (the Privacy Act), but that has not been specifically authorized under criteria established by an Executive Order or an Act of Congress to be kept classified in the interest of national defense or foreign policy.
Sensitive Compartmented Information [CNSSI 4009]	Classified information concerning or derived from intelligence sources, methods, or analytical processes, which is required to be handled within formal access control systems established by the Director of National Intelligence.
Spam	The abuse of electronic messaging systems to indiscriminately send unsolicited bulk messages.
Special Access Program [CNSSI 4009]	A program established for a specific class of classified information that imposes safeguarding and access requirements that exceed those normally required for information at the same classification level.
Spyware	Software that is secretly or surreptitiously installed into an information system to gather information on individuals or organizations without their knowledge; a type of malicious code.
Subject	Generally an individual, process, or device causing information to flow among objects or change to the system state. See *Object*.
Subsystem	A major subdivision or component of an information system consisting of information, information technology, and personnel that performs one or more specific functions.
Supply Chain	A system of organizations, people, activities, information, and resources, possibly international in scope, that provides products or services to consumers.
System	See *Information System*.
System Security Plan [NIST SP 800-18]	Formal document that provides an overview of the security requirements for an information system and describes the security controls in place or planned for meeting those requirements.

System-Specific Security Control	A security control for an information system that has not been designated as a common security control or the portion of a hybrid control that is to be implemented within an information system.
Tailored Security Control Baseline	A set of security controls resulting from the application of tailoring guidance to the security control baseline. See *Tailoring*.
Tailoring	The process by which a security control baseline is modified based on: (i) the application of scoping guidance; (ii) the specification of compensating security controls, if needed; and (iii) the specification of organization-defined parameters in the security controls via explicit assignment and selection statements.
Technical Controls [FIPS 200]	The security controls (i.e., safeguards or countermeasures) for an information system that are primarily implemented and executed by the information system through mechanisms contained in the hardware, software, or firmware components of the system.
Threat [CNSSI 4009, Adapted]	Any circumstance or event with the potential to adversely impact organizational operations (including mission, functions, image, or reputation), organizational assets, individuals, other organizations, or the Nation through an information system via unauthorized access, destruction, disclosure, modification of information, and/or denial of service.
Threat Assessment [CNSSI 4009]	Formal description and evaluation of threat to an information system.
Threat Source [FIPS 200]	The intent and method targeted at the intentional exploitation of a vulnerability or a situation and method that may accidentally trigger a vulnerability. Synonymous with threat agent.
Trusted Path	A mechanism by which a user (through an input device) can communicate directly with the security functions of the information system with the necessary confidence to support the system security policy. This mechanism can only be activated by the user or the security functions of the information system and cannot be imitated by untrusted software.
User [CNSSI 4009, adapted]	Individual, or (system) process acting on behalf of an individual, authorized to access an information system. See *Organizational User* and *Non-Organizational User*.
Vulnerability [CNSSI 4009]	Weakness in an information system, system security procedures, internal controls, or implementation that could be exploited or triggered by a threat source.
Vulnerability Assessment [CNSSI 4009]	Formal description and evaluation of the vulnerabilities in an information system.

APPENDIX C

ACRONYMS

COMMON ABBREVIATIONS

CFR	Code of Federal Regulations
CIO	Chief Information Officer
CISO	Chief Information Security Officer
CNSS	Committee on National Security Systems
CUI	Controlled Unclassified Information
DNS	Domain Name System
DOD	Department of Defense
FIPS	Federal Information Processing Standards
FISMA	Federal Information Security Management Act
HSPD	Homeland Security Presidential Directive
ICS	Industrial Control System
IEEE	Institute of Electrical and Electronics Engineers
IPsec	Internet Protocol Security
ISO/IEC	International Organization for Standardization/International Electrotechnical Commission
NIST	National Institute of Standards and Technology
NSA	National Security Agency
NSTISSI	National Security Telecommunications and Information System Security Instruction
ODNI	Office of the Director of National Intelligence
OMB	Office of Management and Budget
PIV	Personal Identity Verification
PKI	Public Key Infrastructure
RD	Restricted Data
SAISO	Senior Agency Information Security Officer
SAMI	Sources And Methods Information
SBU	Sensitive But Unclassified
SCI	Sensitive Compartmented Information
TSP	Telecommunications Service Priority
VoIP	Voice over Internet Protocol
VPN	Virtual Private Network

APPENDIX D

SECURITY CONTROL BASELINES — SUMMARY
LOW-IMPACT, MODERATE-IMPACT, AND HIGH-IMPACT INFORMATION SYSTEMS

T his appendix contains the security control baselines that represent the starting point in determining the security controls for low-impact, moderate-impact, and high-impact information systems.[71] The three security control baselines are hierarchical in nature with regard to the security controls employed in those baselines.[72] If a security control is selected for one of the baselines, the security control family identifier and control number are listed in the appropriate column. If a control is not used in a particular baseline, the entry is marked "not selected." Control enhancements, when used to supplement security controls, are indicated by the number of the control enhancement. For example, an "IR-2 (1)" in the high baseline entry for the IR-2 security control indicates that the second control from the Incident Response family has been selected along with control enhancement (1). Note that some security controls and enhancements in the security control catalog are not used in any of the baselines in this appendix but are available for use by organizations if needed; for example, when the results of a risk assessment indicate the need for additional controls or control enhancements in order to adequately mitigate risk to organizational operations and organizational assets, individuals, other organizations, and the Nation.

Organizations can use the recommended *priority code* designation associated with each security control in the baselines to assist in making sequencing decisions for control implementation (i.e., a Priority Code 1 [P1] control has a higher priority for implementation than a Priority Code 2 [P2] control; a Priority Code 2 (P2) control has a higher priority for implementation than a Priority Code 3 [P3] control). This recommended sequencing prioritization helps ensure that foundational security controls upon which other controls depend are implemented first, thus enabling organizations to deploy controls in a more structured and timely manner in accordance with available resources. The implementation of security controls by sequence priority code does not imply the achievement of any defined level of risk mitigation until *all* of the security controls in the security plan have been implemented. The priority codes are used only for implementation sequencing, not for making security control selection decisions. Table D-1 summarizes sequence priority codes for the baseline security controls in Table D-2.

TABLE D-1: SECURITY CONTROL PRIORITIZATION CODES

Priority Code	Sequencing	Action
Priority Code 1 (P1)	FIRST	Implement P1 security controls first.
Priority Code 2 (P2)	NEXT	Implement P2 security controls after implementation of P1 controls.
Priority Code 3 (P3)	LAST	Implement P3 security controls after implementation of P1 and P2 controls.
Unspecified Priority Code (P0)	NONE	Security control not selected for baseline.

---

[71] A complete description of all security controls is provided in Appendices F and G. In addition, separate documents for individual security control baselines (listed as Annexes 1, 2, and 3) are available at http://csrc.nist.gov/publications.

[72] The hierarchical nature applies to the security requirements of each control (i.e., the base control plus all of its enhancements) at the low-impact, moderate-impact, and high-impact level in that the control requirements at a particular impact level (e.g., CP-4 *Contingency Plan Testing and Exercises*—Moderate: CP-4 (1)) meets a stronger set of security requirements for that control than the next lower impact level of the same control (e.g., CP-4 *Contingency Plan Testing and Exercises*—Low: CP-4).

In addition to Table D-2, the sequence priority codes and security control baselines are annotated in a priority and baseline allocation summary section below each security control in Appendix F.

TABLE D-2: SECURITY CONTROL BASELINES

CNTL NO.	CONTROL NAME	PRIORITY	CONTROL BASELINES		
			LOW	MOD	HIGH
	Access Control				
AC-1	Access Control Policy and Procedures	P1	AC-1	AC-1	AC-1
AC-2	Account Management	P1	AC-2	AC-2 (1) (2) (3) (4)	AC-2 (1) (2) (3) (4)
AC-3	Access Enforcement	P1	AC-3	AC-3	AC-3
AC-4	Information Flow Enforcement	P1	Not Selected	AC-4	AC-4
AC-5	Separation of Duties	P1	Not Selected	AC-5	AC-5
AC-6	Least Privilege	P1	Not Selected	AC-6 (1) (2)	AC-6 (1) (2)
AC-7	Unsuccessful Login Attempts	P2	AC-7	AC-7	AC-7
AC-8	System Use Notification	P1	AC-8	AC-8	AC-8
AC-9	Previous Logon (Access) Notification	P0	Not Selected	Not Selected	Not Selected
AC-10	Concurrent Session Control	P2	Not Selected	Not Selected	AC-10
AC-11	Session Lock	P3	Not Selected	AC-11	AC-11
AC-12	Session Termination (Withdrawn)	---	---	---	---
AC-13	Supervision and Review—Access Control (Withdrawn)	---	---	---	---
AC-14	Permitted Actions without Identification or Authentication	P1	AC-14	AC-14 (1)	AC-14 (1)
AC-15	Automated Marking (Withdrawn)	---	---	---	---
AC-16	Security Attributes	P0	Not Selected	Not Selected	Not Selected
AC-17	Remote Access	P1	AC-17	AC-17 (1) (2) (3) (4) (5) (7) (8)	AC-17 (1) (2) (3) (4) (5) (7) (8)
AC-18	Wireless Access	P1	AC-18	AC-18 (1)	AC-18 (1) (2) (4) (5)
AC-19	Access Control for Mobile Devices	P1	AC-19	AC-19 (1) (2) (3)	AC-19 (1) (2) (3)
AC-20	Use of External Information Systems	P1	AC-20	AC-20 (1) (2)	AC-20 (1) (2)
AC-21	User-Based Collaboration and Information Sharing	P0	Not Selected	Not Selected	Not Selected
AC-22	Publicly Accessible Content	P2	AC-22	AC-22	AC-22
	Awareness and Training				
AT-1	Security Awareness and Training Policy and Procedures	P1	AT-1	AT-1	AT-1
AT-2	Security Awareness	P1	AT-2	AT-2	AT-2
AT-3	Security Training	P1	AT-3	AT-3	AT-3
AT-4	Security Training Records	P3	AT-4	AT-4	AT-4
AT-5	Contacts with Security Groups and Associations	P0	Not Selected	Not Selected	Not Selected
	Audit and Accountability				
AU-1	Audit and Accountability Policy and Procedures	P1	AU-1	AU-1	AU-1
AU-2	Auditable Events	P1	AU-2	AU-2 (3) (4)	AU-2 (3) (4)

CNTL NO.	CONTROL NAME	PRIORITY	CONTROL BASELINES		
			LOW	MOD	HIGH
AU-3	Content of Audit Records	P1	AU-3	AU-3 (1)	AU-3 (1) (2)
AU-4	Audit Storage Capacity	P1	AU-4	AU-4	AU-4
AU-5	Response to Audit Processing Failures	P1	AU-5	AU-5	AU-5 (1) (2)
AU-6	Audit Review, Analysis, and Reporting	P1	AU-6	AU-6	AU-6 (1)
AU-7	Audit Reduction and Report Generation	P2	Not Selected	AU-7 (1)	AU-7 (1)
AU-8	Time Stamps	P1	AU-8	AU-8 (1)	AU-8 (1)
AU-9	Protection of Audit Information	P1	AU-9	AU-9	AU-9
AU-10	Non-repudiation	P1	Not Selected	Not Selected	AU-10
AU-11	Audit Record Retention	P3	AU-11	AU-11	AU-11
AU-12	Audit Generation	P1	AU-12	AU-12	AU-12 (1)
AU-13	Monitoring for Information Disclosure	P0	Not Selected	Not Selected	Not Selected
AU-14	Session Audit	P0	Not Selected	Not Selected	Not Selected
Security Assessment and Authorization					
CA-1	Security Assessment and Authorization Policies and Procedures	P1	CA-1	CA-1	CA-1
CA-2	Security Assessments	P2	CA-2	CA-2 (1)	CA-2 (1) (2)
CA-3	Information System Connections	P1	CA-3	CA-3	CA-3
CA-4	Security Certification (Withdrawn)	---	---	---	---
CA-5	Plan of Action and Milestones	P3	CA-5	CA-5	CA-5
CA-6	Security Authorization	P3	CA-6	CA-6	CA-6
CA-7	Continuous Monitoring	P3	CA-7	CA-7	CA-7
Configuration Management					
CM-1	Configuration Management Policy and Procedures	P1	CM-1	CM-1	CM-1
CM-2	Baseline Configuration	P1	CM-2	CM-2 (1) (3) (4)	CM-2 (1) (2) (3) (5) (6)
CM-3	Configuration Change Control	P1	Not Selected	CM-3 (2)	CM-3 (1) (2)
CM-4	Security Impact Analysis	P2	CM-4	CM-4	CM-4 (1)
CM-5	Access Restrictions for Change	P1	Not Selected	CM-5	CM-5 (1) (2) (3)
CM-6	Configuration Settings	P1	CM-6	CM-6 (3)	CM-6 (1) (2) (3)
CM-7	Least Functionality	P1	CM-7	CM-7 (1)	CM-7 (1) (2)
CM-8	Information System Component Inventory	P1	CM-8	CM-8 (1) (5)	CM-8 (1) (2) (3) (4) (5)
CM-9	Configuration Management Plan	P1	Not Selected	CM-9	CM-9
Contingency Planning					
CP-1	Contingency Planning Policy and Procedures	P1	CP-1	CP-1	CP-1
CP-2	Contingency Plan	P1	CP-2	CP-2 (1)	CP-2 (1) (2) (3)
CP-3	Contingency Training	P2	CP-3	CP-3	CP-3 (1)
CP-4	Contingency Plan Testing and Exercises	P2	CP-4	CP-4 (1)	CP-4 (1) (2) (4)
CP-5	Contingency Plan Update (Withdrawn)	---	---	---	---
CP-6	Alternate Storage Site	P1	Not Selected	CP-6 (1) (3)	CP-6 (1) (2) (3)
CP-7	Alternate Processing Site	P1	Not Selected	CP-7 (1) (2) (3) (5)	CP-7 (1) (2) (3) (4) (5)

CNTL NO.	CONTROL NAME	PRIORITY	CONTROL BASELINES		
			LOW	MOD	HIGH
CP-8	Telecommunications Services	P1	Not Selected	CP-8 (1) (2)	CP-8 (1) (2) (3) (4)
CP-9	Information System Backup	P1	CP-9	CP-9 (1)	CP-9 (1) (2) (3)
CP-10	Information System Recovery and Reconstitution	P1	CP-10	CP-10 (2) (3)	CP-10 (2) (3) (4)
Identification and Authentication					
IA-1	Identification and Authentication Policy and Procedures	P1	IA-1	IA-1	IA-1
IA-2	Identification and Authentication (Organizational Users)	P1	IA-2 (1)	IA-2 (1) (2) (3) (8)	IA-2 (1) (2) (3) (4) (8) (9)
IA-3	Device Identification and Authentication	P1	Not Selected	IA-3	IA-3
IA-4	Identifier Management	P1	IA-4	IA-4	IA-4
IA-5	Authenticator Management	P1	IA-5 (1)	IA-5 (1) (2) (3)	IA-5 (1) (2) (3)
IA-6	Authenticator Feedback	P1	IA-6	IA-6	IA-6
IA-7	Cryptographic Module Authentication	P1	IA-7	IA-7	IA-7
IA-8	Identification and Authentication (Non-Organizational Users)	P1	IA-8	IA-8	IA-8
Incident Response					
IR-1	Incident Response Policy and Procedures	P1	IR-1	IR-1	IR-1
IR-2	Incident Response Training	P2	IR-2	IR-2	IR-2 (1) (2)
IR-3	Incident Response Testing and Exercises	P2	Not Selected	IR-3	IR-3 (1)
IR-4	Incident Handling	P1	IR-4	IR-4 (1)	IR-4 (1)
IR-5	Incident Monitoring	P1	IR-5	IR-5	IR-5 (1)
IR-6	Incident Reporting	P1	IR-6	IR-6 (1)	IR-6 (1)
IR-7	Incident Response Assistance	P3	IR-7	IR-7 (1)	IR-7 (1)
IR-8	Incident Response Plan	P1	IR-8	IR-8	IR-8
Maintenance					
MA-1	System Maintenance Policy and Procedures	P1	MA-1	MA-1	MA-1
MA-2	Controlled Maintenance	P2	MA-2	MA-2 (1)	MA-2 (1) (2)
MA-3	Maintenance Tools	P2	Not Selected	MA-3 (1) (2)	MA-3 (1) (2) (3)
MA-4	Non-Local Maintenance	P1	MA-4	MA-4 (1) (2)	MA-4 (1) (2) (3)
MA-5	Maintenance Personnel	P1	MA-5	MA-5	MA-5
MA-6	Timely Maintenance	P1	Not Selected	MA-6	MA-6
Media Protection					
MP-1	Media Protection Policy and Procedures	P1	MP-1	MP-1	MP-1
MP-2	Media Access	P1	MP-2	MP-2 (1)	MP-2 (1)
MP-3	Media Marking	P1	Not Selected	MP-3	MP-3
MP-4	Media Storage	P1	Not Selected	MP-4	MP-4
MP-5	Media Transport	P1	Not Selected	MP-5 (2) (4)	MP-5 (2) (3) (4)
MP-6	Media Sanitization	P1	MP-6	MP-6	MP-6 (1) (2) (3)
Physical and Environmental Protection					
PE-1	Physical and Environmental Protection Policy and Procedures	P1	PE-1	PE-1	PE-1
PE-2	Physical Access Authorizations	P1	PE-2	PE-2	PE-2
PE-3	Physical Access Control	P1	PE-3	PE-3	PE-3 (1)

CNTL NO.	CONTROL NAME	PRIORITY	CONTROL BASELINES		
			LOW	MOD	HIGH
PE-4	Access Control for Transmission Medium	P1	Not Selected	PE-4	PE-4
PE-5	Access Control for Output Devices	P1	Not Selected	PE-5	PE-5
PE-6	Monitoring Physical Access	P1	PE-6	PE-6 (1)	PE-6 (1) (2)
PE-7	Visitor Control	P1	PE-7	PE-7 (1)	PE-7 (1)
PE-8	Access Records	P3	PE-8	PE-8	PE-8 (1) (2)
PE-9	Power Equipment and Power Cabling	P1	Not Selected	PE-9	PE-9
PE-10	Emergency Shutoff	P1	Not Selected	PE-10	PE-10
PE-11	Emergency Power	P1	Not Selected	PE-11	PE-11 (1)
PE-12	Emergency Lighting	P1	PE-12	PE-12	PE-12
PE-13	Fire Protection	P1	PE-13	PE-13 (1) (2) (3)	PE-13 (1) (2) (3)
PE-14	Temperature and Humidity Controls	P1	PE-14	PE-14	PE-14
PE-15	Water Damage Protection	P1	PE-15	PE-15	PE-15 (1)
PE-16	Delivery and Removal	P1	PE-16	PE-16	PE-16
PE-17	Alternate Work Site	P1	Not Selected	PE-17	PE-17
PE-18	Location of Information System Components	P2	Not Selected	PE-18	PE-18 (1)
PE-19	Information Leakage	P0	Not Selected	Not Selected	Not Selected
Planning					
PL-1	Security Planning Policy and Procedures	P1	PL-1	PL-1	PL-1
PL-2	System Security Plan	P1	PL-2	PL-2	PL-2
PL-3	System Security Plan Update (Withdrawn)	---	---	---	---
PL-4	Rules of Behavior	P1	PL-4	PL-4	PL-4
PL-5	Privacy Impact Assessment	P1	PL-5	PL-5	PL-5
PL-6	Security-Related Activity Planning	P3	Not Selected	PL-6	PL-6
Personnel Security					
PS-1	Personnel Security Policy and Procedures	P1	PS-1	PS-1	PS-1
PS-2	Position Categorization	P1	PS-2	PS-2	PS-2
PS-3	Personnel Screening	P1	PS-3	PS-3	PS-3
PS-4	Personnel Termination	P2	PS-4	PS-4	PS-4
PS-5	Personnel Transfer	P2	PS-5	PS-5	PS-5
PS-6	Access Agreements	P3	PS-6	PS-6	PS-6
PS-7	Third-Party Personnel Security	P1	PS-7	PS-7	PS-7
PS-8	Personnel Sanctions	P3	PS-8	PS-8	PS-8
Risk Assessment					
RA-1	Risk Assessment Policy and Procedures	P1	RA-1	RA-1	RA-1
RA-2	Security Categorization	P1	RA-2	RA-2	RA-2
RA-3	Risk Assessment	P1	RA-3	RA-3	RA-3
RA-4	Risk Assessment Update (Withdrawn)	---	---	---	---
RA-5	Vulnerability Scanning	P1	RA-5	RA-5 (1)	RA-5 (1) (2) (3) (4) (5) (7)
System and Services Acquisition					
SA-1	System and Services Acquisition Policy and Procedures	P1	SA-1	SA-1	SA-1
SA-2	Allocation of Resources	P1	SA-2	SA-2	SA-2

CNTL NO.	CONTROL NAME	PRIORITY	CONTROL BASELINES		
			LOW	MOD	HIGH
SA-3	Life Cycle Support	P1	SA-3	SA-3	SA-3
SA-4	Acquisitions	P1	SA-4	SA-4 (1) (4)	SA-4 (1) (2) (4)
SA-5	Information System Documentation	P2	SA-5	SA-5 (1) (3)	SA-5 (1) (2) (3)
SA-6	Software Usage Restrictions	P1	SA-6	SA-6	SA-6
SA-7	User-Installed Software	P1	SA-7	SA-7	SA-7
SA-8	Security Engineering Principles	P1	Not Selected	SA-8	SA-8
SA-9	External Information System Services	P1	SA-9	SA-9	SA-9
SA-10	Developer Configuration Management	P1	Not Selected	SA-10	SA-10
SA-11	Developer Security Testing	P2	Not Selected	SA-11	SA-11
SA-12	Supply Chain Protection	P1	Not Selected	Not Selected	SA-12
SA-13	Trustworthiness	P1	Not Selected	Not Selected	SA-13
SA-14	Critical Information System Components	P0	Not Selected	Not Selected	Not Selected
System and Communications Protection					
SC-1	System and Communications Protection Policy and Procedures	P1	SC-1	SC-1	SC-1
SC-2	Application Partitioning	P1	Not Selected	SC-2	SC-2
SC-3	Security Function Isolation	P1	Not Selected	Not Selected	SC-3
SC-4	Information in Shared Resources	P1	Not Selected	SC-4	SC-4
SC-5	Denial of Service Protection	P1	SC-5	SC-5	SC-5
SC-6	Resource Priority	P0	Not Selected	Not Selected	Not Selected
SC-7	Boundary Protection	P1	SC-7	SC-7 (1) (2) (3) (4) (5) (7)	SC-7 (1) (2) (3) (4) (5) (6) (7) (8)
SC-8	Transmission Integrity	P1	Not Selected	SC-8 (1)	SC-8 (1)
SC-9	Transmission Confidentiality	P1	Not Selected	SC-9 (1)	SC-9 (1)
SC-10	Network Disconnect	P2	Not Selected	SC-10	SC-10
SC-11	Trusted Path	P0	Not Selected	Not Selected	Not Selected
SC-12	Cryptographic Key Establishment and Management	P1	SC-12	SC-12	SC-12 (1)
SC-13	Use of Cryptography	P1	SC-13	SC-13	SC-13
SC-14	Public Access Protections	P1	SC-14	SC-14	SC-14
SC-15	Collaborative Computing Devices	P1	SC-15	SC-15	SC-15
SC-16	Transmission of Security Attributes	P0	Not Selected	Not Selected	Not Selected
SC-17	Public Key Infrastructure Certificates	P1	Not Selected	SC-17	SC-17
SC-18	Mobile Code	P1	Not Selected	SC-18	SC-18
SC-19	Voice Over Internet Protocol	P1	Not Selected	SC-19	SC-19
SC-20	Secure Name /Address Resolution Service (Authoritative Source)	P1	SC-20 (1)	SC-20 (1)	SC-20 (1)
SC-21	Secure Name /Address Resolution Service (Recursive or Caching Resolver)	P1	Not Selected	Not Selected	SC-21
SC-22	Architecture and Provisioning for Name/Address Resolution Service	P1	Not Selected	SC-22	SC-22
SC-23	Session Authenticity	P1	Not Selected	SC-23	SC-23
SC-24	Fail in Known State	P1	Not Selected	Not Selected	SC-24
SC-25	Thin Nodes	P0	Not Selected	Not Selected	Not Selected

CNTL NO.	CONTROL NAME	PRIORITY	CONTROL BASELINES		
			LOW	MOD	HIGH
SC-26	Honeypots	P0	Not Selected	Not Selected	Not Selected
SC-27	Operating System-Independent Applications	P0	Not Selected	Not Selected	Not Selected
SC-28	Protection of Information at Rest	P1	Not Selected	SC-28	SC-28
SC-29	Heterogeneity	P0	Not Selected	Not Selected	Not Selected
SC-30	Virtualization Techniques	P0	Not Selected	Not Selected	Not Selected
SC-31	Covert Channel Analysis	P0	Not Selected	Not Selected	Not Selected
SC-32	Information System Partitioning	P1	Not Selected	SC-32	SC-32
SC-33	Transmission Preparation Integrity	P0	Not Selected	Not Selected	Not Selected
SC-34	Non-Modifiable Executable Programs	P0	Not Selected	Not Selected	Not Selected
System and Information Integrity					
SI-1	System and Information Integrity Policy and Procedures	P1	SI-1	SI-1	SI-1
SI-2	Flaw Remediation	P1	SI-2	SI-2 (2)	SI-2 (1) (2)
SI-3	Malicious Code Protection	P1	SI-3	SI-3 (1) (2) (3)	SI-3 (1) (2) (3)
SI-4	Information System Monitoring	P1	Not Selected	SI-4 (2) (4) (5) (6)	SI-4 (2) (4) (5) (6)
SI-5	Security Alerts, Advisories, and Directives	P1	SI-5	SI-5	SI-5 (1)
SI-6	Security Functionality Verification	P1	Not Selected	Not Selected	SI-6
SI-7	Software and Information Integrity	P1	Not Selected	SI-7 (1)	SI-7 (1) (2)
SI-8	Spam Protection	P1	Not Selected	SI-8	SI-8 (1)
SI-9	Information Input Restrictions	P2	Not Selected	SI-9	SI-9
SI-10	Information Input Validation	P1	Not Selected	SI-10	SI-10
SI-11	Error Handling	P2	Not Selected	SI-11	SI-11
SI-12	Information Output Handling and Retention	P2	SI-12	SI-12	SI-12
SI-13	Predictable Failure Prevention	P0	Not Selected	Not Selected	Not Selected
Program Management					
PM-1	Information Security Program Plan	P1			
PM-2	Senior Information Security Officer	P1			
PM-3	Information Security Resources	P1			
PM-4	Plan of Action and Milestones Process	P1			
PM-5	Information System Inventory	P1			
PM-6	Information Security Measures of Performance	P1	**Deployed organization-wide Supporting all baselines**		
PM-7	Enterprise Architecture	P1			
PM-8	Critical Infrastructure Plan	P1			
PM-9	Risk Management Strategy	P1			
PM-10	Security Authorization Process	P1			
PM-11	Mission/Business Process Definition	P1			

APPENDIX E

MINIMUM ASSURANCE REQUIREMENTS
LOW-IMPACT, MODERATE-IMPACT, AND HIGH-IMPACT INFORMATION SYSTEMS

T he minimum assurance requirements for security controls described in the security control catalog are listed below. The assurance requirements are directed at the activities and actions that security control developers and implementers[73] define and apply to increase the level of confidence that the controls are implemented correctly, operating as intended, and producing the desired outcome with respect to meeting the security requirements for the information system. The assurance requirements are applied on a control-by-control basis. The requirements are grouped by information system impact level (i.e., low, moderate, and high) since the requirements apply to each control within the respective impact level. Using a format similar to security controls, assurance requirements are followed by supplemental guidance that provides additional detail and explanation of how the requirements are to be applied. Bolded text indicates requirements that appear for the first time at a particular impact level.

Low-Impact Information Systems

Assurance Requirement: **The security control is in effect and meets explicitly identified functional requirements in the control statement.**

Supplemental Guidance: For security controls in low-impact information systems, the focus is on the controls being in place with the expectation that no obvious errors exist and that, as flaws are discovered, they are addressed in a timely manner.

Moderate-Impact Information Systems

Assurance Requirement: The security control is in effect and meets explicitly identified functional requirements in the control statement. **The control developer/implementer provides a description of the functional properties of the control with sufficient detail to permit analysis and testing of the control. The control developer/implementer includes as an integral part of the control, assigned responsibilities and specific actions supporting increased confidence that when the control is implemented, it will meet its required function or purpose. These actions include, for example, requiring the development of records with structure and content suitable to facilitate making this determination.**

Supplemental Guidance: For security controls in moderate-impact information systems, the focus is on actions supporting increased confidence in the correct implementation and operation of the control. While flaws are still likely to be uncovered (and addressed expeditiously), the control developer/implementer incorporates, as part of the control, specific capabilities and produces specific documentation supporting increased confidence that the control meets its required function or purpose. This documentation is also needed by assessors to analyze and test the functional properties of the control as part of the overall assessment of the control.

Note: This level of assurance is not intended to protect a moderate-impact information system against high-end threat agents (i.e., threat agents that are highly skilled, highly motivated, and well-resourced). When such protection is required, the section below entitled *Additional Assurance Requirements for Moderate-Impact and High-Impact Information Systems* applies.

---

[73] In this context, a developer/implementer is an individual or group of individuals responsible for the development or implementation of security controls. This may include in addition to organizational personnel, for example, hardware and software vendors providing the controls and contractors implementing the controls.

High-Impact Information Systems

<u>Assurance Requirement</u>: The security control is in effect and meets explicitly identified functional requirements in the control statement. The control developer/implementer provides a description of the functional properties **and design/implementation** of the control with sufficient detail to permit analysis and testing of the control (**including functional interfaces among control components**). The control developer/implementer includes as an integral part of the control, assigned responsibilities and specific actions supporting increased confidence that when the control is implemented, it will **continuously and consistently (i.e., across the information system)** meet its required function or purpose **and support improvement in the effectiveness of the control**. These actions include, for example, requiring the development of records with structure and content suitable to facilitate making this determination.

<u>Supplemental Guidance</u>: For security controls in high-impact information systems, the focus is expanded to require, within the control, the capabilities that are needed to support ongoing consistent operation of the control and continuous improvement in the control's effectiveness. The developer/implementer is expected to expend significant effort on the design, development, implementation, and component/integration testing of the controls and to produce associated design and implementation documentation to support these activities. This documentation is also needed by assessors to analyze and test the internal components of the control as part of the overall assessment of the control.

Note: This level of assurance is not intended to protect a high-impact information system against high-end threat agents (i.e., threat agents that are highly skilled, highly motivated, and well-resourced). When such protection is required, the section below entitled *Additional Assurance Requirements for Moderate-Impact and High-Impact Information Systems* applies.

Additional Assurance Requirements for Moderate-Impact and High-Impact Information Systems

<u>Assurance Requirement</u>: The security control is in effect and meets explicitly identified functional requirements in the control statement. The control developer/implementer provides a description of the functional properties and design/implementation of the control with sufficient detail to permit analysis and testing of the control. The control developer/implementer includes as an integral part of the control, actions supporting increased confidence that when the control is implemented, it will continuously and consistently (i.e., across the information system) meet its required function or purpose and support improvement in the effectiveness of the control. These actions include requiring the development of records with structure and content suitable to facilitate making this determination. **The control is developed in a manner that supports a high degree of confidence that the control is complete, consistent, and correct.**

<u>Supplemental Guidance</u>: The additional high assurance requirements are intended to supplement the minimum assurance requirements for moderate-impact and high-impact information systems, when appropriate, in order to protect against threats from highly skilled, highly motivated, and well-resourced threat agents. This level of protection is necessary for those information systems where the organization is not willing to accept the risks associated with the type of threat agents cited above.

SECURITY CONTROL CATALOG
SECURITY CONTROLS, ENHANCEMENTS, AND SUPPLEMENTAL GUIDANCE

The catalog of security controls in this appendix provides a range of safeguards and countermeasures for organizations and information systems. The organization of the security control catalog, the structure of the controls, and the concept of allocating security controls and control enhancements to the initial baselines in Appendix D are described in Chapter Two. The security controls in the catalog are expected to change over time, as controls are withdrawn, revised and added. In order to maintain stability in security plans and automated tools supporting the implementation of NIST Special Publication 800-53, security controls and control enhancements will not be renumbered each time a control or enhancement is withdrawn. Notations of security controls and controls enhancements that have been withdrawn will be maintained in the catalog for historical purposes.

About the Catalog

Security controls and control enhancements in Appendices F and G are generally designed to be policy-neutral and technology/implementation independent. Additional information about security controls and control enhancements can be provided in two ways:

- By establishing specific values in the variable sections of selected security controls (i.e., *assignment* and *selection* statements); and

- By specifying security control implementation detail (e.g., platform dependencies) in the associated security plan for the information system or security program plan for the organization.

Assignment and selection statements provide organizations with the capability to specialize security controls and control enhancements based on organizational security requirements and/or requirements originating in federal laws, Executive Orders, directives, policies, regulations, standards, or guidelines. Security control enhancements are used to strengthen or broaden the fundamental security capability described in the base control and are not used as a substitute for using assignment or selection statements to add greater specificity to the control. The first security control in each family (a.k.a. the *dash one* control) generates the requirement for policy and procedures that are needed for the effective implementation of the other security controls and control enhancements in the family. Therefore, the individual controls/enhancements in the family typically do not call for the development of such policy and procedures.

Security controls and control enhancements are employed in federal information systems in accordance with the risk management guidance provided in NIST Special Publication 800-39 as summarized in Chapter Three of this publication. This guidance includes selecting baseline security controls (see Appendix D) in accordance with the FIPS 199 security category of the information system and the FIPS 200 system impact level, and subsequently tailoring the baseline. The tailored security control baseline represents the minimum controls for low-impact, moderate-impact, and high-impact information systems, respectively. There are additional security controls and control enhancements that appear in the catalog that are not used in any of the baselines. These additional controls and control enhancements are available to organizations and can be used in supplementing the tailored baselines to achieve the needed level of protection in accordance with an organizational assessment of risk. Moreover, security controls and control enhancements contained in higher-level baselines can also be used in lower-level baselines, if deemed appropriate, to provide additional protection measures.

Beginning with NIST Special Publication 800-53, Revision 3, the supplemental guidance sections for security controls and control enhancements contain no requirements or references to FIPS or NIST Special Publications. NIST publications are included in a new *References* section that has been added to the general description and content of the security control specification. In addition, minimum and maximum values (e.g., testing contingency plans *at least annually*) have been removed from the assignment statements in security controls. Organizations should consult specific federal laws, Executive Orders, directives, policies, regulations, standards, or guidelines as the definitive sources for such information. Removal of minimum and maximum values from the security controls does not obviate the need of organizations to comply with requirements in the controlling source publications.

Finally, in support of the Joint Task Force Transformation Initiative to develop a unified information security framework for the federal government, security controls for national security systems are included in the security control catalog. The inclusion of these security controls is not intended to impose security requirements on organizations that operate national security systems; rather, the controls are available to use on a voluntary basis with the approval of appropriate federal officials exercising policy authority over such systems. In addition, the security control priorities and security control baselines listed in Appendix D and in the priority and baseline allocation summary boxes below each security control in Appendix F, apply to nonnational security systems *only* unless otherwise directed by the aforementioned federal officials with national security policy authority.

FAMILY: ACCESS CONTROL   **CLASS:** TECHNICAL

AC-1   **ACCESS CONTROL POLICY AND PROCEDURES**

Control: The organization develops, disseminates, and reviews/updates [*Assignment: organization-defined frequency*]:

a. A formal, documented access control policy that addresses purpose, scope, roles, responsibilities, management commitment, coordination among organizational entities, and compliance; and

b. Formal, documented procedures to facilitate the implementation of the access control policy and associated access controls.

Supplemental Guidance: This control is intended to produce the policy and procedures that are required for the effective implementation of selected security controls and control enhancements in the access control family. The policy and procedures are consistent with applicable federal laws, Executive Orders, directives, policies, regulations, standards, and guidance. Existing organizational policies and procedures may make the need for additional specific policies and procedures unnecessary. The access control policy can be included as part of the general information security policy for the organization. Access control procedures can be developed for the security program in general and for a particular information system, when required. The organizational risk management strategy is a key factor in the development of the access control policy. Related control: PM-9.

Control Enhancements: None.

References: NIST Special Publications 800-12, 800-100.

Priority and Baseline Allocation:

P1	**LOW** AC-1	**MOD** AC-1	**HIGH** AC-1

AC-2   **ACCOUNT MANAGEMENT**

Control: The organization manages information system accounts, including:

a. Identifying account types (i.e., individual, group, system, application, guest/anonymous, and temporary);

b. Establishing conditions for group membership;

c. Identifying authorized users of the information system and specifying access privileges;

d. Requiring appropriate approvals for requests to establish accounts;

e. Establishing, activating, modifying, disabling, and removing accounts;

f. Specifically authorizing and monitoring the use of guest/anonymous and temporary accounts;

g. Notifying account managers when temporary accounts are no longer required and when information system users are terminated, transferred, or information system usage or need-to-know/need-to-share changes;

h. Deactivating: (i) temporary accounts that are no longer required; and (ii) accounts of terminated or transferred users;

i. Granting access to the system based on: (i) a valid access authorization; (ii) intended system usage; and (iii) other attributes as required by the organization or associated missions/business functions; and

j. Reviewing accounts [*Assignment: organization-defined frequency*].

Supplemental Guidance: The identification of authorized users of the information system and the specification of access privileges is consistent with the requirements in other security controls in the security plan. Users requiring administrative privileges on information system accounts receive additional scrutiny by organizational officials responsible for approving such accounts and privileged access. Related controls: AC-3, AC-4, AC-5, AC-6, AC-10, AC-17, AC-19, AC-20, AU-9, IA-4, IA-5, CM-5, CM-6, MA-3, MA-4, MA-5, SA-7, SC-13, SI-9.

Control Enhancements:

(1)　The organization employs automated mechanisms to support the management of information system accounts.

(2)　The information system automatically terminates temporary and emergency accounts after [*Assignment: organization-defined time period for each type of account*].

(3)　The information system automatically disables inactive accounts after [*Assignment: organization- defined time period*].

(4)　The information system automatically audits account creation, modification, disabling, and termination actions and notifies, as required, appropriate individuals.

(5)　The organization:

(a)　Requires that users log out when [*Assignment: organization defined time-period of expected inactivity and/or description of when to log out*];

(b)　Determines normal time-of-day and duration usage for information system

accounts; (c)　Monitors for atypical usage of information system accounts; and

(d)　Reports atypical usage to designated organizational officials.

(6)　The information system dynamically manages user privileges and associated access authorizations.

Enhancement Supplemental Guidance: In contrast to conventional access control approaches which employ static information system accounts and predefined sets of user privileges, many service-oriented architecture implementations rely on run time access control decisions facilitated by dynamic privilege management. While user identities remain relatively constant over time, user privileges may change more frequently based on the ongoing mission/business requirements and operational needs of the organization.

(7)　The organization:

(a)　Establishes and administers privileged user accounts in accordance with a role-based access scheme that organizes information system and network privileges into roles; and

(b)　Tracks and monitors privileged role assignments.

Enhancement Supplemental Guidance: Privileged roles include, for example, key management, network and system administration, database administration, web administration.

References: None.

Priority and Baseline Allocation:

P1	**LOW** AC-2	**MOD** AC-2 (1) (2) (3) (4)	**HIGH** AC-2 (1) (2) (3) (4)

AC-3　ACCESS ENFORCEMENT

Control: The information system enforces approved authorizations for logical access to the system in accordance with applicable policy.

Supplemental Guidance: Access control policies (e.g., identity-based policies, role-based policies, attribute-based policies) and access enforcement mechanisms (e.g., access control lists, access control matrices, cryptography) are employed by organizations to control access between users (or processes acting on behalf of users) and objects (e.g., devices, files, records, processes, programs, domains) in the information system. In addition to enforcing authorized access at the information-system level, access enforcement mechanisms are employed at the application level, when necessary, to provide increased information security for the organization. Consideration is given to the implementation of an audited, explicit override of automated mechanisms in the event of emergencies or other serious events. If encryption of stored information is employed as an access enforcement mechanism, the cryptography used is FIPS 140-2 (as amended) compliant. For classified information, the cryptography used is largely dependent on the classification level of the information and the clearances of the individuals having access to the information. Mechanisms implemented by AC-3 are configured to enforce authorizations determined by other security controls. Related controls: AC-2, AC-4, AC-5, AC-6, AC-16, AC-17, AC-18, AC-19, AC-20, AC-21, AC-22, AU-9, CM-5, CM-6, MA-3, MA-4, MA-5, SA-7, SC-13, SI-9.

Control Enhancements:

(1)   [Withdrawn: Incorporated into AC-6].

(2)   **The information system enforces dual authorization, based on organizational policies and procedures for [*Assignment: organization-defined privileged commands*].**

Enhancement Supplemental Guidance: Dual authorization mechanisms require two forms of approval to execute. The organization does not employ dual authorization mechanisms when an immediate response is necessary to ensure public and environmental safety.

(3)   **The information system enforces [*Assignment: organization-defined nondiscretionary access control policies*] over [*Assignment: organization-defined set of users and resources*] where the policy rule set for each policy specifies:**

(a)   **Access control information (i.e., attributes) employed by the policy rule set (e.g., position, nationality, age, project, time of day); and**

(b)   **Required relationships among the access control information to permit access.**

Enhancement Supplemental Guidance: Nondiscretionary access control policies that may be implemented by organizations include, for example, Attribute-Based Access Control, Mandatory Access Control, and Originator Controlled Access Control. Nondiscretionary access control policies may be employed by organizations in addition to the employment of discretionary access control policies.

For Mandatory Access Control (MAC): Policy establishes coverage over all subjects and objects under its control to ensure that each user receives only that information to which the user is authorized access based on classification of the information, and on user clearance and formal access authorization. The information system assigns appropriate security attributes (e.g., labels/security domains/types) to subjects and objects, and uses these attributes as the basis for MAC decisions. The Bell-LaPadula security model defines allowed access with regard to an organization-defined set of strictly hierarchical security levels as follows: A subject can read an object only if the security level of the subject dominates the security level of the object and a subject can write to an object only if two conditions are met: the security level of the object dominates the security level of the subject, and the security level of the user's clearance dominates the security level of the object (no read up, no write down).

For Role-Based Access Control (RBAC): Policy establishes coverage over all users and resources to ensure that access rights are grouped by role name, and access to resources is restricted to users who have been authorized to assume the associated role.

(4)   **The information system enforces a Discretionary Access Control (DAC) policy that:**

(a)   **Allows users to specify and control sharing by named individuals or groups of individuals, or by both;**

(b)   **Limits propagation of access rights; and**

(c)   **Includes or excludes access to the granularity of a single user.**

(5)   **The information system prevents access to [*Assignment: organization-defined security-relevant information*] except during secure, nonoperable system states.**

Enhancement Supplemental Guidance: Security-relevant information is any information within the information system that can potentially impact the operation of security functions in a manner that could result in failure to enforce the system security policy or maintain isolation of code and data. Filtering rules for routers and firewalls, cryptographic key management information, key configuration parameters for security services, and access control lists are examples of security-relevant information. Secure, nonoperable system states are states in which the information system is not performing mission/business-related processing (e.g., the system is off-line for maintenance, troubleshooting, boot-up, shutdown).

(6)   **The organization encrypts or stores off-line in a secure location [*Assignment: organization-defined user and/or system information*].**

Enhancement Supplemental Guidance: The use of encryption by the organization reduces the probability of unauthorized disclosure of information and can also detect unauthorized changes to information. Removing information from online storage to offline storage eliminates the possibility of individuals gaining unauthorized access via a network. Related control: MP-4.

References: None.

Priority and Baseline Allocation:

P1	LOW AC-3	MOD AC-3	HIGH AC-3

AC-4   INFORMATION FLOW ENFORCEMENT

Control: The information system enforces approved authorizations for controlling the flow of information within the system and between interconnected systems in accordance with applicable policy.

Supplemental Guidance: Information flow control regulates where information is allowed to travel within an information system and between information systems (as opposed to who is allowed to access the information) and without explicit regard to subsequent accesses to that information. A few examples of flow control restrictions include: keeping export controlled information from being transmitted in the clear to the Internet, blocking outside traffic that claims to be from within the organization, and not passing any web requests to the Internet that are not from the internal web proxy. Information flow control policies and enforcement mechanisms are commonly employed by organizations to control the flow of information between designated sources and destinations (e.g., networks, individuals, devices) within information systems and between interconnected systems. Flow control is based on the characteristics of the information and/or the information path. Specific examples of flow control enforcement can be found in boundary protection devices (e.g., proxies, gateways, guards, encrypted tunnels, firewalls, and routers) that employ rule sets or establish configuration settings that restrict information system services, provide a packet-filtering capability based on header information, or message-filtering capability based on content (e.g., using key word searches or document characteristics). Mechanisms implemented by AC-4 are configured to enforce authorizations determined by other security controls. Related controls: AC-17, AC-19, AC-21, CM-7, SA-8, SC-2, SC-5, SC-7, SC-18.

Control Enhancements:

(1)   **The information system enforces information flow control using explicit security attributes on information, source, and destination objects as a basis for flow control decisions.**

Enhancement Supplemental Guidance: Information flow enforcement mechanisms compare security attributes on all information (data content and data structure), source and destination objects, and respond appropriately (e.g., block, quarantine, alert administrator) when the mechanisms encounter information flows not explicitly allowed by the information flow policy. Information flow enforcement using explicit security attributes can be used, for example, to control the release of certain types of information.

(2)   **The information system enforces information flow control using protected processing domains (e.g., domain type-enforcement) as a basis for flow control decisions.**

(3)   The information system enforces dynamic information flow control based on policy that allows or disallows information flows based on changing conditions or operational considerations.

(4)   The information system prevents encrypted data from bypassing content-checking mechanisms.

(5)   The information system enforces [*Assignment: organization-defined limitations on the embedding of data types within other data types*].

(6)   The information system enforces information flow control on metadata.

(7)   The information system enforces [*Assignment: organization-defined one-way flows*] using hardware mechanisms.

(8)   The information system enforces information flow control using [*Assignment: organization-defined security policy filters*] as a basis for flow control decisions.

Enhancement Supplemental Guidance: Organization-defined security policy filters include, for example, dirty word filters, file type checking filters, structured data filters, unstructured data filters, metadata content filters, and hidden content filters. Structured data permits the interpretation of its content by virtue of atomic elements that are understandable by an application and indivisible. Unstructured data refers to masses of (usually) digital information that does not have a data structure or has a data structure that is not easily readable by a machine. Unstructured data consists of two basic categories: (i) bitmap objects that are inherently non language-based (i.e., image, video, or audio files); and (ii) textual objects that are based on a written or printed language (i.e., commercial off-the-shelf word processing documents, spreadsheets, or emails).

(9)   The information system enforces the use of human review for [*Assignment: organization-defined security policy filters*] when the system is not capable of making an information flow control decision.

(10) The information system provides the capability for a privileged administrator to enable/disable [*Assignment: organization-defined security policy filters*].

(11) The information system provides the capability for a privileged administrator to configure [*Assignment: organization-defined security policy filters*] to support different security policies.

Enhancement Supplemental Guidance: For example, to reflect changes in the security policy, an administrator can change the list of "dirty words" that the security policy mechanism checks in accordance with the definitions provided by the organization.

(12) The information system, when transferring information between different security domains, identifies information flows by data type specification and usage.

Enhancement Supplemental Guidance: Data type specification and usage include, for example, using file naming to reflect type of data and limiting data transfer based on file type.

(13) The information system, when transferring information between different security domains, decomposes information into policy-relevant subcomponents for submission to policy enforcement mechanisms.

Enhancement Supplemental Guidance: Policy enforcement mechanisms include the filtering and/or sanitization rules that are applied to information prior to transfer to a different security domain. Parsing transfer files facilitates policy decisions on source, destination, certificates, classification, subject, attachments, and other information security-related component differentiators. Policy rules for cross domain transfers include, for example, limitations on embedding components/information types within other components/information types, prohibiting more than two-levels of embedding, and prohibiting the transfer of archived information types.

(14) The information system, when transferring information between different security domains, implements policy filters that constrain data structure and content to [*Assignment: organization-defined information security policy requirements*].

Enhancement Supplemental Guidance: Constraining file lengths, allowed enumerations, character sets, schemas, and other data object attributes reduces the range of potential malicious and/or unsanctioned content. Examples of constraints include ensuring that: (i) character data fields only contain printable ASCII; (ii) character data fields only contain alpha-numeric characters;

(iii) character data fields do not contain special characters; or (iv) maximum field sizes and file lengths are enforced based upon organization-defined security policy.

(15) **The information system, when transferring information between different security domains, detects unsanctioned information and prohibits the transfer of such information in accordance with the security policy.**

Enhancement Supplemental Guidance: Actions to support this enhancement include: checking all transferred information for malware, implementing dirty word list searches on transferred information, and applying the same protection measures to metadata (e.g., security attributes) that is applied to the information payload.

(16) **The information system enforces security policies regarding information on interconnected systems.**

Enhancement Supplemental Guidance: Transferring information between interconnected information systems of differing security policies introduces risk that such transfers violate one or more policies. While security policy violations may not be absolutely prohibited, policy guidance from information owners/stewards is implemented at the policy enforcement point between the interconnected systems. Specific architectural solutions are mandated, when required, to reduce the potential for undiscovered vulnerabilities. Architectural solutions include, for example: (i) prohibiting information transfers between interconnected systems (i.e. implementing access only, one way transfer mechanisms); (ii) employing hardware mechanisms to enforce unitary information flow directions; and (iii) implementing fully tested, re-grading mechanisms to reassign security attributes and associated security labels.

(17) **The information system:**

(a) **Uniquely identifies and authenticates source and destination domains for information transfer;**

(b) **Binds security attributes to information to facilitate information flow policy enforcement; and**

(c) **Tracks problems associated with the security attribute binding and information transfer.**

Enhancement Supplemental Guidance: Attribution is a critical component of a security concept of operations. The ability to identify source and destination points for information flowing in an information system, allows forensic reconstruction of events when required, and increases policy compliance by attributing policy violations to specific organizations/individuals. Means to enforce this enhancement include ensuring that the information system resolution labels distinguish between information systems and organizations, and between specific system components or individuals involved in preparing, sending, receiving, or disseminating information.

References: None.

Priority and Baseline Allocation:

P1	**LOW** Not Selected	**MOD** AC-4	**HIGH** AC-4

AC-5   SEPARATION OF DUTIES

Control: The organization:

a. Separates duties of individuals as necessary, to prevent malevolent activity without collusion;

b. Documents separation of duties; and

c. Implements separation of duties through assigned information system access authorizations.

Supplemental Guidance: Examples of separation of duties include: (i) mission functions and distinct information system support functions are divided among different individuals/roles; (ii) different individuals perform information system support functions (e.g., system management, systems programming, configuration management, quality assurance and testing, network security); (iii) security personnel who administer access control functions do not administer audit functions; and (iv) different administrator accounts for different roles. Access authorizations defined in this control are implemented by control AC-3. Related controls: AC-3.

Control Enhancements: None.

References: None.

Priority and Baseline Allocation:

P1	**LOW** Not Selected	**MOD** AC-5	**HIGH** AC-5

AC-6   LEAST PRIVILEGE

Control: The organization employs the concept of least privilege, allowing only authorized accesses for users (and processes acting on behalf of users) which are necessary to accomplish assigned tasks in accordance with organizational missions and business functions.

Supplemental Guidance: The access authorizations defined in this control are largely implemented by control AC-3. The organization employs the concept of least privilege for specific duties and information systems (including specific ports, protocols, and services) in accordance with risk assessments as necessary to adequately mitigate risk to organizational operations and assets, individuals, other organizations, and the Nation. Related controls: AC-2, AC-3, CM-7.

Control Enhancements:

(1)   The organization explicitly authorizes access to [*Assignment: organization-defined list of security functions (deployed in hardware, software, and firmware) and security-relevant information*].

Enhancement Supplemental Guidance: Establishing system accounts, configuring access authorizations (i.e., permissions, privileges), setting events to be audited, and setting intrusion detection parameters are examples of security functions. Explicitly authorized personnel include, for example, security administrators, system and network administrators, system security officers, system maintenance personnel, system programmers, and other privileged users. Related control: AC-17.

(2)   The organization requires that users of information system accounts, or roles, with access to [*Assignment: organization-defined list of security functions or security-relevant information*], use non-privileged accounts, or roles, when accessing other system functions, and if feasible, audits any use of privileged accounts, or roles, for such functions.

Enhancement Supplemental Guidance: This control enhancement is intended to limit exposure due to operating from within a privileged account or role. The inclusion of *role* is intended to address those situations where an access control policy such as *Role Based Access Control (RBAC)* is being implemented and where a change of role provides the same degree of assurance in the change of access authorizations for both the user and all processes acting on behalf of the user as would be provided by a change between a privileged and non-privileged account. Audit of privileged activity may require physical separation employing information systems on which the user does not have privileged access.

(3)   The organization authorizes network access to [*Assignment: organization-defined privileged commands*] only for compelling operational needs and documents the rationale for such access in the security plan for the information system.

(4)   The information system provides separate processing domains to enable finer-grained allocation of user privileges.

Enhancement Supplemental Guidance: Employing virtualization techniques to allow greater privilege within a virtual machine while restricting privilege to the underlying actual machine is an example of providing separate processing domains for finer-grained allocation of user privileges.

(5)   **The organization limits authorization to super user accounts on the information system to designated system administration personnel.**

Enhancement Supplemental Guidance: Super user accounts are typically described as "root" or "administrator" for various types of commercial off-the-shelf operating systems. Configuring organizational information systems (e.g., notebook/laptop computers, servers, workstations) such that day-to-day users are not authorized access to super user accounts is an example of limiting system authorization. The organization may differentiate in the application of this control enhancement between allowed privileges for local information system accounts and for domain accounts provided the organization retains the ability to control the configuration of the system with regard to key security parameters and as otherwise necessary to sufficiently mitigate risk.

(6)   **The organization prohibits privileged access to the information system by non-organizational users.**

Enhancement Supplemental Guidance: A qualified organizational user may be advised by a non-organizational user, if necessary.

References: None.

Priority and Baseline Allocation:

P1	**LOW** Not Selected	**MOD** AC-6 (1) (2)	**HIGH** AC-6 (1) (2)

AC-7   UNSUCCESSFUL LOGIN ATTEMPTS

Control: The information system:

a.   Enforces a limit of [*Assignment: organization-defined number*] consecutive invalid access attempts by a user during a [*Assignment: organization-defined time period*]; and

b.   Automatically [*Selection: locks the account/node for an [Assignment: organization-defined time period]; locks the account/node until released by an administrator; delays next login prompt according to [Assignment: organization-defined delay algorithm]*]] when the maximum number of unsuccessful attempts is exceeded. The control applies regardless of whether the login occurs via a local or network connection.

Supplemental Guidance: Due to the potential for denial of service, automatic lockouts initiated by the information system are usually temporary and automatically release after a predetermined time period established by the organization. If a delay algorithm is selected, the organization may chose to employ different algorithms for different information system components based on the capabilities of those components. Response to unsuccessful login attempts may be implemented at both the operating system and the application levels. This control applies to all accesses other than those accesses explicitly identified and documented by the organization in AC-14.

Control Enhancements:

(1)   **The information system automatically locks the account/node until released by an administrator when the maximum number of unsuccessful attempts is exceeded.**

(2)   **The information system provides additional protection for mobile devices accessed via login by purging information from the device after [*Assignment: organization-defined number*] consecutive, unsuccessful login attempts to the device.**

Enhancement Supplemental Guidance: This enhancement applies only to mobile devices for which a login occurs (e.g., personal digital assistants) and not to mobile devices accessed without a login such as removable media. In certain situations, this enhancement may not apply to mobile devices if the information on the device is encrypted with sufficiently strong encryption mechanisms, making purging unnecessary. The login is to the mobile device, not to any one account on the device. Therefore, a successful login to any account on the mobile device resets the unsuccessful login count to zero.

References: None.

Priority and Baseline Allocation:

P2	LOW AC-7	MOD AC-7	HIGH AC-7

AC-8   SYSTEM USE NOTIFICATION

Control: The information system:

a. Displays an approved system use notification message or banner before granting access to the system that provides privacy and security notices consistent with applicable federal laws, Executive Orders, directives, policies, regulations, standards, and guidance and states that: (i) users are accessing a U.S. Government information system; (ii) system usage may be monitored, recorded, and subject to audit; (iii) unauthorized use of the system is prohibited and subject to criminal and civil penalties; and (iv) use of the system indicates consent to monitoring and recording;

b. Retains the notification message or banner on the screen until users take explicit actions to log on to or further access the information system; and

c. For publicly accessible systems: (i) displays the system use information when appropriate, before granting further access; (ii) displays references, if any, to monitoring, recording, or auditing that are consistent with privacy accommodations for such systems that generally prohibit those activities; and (iii) includes in the notice given to public users of the information system, a description of the authorized uses of the system.

Supplemental Guidance: System use notification messages can be implemented in the form of warning banners displayed when individuals log in to the information system. System use notification is intended only for information system access that includes an interactive login interface with a human user and is not intended to require notification when an interactive interface does not exist.

Control Enhancements: None.

References: None.

Priority and Baseline Allocation:

P1	LOW AC-8	MOD AC-8	HIGH AC-8

AC-9   PREVIOUS LOGON (ACCESS) NOTIFICATION

Control: The information system notifies the user, upon successful logon (access), of the date and time of the last logon (access).

Supplemental Guidance: This control is intended to cover both traditional logons to information systems and general accesses to information systems that occur in other types of architectural configurations (e.g., service oriented architectures).

Control Enhancements:

(1) The information system notifies the user, upon successful logon/access, of the number of unsuccessful logon/access attempts since the last successful logon/access.

(2)   The information system notifies the user of the number of [*Selection: successful logins/accesses; unsuccessful login/access attempts; both*] during [*Assignment: organization-defined time period*].

(3)   The information system notifies the user of [*Assignment: organization-defined set of security- related changes to the user's account*] during [*Assignment: organization-defined time period*].

References: None.

Priority and Baseline Allocation:

P0	**LOW** Not Selected	**MOD** Not Selected	**HIGH** Not Selected

AC-10   CONCURRENT SESSION CONTROL

Control: The information system limits the number of concurrent sessions for each system account to [*Assignment: organization-defined number*].

Supplemental Guidance: The organization may define the maximum number of concurrent sessions for an information system account globally, by account type, by account, or a combination. This control addresses concurrent sessions for a given information system account and does not address concurrent sessions by a single user via multiple system accounts.

Control Enhancements: None.

References: None.

Priority and Baseline Allocation:

P2	**LOW** Not Selected	**MOD** Not Selected	**HIGH** AC-10

AC-11   SESSION LOCK

Control: The information system:

a.   Prevents further access to the system by initiating a session lock after [*Assignment: organization-defined time period*] of inactivity or upon receiving a request from a user; and

b.   Retains the session lock until the user reestablishes access using established identification and authentication procedures.

Supplemental Guidance: A session lock is a temporary action taken when a user stops work and moves away from the immediate physical vicinity of the information system but does not want to log out because of the temporary nature of the absence. The session lock is implemented at the point where session activity can be determined. This is typically at the operating system-level, but may be at the application-level. A session lock is not a substitute for logging out of the information system, for example, if the organization requires users to log out at the end of the workday.

Control Enhancements:

(1)   The information system session lock mechanism, when activated on a device with a display screen, places a publically viewable pattern onto the associated display, hiding what was previously visible on the screen.

References: OMB Memorandum 06-16.

Priority and Baseline Allocation:

P3	**LOW** Not Selected	**MOD** AC-11	**HIGH** AC-11

AC-12   SESSION TERMINATION

[Withdrawn: Incorporated into SC-10].

AC-13   SUPERVISION AND REVIEW — ACCESS CONTROL

[Withdrawn: Incorporated into AC-2 and AU-6].

AC-14   PERMITTED ACTIONS WITHOUT IDENTIFICATION OR AUTHENTICATION

Control: The organization:

a. Identifies specific user actions that can be performed on the information system without identification or authentication; and

b. Documents and provides supporting rationale in the security plan for the information system, user actions not requiring identification and authentication.

Supplemental Guidance: This control is intended for those specific instances where an organization determines that no identification and authentication is required; it is not, however, mandating that such instances exist in given information system. The organization may allow a limited number of user actions without identification and authentication (e.g., when individuals access public websites or other publicly accessible federal information systems such as http://www.usa.gov). Organizations also identify any actions that normally require identification or authentication but may under certain circumstances (e.g., emergencies), allow identification or authentication mechanisms to be bypassed. Such bypass may be, for example, via a software-readable physical switch that commands bypass of the login functionality and is protected from accidental or unmonitored use. This control does not apply to situations where identification and authentication have already occurred and are not being repeated, but rather to situations where identification and/or authentication have not yet occurred. Related control: CP-2, IA-2.

Control Enhancements:

(1) **The organization permits actions to be performed without identification and authentication only to the extent necessary to accomplish mission/business objectives.**

References: None.

Priority and Baseline Allocation:

P1	**LOW** AC-14	**MOD** AC-14 (1)	**HIGH** AC-14 (1)

AC-15   AUTOMATED MARKING

[Withdrawn: Incorporated into MP-3].

AC-16   SECURITY ATTRIBUTES

Control: The information system supports and maintains the binding of [*Assignment: organization-defined security attributes*] to information in storage, in process, and in transmission.

Supplemental Guidance: Security attributes are abstractions representing the basic properties or characteristics of an entity (e.g., subjects and objects) with respect to safeguarding information. These attributes are typically associated with internal data structures (e.g., records, buffers, files) within the information system and are used to enable the implementation of access control and flow control policies, reflect special dissemination, handling or distribution instructions, or support other aspects of the information security policy. The term security label is often used to associate a set of security attributes with a specific information object as part of the data structure for that object (e.g., user access privileges, nationality, affiliation as contractor). Related controls: AC-3, AC-4, SC-16, MP-3.

Control Enhancements:

(1)   **The information system dynamically reconfigures security attributes in accordance with an identified security policy as information is created and combined.**

(2)   **The information system allows authorized entities to change security attributes.**

(3)   **The information system maintains the binding of security attributes to information with sufficient assurance that the information--attribute association can be used as the basis for automated policy actions.**

Enhancement Supplemental Guidance: Examples of automated policy actions include automated access control decisions (e.g., Mandatory Access Control decisions), or decisions to release (or not release) information (e.g., information flows via cross domain systems).

(4)   **The information system allows authorized users to associate security attributes with information.**

Enhancement Supplemental Guidance: The support provided by the information system can vary from prompting users to select security attributes to be associated with specific information objects, to ensuring that the combination of attributes selected is valid.

(5)   **The information system displays security attributes in human-readable form on each object output from the system to system output devices to identify [*Assignment: organization-identified set of special dissemination, handling, or distribution instructions*] using [*Assignment: organization- identified human readable, standard naming conventions*].**

Enhancement Supplemental Guidance: Objects output from the information system include, for example, pages, screens, or equivalent. Output devices include, for example, printers and video displays on computer terminals, monitors, screens on notebook/laptop computers and personal digital assistants.

References: None.

Priority and Baseline Allocation:

P0	LOW	Not Selected	MOD	Not Selected	HIGH	Not Selected

AC-17   REMOTE ACCESS

Control: The organization:

a.   Documents allowed methods of remote access to the information system;

b.   Establishes usage restrictions and implementation guidance for each allowed remote access method;

c.   Monitors for unauthorized remote access to the information system;

d.   Authorizes remote access to the information system prior to connection; and

e.   Enforces requirements for remote connections to the information system.

Supplemental Guidance: This control requires explicit authorization prior to allowing remote access to an information system without specifying a specific format for that authorization. For example, while the organization may deem it appropriate to use a system interconnection agreement to authorize a given remote access, such agreements are not required by this control. Remote access is any access to an organizational information system by a user (or process acting on behalf of a user) communicating through an external network (e.g., the Internet). Examples of remote access methods include dial-up, broadband, and wireless (see AC-18 for wireless access). A virtual private network when adequately provisioned with appropriate security controls, is considered an internal network (i.e., the organization establishes a network connection between organization-controlled endpoints in a manner that does not require the organization to depend on external networks to protect the confidentiality or integrity of information transmitted across the network). Remote access controls are applicable to information systems other than public web servers or systems specifically designed for public access. Enforcing access restrictions associated with remote connections is accomplished by control AC-3. Related controls: AC-3, AC-18, AC-20, IA-2, IA-3, IA-8, MA-4.

Control Enhancements:

(1) **The organization employs automated mechanisms to facilitate the monitoring and control of remote access methods.**

Enhancement Supplemental Guidance: Automated monitoring of remote access sessions allows organizations to audit user activities on a variety of information system components (e.g., servers, workstations, notebook/laptop computers) and to ensure compliance with remote access policy.

(2) **The organization uses cryptography to protect the confidentiality and integrity of remote access sessions.**

Enhancement Supplemental Guidance: The encryption strength of mechanism is selected based on the security categorization of the information. Related controls: SC-8, SC-9, SC-13.

(3) **The information system routes all remote accesses through a limited number of managed access control points.**

Enhancement Supplemental Guidance: Related control: SC-7.

(4) **The organization authorizes the execution of privileged commands and access to security-relevant information via remote access only for compelling operational needs and documents the rationale for such access in the security plan for the information system.**

Enhancement Supplemental Guidance: Related control: AC-6.

(5) **The organization monitors for unauthorized remote connections to the information system [*Assignment: organization-defined frequency*], and takes appropriate action if an unauthorized connection is discovered.**

(6) **The organization ensures that users protect information about remote access mechanisms from unauthorized use and disclosure.**

(7) **The organization ensures that remote sessions for accessing [*Assignment: organization-defined list of security functions and security-relevant information*] employ [*Assignment: organization- defined additional security measures*] and are audited.**

Enhancement Supplemental Guidance: Additional security measures are typically above and beyond standard bulk or session layer encryption (e.g., Secure Shell [SSH], Virtual Private Networking [VPN] with blocking mode enabled). Related controls: SC-8, SC-9.

(8) **The organization disables [*Assignment: organization-defined networking protocols within the information system deemed to be nonsecure*] except for explicitly identified components in support of specific operational requirements.**

Enhancement Supplemental Guidance: The organization can either make a determination of the relative security of the networking protocol or base the security decision on the assessment of other entities. Bluetooth and peer-to-peer networking are examples of less than secure networking protocols.

References: NIST Special Publications 800-46, 800-77, 800-113, 800-114, 800-121.

Priority and Baseline Allocation:

| P1 | **LOW** AC-17 | **MOD** AC-17 (1) (2) (3) (4) (5) (7) (8) | **HIGH** AC-17 (1) (2) (3) (4) (5) (7) (8) |

AC-18   WIRELESS ACCESS

Control: The organization:

a. Establishes usage restrictions and implementation guidance for wireless access;

b. Monitors for unauthorized wireless access to the information system;

c. Authorizes wireless access to the information system prior to connection; and

d. Enforces requirements for wireless connections to the information system.

Supplemental Guidance: Wireless technologies include, but are not limited to, microwave, satellite, packet radio (UHF/VHF), 802.11x, and Bluetooth. Wireless networks use authentication protocols (e.g., EAP/TLS, PEAP), which provide credential protection and mutual authentication. In certain situations, wireless signals may radiate beyond the confines and control of organization-controlled facilities. Related controls: AC-3, IA-2, IA-3, IA-8.

Control Enhancements:

(1)   **The information system protects wireless access to the system using authentication and encryption.**

Enhancement Supplemental Guidance: Authentication applies to user, device, or both as necessary. Related control: SC-13.

(2)   **The organization monitors for unauthorized wireless connections to the information system, including scanning for unauthorized wireless access points [*Assignment: organization-defined frequency*], and takes appropriate action if an unauthorized connection is discovered.**

Enhancement Supplemental Guidance: Organizations proactively search for unauthorized wireless connections including the conduct of thorough scans for unauthorized wireless access points. The scan is not necessarily limited to only those areas within the facility containing the information systems, yet is conducted outside of those areas only as needed to verify that unauthorized wireless access points are not connected to the system.

(3)   **The organization disables, when not intended for use, wireless networking capabilities internally embedded within information system components prior to issuance and deployment.**

(4)   **The organization does not allow users to independently configure wireless networking capabilities. (5)   The organization confines wireless communications to organization-controlled boundaries.**

Enhancement Supplemental Guidance: Actions that may be taken by the organization to confine wireless communications to organization-controlled boundaries include: (i) reducing the power of the wireless transmission such that it cannot transit the physical perimeter of the organization; (ii) employing measures such as TEMPEST to control wireless emanations; and (iii) configuring the wireless access such that it is point to point in nature.

References: NIST Special Publications 800-48, 800-94, 800-97.

Priority and Baseline Allocation:

P1	**LOW** AC-18	**MOD** AC-18 (1)	**HIGH** AC-18 (1) (2) (4) (5)

AC-19   ACCESS CONTROL FOR MOBILE DEVICES

Control: The organization:

a. Establishes usage restrictions and implementation guidance for organization-controlled mobile devices;

b. Authorizes connection of mobile devices meeting organizational usage restrictions and implementation guidance to organizational information systems;

c. Monitors for unauthorized connections of mobile devices to organizational information systems;

d. Enforces requirements for the connection of mobile devices to organizational information systems;

e. Disables information system functionality that provides the capability for automatic execution of code on mobile devices without user direction;

f. Issues specially configured mobile devices to individuals traveling to locations that the organization deems to be of significant risk in accordance with organizational policies and procedures; and

g. Applies [*Assignment: organization-defined inspection and preventative measures*] to mobile devices returning from locations that the organization deems to be of significant risk in accordance with organizational policies and procedures.

Supplemental Guidance: Mobile devices include portable storage media (e.g., USB memory sticks, external hard disk drives) and portable computing and communications devices with information storage capability (e.g., notebook/laptop computers, personal digital assistants, cellular telephones, digital cameras, and audio recording devices). Organization-controlled mobile devices include those devices for which the organization has the authority to specify and the ability to enforce specific security requirements. Usage restrictions and implementation guidance related to mobile devices include, for example, configuration management, device identification and authentication, implementation of mandatory protective software (e.g., malicious code detection, firewall), scanning devices for malicious code, updating virus protection software, scanning for critical software updates and patches, conducting primary operating system (and possibly other resident software) integrity checks, and disabling unnecessary hardware (e.g., wireless, infrared). Examples of information system functionality that provide the capability for automatic execution of code are AutoRun and AutoPlay.

Organizational policies and procedures for mobile devices used by individuals departing on and returning from travel include, for example, determining which locations are of concern, defining required configurations for the devices, ensuring that the devices are configured as intended before travel is initiated, and applying specific measures to the device after travel is completed. Specially configured mobile devices include, for example, computers with sanitized hard drives, limited applications, and additional hardening (e.g., more stringent configuration settings). Specified measures applied to mobile devices upon return from travel include, for example, examining the device for signs of physical tampering and purging/reimaging the hard disk drive. Protecting information residing on mobile devices is covered in the media protection family. Related controls: MP-4, MP-5.

Control Enhancements:

(1) **The organization restricts the use of writable, removable media in organizational information systems.**

(2) **The organization prohibits the use of personally owned, removable media in organizational information systems.**

(3) **The organization prohibits the use of removable media in organizational information systems when the media has no identifiable owner.**

Enhancement Supplemental Guidance: An identifiable owner (e.g., individual, organization, or project) for removable media helps to reduce the risk of using such technology by assigning responsibility and accountability for addressing known vulnerabilities in the media (e.g., malicious code insertion).

(4) **The organization:**

(a) **Prohibits the use of unclassified mobile devices in facilities containing information systems processing, storing, or transmitting classified information unless specifically permitted by the appropriate authorizing official(s); and**

(b)   Enforces the following restrictions on individuals permitted to use mobile devices in facilities containing information systems processing, storing, or transmitting classified information:

- Connection of unclassified mobile devices to classified information systems is prohibited;

- Connection of unclassified mobile devices to unclassified information systems requires approval from the appropriate authorizing official(s);

- Use of internal or external modems or wireless interfaces within the mobile devices is prohibited; and

- Mobile devices and the information stored on those devices are subject to random reviews/inspections by [*Assignment: organization-defined security officials*], and if classified information is found, the incident handling policy is followed.

References: NIST Special Publications 800-114, 800-124.

Priority and Baseline Allocation:

P1	LOW AC-19	MOD AC-19 (1) (2) (3)	HIGH AC-19 (1) (2) (3)

AC-20   USE OF EXTERNAL INFORMATION SYSTEMS

Control: The organization establishes terms and conditions, consistent with any trust relationships established with other organizations owning, operating, and/or maintaining external information systems, allowing authorized individuals to:

a.   Access the information system from the external information systems; and

b.   Process, store, and/or transmit organization-controlled information using the external information systems.

Supplemental Guidance: External information systems are information systems or components of information systems that are outside of the authorization boundary established by the organization and for which the organization typically has no direct supervision and authority over the application of required security controls or the assessment of security control effectiveness. External information systems include, but are not limited to: (i) personally owned information systems (e.g., computers, cellular telephones, or personal digital assistants); (ii) privately owned computing and communications devices resident in commercial or public facilities (e.g., hotels, convention centers, or airports); (iii) information systems owned or controlled by nonfederal governmental organizations; and (iv) federal information systems that are not owned by, operated by, or under the direct supervision and authority of the organization. For some external systems, in particular those systems operated by other federal agencies, including organizations subordinate to those agencies, the trust relationships that have been established between those organizations and the originating organization may be such, that no explicit terms and conditions are required. In effect, the information systems of these organizations would not be considered external. These situations typically occur when, for example, there is some pre-existing sharing or trust agreement (either implicit or explicit) established between federal agencies and/or organizations subordinate to those agencies, or such trust agreements are specified by applicable laws, Executive Orders, directives, or policies. Authorized individuals include organizational personnel, contractors, or any other individuals with authorized access to the organizational information system and over which the organization has the authority to impose rules of behavior with regard to system access. The restrictions that an organization imposes on authorized individuals need not be uniform, as those restrictions are likely to vary depending upon the trust relationships between organizations. Thus, an organization might impose more stringent security restrictions on a contractor than on a state, local, or tribal government.

This control does not apply to the use of external information systems to access public interfaces to organizational information systems and information (e.g., individuals accessing federal information through www.usa.gov). The organization establishes terms and conditions for the use of external information systems in accordance with organizational security policies and procedures. The terms and conditions address as a minimum; (i) the types of applications that can be accessed on the organizational information system from the external information system; and (ii) the maximum security categorization of information that can be processed, stored, and transmitted on the external information system. This control defines access authorizations enforced by AC-3, rules of behavior requirements enforced by PL-4, and session establishment rules enforced by AC-17. Related controls: AC-3, AC-17, PL-4.

Control Enhancements:

(1)   **The organization permits authorized individuals to use an external information system to access the information system or to process, store, or transmit organization-controlled information only when the organization:**

    (a)   **Can verify the implementation of required security controls on the external system as specified in the organization's information security policy and security plan; or**

    (b)   **Has approved information system connection or processing agreements with the organizational entity hosting the external information system.**

(2)   **The organization limits the use of organization-controlled portable storage media by authorized individuals on external information systems.**

Enhancement Supplemental Guidance: Limits on the use of organization-controlled portable storage media in external information systems can include, for example, complete prohibition of the use of such devices or restrictions on how the devices may be used and under what conditions the devices may be used.

References: FIPS Publication 199.

Priority and Baseline Allocation:

P1	LOW AC-20	MOD AC-20 (1) (2)	HIGH AC-20 (1) (2)

AC-21   USER-BASED COLLABORATION AND INFORMATION SHARING

Control: The organization:

a.   Facilitates information sharing by enabling authorized users to determine whether access authorizations assigned to the sharing partner match the access restrictions on the information for [*Assignment: organization-defined information sharing circumstances where user discretion is required*]; and

b.   Employs [*Assignment: list of organization-defined information sharing circumstances and automated mechanisms or manual processes required*] to assist users in making information sharing/collaboration decisions.

Supplemental Guidance: The control applies to information that may be restricted in some manner (e.g., privileged medical, contract-sensitive, proprietary, personally identifiable information, special access programs/compartments) based on some formal or administrative determination. Depending on the information-sharing circumstance, the sharing partner may be defined at the individual, group, or organization level and information may be defined by specific content, type, or security categorization. Related control: AC-3.

Control Enhancements:

(1)   **The information system employs automated mechanisms to enable authorized users to make information-sharing decisions based on access authorizations of sharing partners and access restrictions on information to be shared.**

References: None.

Priority and Baseline Allocation:

P0	**LOW** Not Selected	**MOD** Not Selected	**HIGH** Not Selected

AC-22   PUBLICLY ACCESSIBLE CONTENT

Control: The organization:

a.   Designates individuals authorized to post information onto an organizational information system that is publicly accessible;

b.   Trains authorized individuals to ensure that publicly accessible information does not contain nonpublic information;

c.   Reviews the proposed content of publicly accessible information for nonpublic information prior to posting onto the organizational information system;

d.   Reviews the content on the publicly accessible organizational information system for nonpublic information [*Assignment: organization-defined frequency*]; and

e.   Removes nonpublic information from the publicly accessible organizational information system, if discovered.

Supplemental Guidance: Nonpublic information is any information for which the general public is not authorized access in accordance with federal laws, Executive Orders, directives, policies, regulations, standards, or guidance. Information protected under the Privacy Act and vendor proprietary information are examples of nonpublic information. This control addresses posting information on an organizational information system that is accessible to the general public, typically without identification or authentication. The posting of information on non-organization information systems is covered by appropriate organizational policy. Related controls: AC-3, AU-13.

Control Enhancements: None.

References: None.

Priority and Baseline Allocation:

P2	**LOW** AC-22	**MOD** AC-22	**HIGH** AC-22

FAMILY: AWARENESS AND TRAINING   **CLASS:** OPERATIONAL

AT-1   **SECURITY AWARENESS AND TRAINING POLICY AND PROCEDURES**

Control: The organization develops, disseminates, and reviews/updates [*Assignment: organization-defined frequency*]:

a.   A formal, documented security awareness and training policy that addresses purpose, scope, roles, responsibilities, management commitment, coordination among organizational entities, and compliance; and

b.   Formal, documented procedures to facilitate the implementation of the security awareness and training policy and associated security awareness and training controls.

Supplemental Guidance: This control is intended to produce the policy and procedures that are required for the effective implementation of selected security controls and control enhancements in the security awareness and training family. The policy and procedures are consistent with applicable federal laws, Executive Orders, directives, policies, regulations, standards, and guidance. Existing organizational policies and procedures may make the need for additional specific policies and procedures unnecessary. The security awareness and training policy can be included as part of the general information security policy for the organization. Security awareness and training procedures can be developed for the security program in general and for a particular information system, when required. The organizational risk management strategy is a key factor in the development of the security awareness and training policy. Related control: PM-9.

Control Enhancements: None.

References: NIST Special Publications 800-12, 800-16, 800-50, 800-100.

Priority and Baseline Allocation:

P1	**LOW** AT-1	**MOD** AT-1	**HIGH** AT-1

AT-2   **SECURITY AWARENESS**

Control: The organization provides basic security awareness training to all information system users (including managers, senior executives, and contractors) as part of initial training for new users, when required by system changes, and [*Assignment: organization-defined frequency*] thereafter.

Supplemental Guidance: The organization determines the appropriate content of security awareness training and security awareness techniques based on the specific requirements of the organization and the information systems to which personnel have authorized access. The content includes a basic understanding of the need for information security and user actions to maintain security and to respond to suspected security incidents. The content also addresses awareness of the need for operations security as it relates to the organization's information security program. Security awareness techniques can include, for example, displaying posters, offering supplies inscribed with security reminders, generating email advisories/notices from senior organizational officials, displaying logon screen messages, and conducting information security awareness events.

Control Enhancements:

(1)   **The organization includes practical exercises in security awareness training that simulate actual cyber attacks.**

Enhancement Supplemental Guidance: Practical exercises may include, for example, no-notice social engineering attempts to collect information, gain unauthorized access, or simulate the adverse impact of opening malicious email attachments or invoking malicious web links.

References: C.F.R. Part 5 Subpart C (5 C.F.R 930.301); NIST Special Publication 800-50.

Priority and Baseline Allocation:

P1	LOW AT-2	MOD AT-2	HIGH AT-2

AT-3   SECURITY TRAINING

Control: The organization provides role-based security-related training: (i) before authorizing access to the system or performing assigned duties; (ii) when required by system changes; and (iii) [*Assignment: organization-defined frequency*] thereafter.

Supplemental Guidance: The organization determines the appropriate content of security training based on assigned roles and responsibilities and the specific requirements of the organization and the information systems to which personnel have authorized access. In addition, the organization provides information system managers, system and network administrators, personnel performing independent verification and validation activities, security control assessors, and other personnel having access to system-level software, adequate security-related technical training to perform their assigned duties. Organizational security training addresses management, operational, and technical roles and responsibilities covering physical, personnel, and technical safeguards and countermeasures. The organization also provides the training necessary for these individuals to carry out their responsibilities related to operations security within the context of the organization's information security program. Related controls: AT-2, SA-3.

Control Enhancements:

(1) **The organization provides employees with initial and [*Assignment: organization-defined frequency*] training in the employment and operation of environmental controls.**

Enhancement Supplemental Guidance: Environmental controls include, for example, fire suppression and detection devices/systems, sprinkler systems, handheld fire extinguishers, fixed fire hoses, smoke detectors, temperature/humidity, HVAC, and power within the facility.

(2) **The organization provides employees with initial and [*Assignment: organization-defined frequency*] training in the employment and operation of physical security controls.**

Enhancement Supplemental Guidance: Physical security controls include, for example, physical access control devices, physical intrusion alarms, monitoring and surveillance equipment, and security guards (deployment and operating procedures).

References: C.F.R. Part 5 Subpart C (5 C.F.R 930.301); NIST Special Publications 800-16, 800-50.

Priority and Baseline Allocation:

P1	LOW AT-3	MOD AT-3	HIGH AT-3

AT-4   SECURITY TRAINING RECORDS

Control: The organization:

a. Documents and monitors individual information system security training activities including basic security awareness training and specific information system security training; and

b. Retains individual training records for [*Assignment: organization-defined time period*].

Supplemental Guidance: While an organization may deem that organizationally mandated individual training programs and the development of individual training plans are necessary, this control does not mandate either. Documentation for specialized training may be maintained by individual supervisors at the option of the organization.

Control Enhancements: None.

References: None.

Priority and Baseline Allocation:

P3	LOW AT-4	MOD AT-4	HIGH AT-4

AT-5   CONTACTS WITH SECURITY GROUPS AND ASSOCIATIONS

Control: The organization establishes and institutionalizes contact with selected groups and associations within the security community:

- To facilitate ongoing security education and training for organizational personnel;

- To stay up to date with the latest recommended security practices, techniques, and technologies; and

- To share current security-related information including threats, vulnerabilities, and incidents.

Supplemental Guidance: Ongoing contact with security groups and associations is of paramount importance in an environment of rapid technology changes and dynamic threats. Security groups and associations can include, for example, special interest groups, specialized forums, professional associations, news groups, and/or peer groups of security professionals in similar organizations. The groups and associations selected are consistent with the organization's mission/business requirements. Information-sharing activities regarding threats, vulnerabilities, and incidents related to information systems are consistent with applicable federal laws, Executive Orders, directives, policies, regulations, standards, and guidance.

Control Enhancements: None.

References: None.

Priority and Baseline Allocation:

P0	LOW Not Selected	MOD Not Selected	HIGH Not Selected

FAMILY: AUDIT AND ACCOUNTABILITY   **CLASS:** TECHNICAL

AU-1   **AUDIT AND ACCOUNTABILITY POLICY AND PROCEDURES**

Control: The organization develops, disseminates, and reviews/updates [*Assignment: organization-defined frequency*]:

a. A formal, documented audit and accountability policy that addresses purpose, scope, roles, responsibilities, management commitment, coordination among organizational entities, and compliance; and

b. Formal, documented procedures to facilitate the implementation of the audit and accountability policy and associated audit and accountability controls.

Supplemental Guidance: This control is intended to produce the policy and procedures that are required for the effective implementation of selected security controls and control enhancements in the audit and accountability family. The policy and procedures are consistent with applicable federal laws, Executive Orders, directives, policies, regulations, standards, and guidance. Existing organizational policies and procedures may make the need for additional specific policies and procedures unnecessary. The audit and accountability policy can be included as part of the general information security policy for the organization. Audit and accountability procedures can be developed for the security program in general and for a particular information system, when required. The organizational risk management strategy is a key factor in the development of the audit and accountability policy. Related control: PM-9.

Control Enhancements: None.

References: NIST Special Publications 800-12, 800-100.

Priority and Baseline Allocation:

P1	**LOW** AU-1	**MOD** AU-1	**HIGH** AU-1

AU-2   **AUDITABLE EVENTS**

Control: The organization:

a. Determines, based on a risk assessment and mission/business needs, that the information system must be capable of auditing the following events: [*Assignment: organization-defined list of auditable events*];

b. Coordinates the security audit function with other organizational entities requiring audit-related information to enhance mutual support and to help guide the selection of auditable events;

c. Provides a rationale for why the list of auditable events are deemed to be adequate to support after-the-fact investigations of security incidents; and

d. Determines, based on current threat information and ongoing assessment of risk, that the following events are to be audited within the information system: [*Assignment: organization-defined subset of the auditable events defined in AU-2 a. to be audited along with the frequency of (or situation requiring) auditing for each identified event*].

Supplemental Guidance: The purpose of this control is for the organization to identify events which need to be auditable as significant and relevant to the security of the information system; giving an overall system requirement in order to meet ongoing and specific audit needs. To balance auditing requirements with other information system needs, this control also requires identifying that subset of *auditable* events that are to be *audited* at a given point in time. For example, the organization may determine that the information system must have the capability to log every file access both successful and unsuccessful, but not activate that capability except for specific circumstances due to the extreme burden on system performance. In addition, audit records can be generated at various levels of abstraction, including at the packet level as information traverses the network. Selecting the right level of abstraction for audit record generation is a critical aspect of an audit capability and can facilitate the identification of root causes to problems. Related control: AU-3.

Control Enhancements:

(1)   [Withdrawn: Incorporated into AU-12].

(2)   [Withdrawn: Incorporated into AU-12].

(3)   **The organization reviews and updates the list of auditable events [*Assignment: organization- defined frequency*].**

       Enhancement Supplemental Guidance: The list of auditable events is defined in AU-2.

(4)   **The organization includes execution of privileged functions in the list of events to be audited by the information system.**

References: NIST Special Publication 800-92; Web: CSRC.NIST.GOV/PCIG/CIG.HTML.

Priority and Baseline Allocation:

P1	**LOW** AU-2	**MOD** AU-2 (3) (4)	**HIGH** AU-2 (3) (4)

AU-3   CONTENT OF AUDIT RECORDS

Control: The information system produces audit records that contain sufficient information to, at a minimum, establish what type of event occurred, when (date and time) the event occurred, where the event occurred, the source of the event, the outcome (success or failure) of the event, and the identity of any user/subject associated with the event.

Supplemental Guidance: Audit record content that may be necessary to satisfy the requirement of this control, includes, for example, time stamps, source and destination addresses, user/process identifiers, event descriptions, success/fail indications, filenames involved, and access control or flow control rules invoked. Related controls: AU-2, AU-8.

Control Enhancements:

(1)   **The information system includes [*Assignment: organization-defined additional, more detailed information*] in the audit records for audit events identified by type, location, or subject.**

       Enhancement Supplemental Guidance: An example of detailed information that the organization may require in audit records is full-text recording of privileged commands or the individual identities of group account users.

(2)   **The organization centrally manages the content of audit records generated by [*Assignment: organization-defined information system components*].**

References: None.

Priority and Baseline Allocation:

P1	**LOW** AU-3	**MOD** AU-3 (1)	**HIGH** AU-3 (1) (2)

AU-4   AUDIT STORAGE CAPACITY

Control: The organization allocates audit record storage capacity and configures auditing to reduce the likelihood of such capacity being exceeded.

Supplemental Guidance: The organization considers the types of auditing to be performed and the audit processing requirements when allocating audit storage capacity. Related controls: AU-2, AU-5, AU-6, AU-7, SI-4.

Control Enhancements: None.

References: None.

Priority and Baseline Allocation:

P1	LOW　AU-4	MOD　AU-4	HIGH　AU-4

AU-5　RESPONSE TO AUDIT PROCESSING FAILURES

Control: The information system:

a.　Alerts designated organizational officials in the event of an audit processing failure; and

b.　Takes the following additional actions: [*Assignment: organization-defined actions to be taken (e.g., shut down information system, overwrite oldest audit records, stop generating audit records)*].

Supplemental Guidance: Audit processing failures include, for example, software/hardware errors, failures in the audit capturing mechanisms, and audit storage capacity being reached or exceeded. Related control: AU-4.

Control Enhancements:

(1)　The information system provides a warning when allocated audit record storage volume reaches [*Assignment: organization-defined percentage*] of maximum audit record storage capacity.

(2)　The information system provides a real-time alert when the following audit failure events occur: [*Assignment: organization-defined audit failure events requiring real-time alerts*].

(3)　The information system enforces configurable traffic volume thresholds representing auditing capacity for network traffic and [*Selection: rejects or delays*] network traffic above those thresholds.

(4)　The information system invokes a system shutdown in the event of an audit failure, unless an alternative audit capability exists.

References: None.

Priority and Baseline Allocation:

P1	LOW　AU-5	MOD　AU-5	HIGH　AU-5 (1) (2)

AU-6　AUDIT REVIEW, ANALYSIS, AND REPORTING

Control: The organization:

a.　Reviews and analyzes information system audit records [*Assignment: organization-defined frequency*] for indications of inappropriate or unusual activity, and reports findings to designated organizational officials; and

b.　Adjusts the level of audit review, analysis, and reporting within the information system when there is a change in risk to organizational operations, organizational assets, individuals, other organizations, or the Nation based on law enforcement information, intelligence information, or other credible sources of information.

Supplemental Guidance: Related control: AU-7.

Control Enhancements:

(1)   The information system integrates audit review, analysis, and reporting processes to support organizational processes for investigation and response to suspicious activities.

(2)   [Withdrawn: Incorporated into SI-4].

(3)   The organization analyzes and correlates audit records across different repositories to gain organization-wide situational awareness.

(4)   The information system centralizes the review and analysis of audit records from multiple components within the system.

Enhancement Supplemental Guidance: An example of an automated mechanism for centralized review and analysis is a Security Information Management (SIM) product. Related control: AU-2.

(5)   The organization integrates analysis of audit records with analysis of vulnerability scanning information, performance data, and network monitoring information to further enhance the ability to identify inappropriate or unusual activity.

Enhancement Supplemental Guidance: A Security Event/Information Management system tool can facilitate audit record aggregation and consolidation from multiple information system components as well as audit record correlation and analysis. The use of standardized audit record analysis scripts developed by the organization (with localized script adjustments, as necessary), provides a more cost-effective approach for analyzing audit record information collected. The correlation of audit record information with vulnerability scanning information is important in determining the veracity of the vulnerability scans and correlating attack detection events with scanning results. Related control: AU-7, RA-5, SI-4.

(6)   The organization correlates information from audit records with information obtained from monitoring physical access to further enhance the ability to identify suspicious, inappropriate, unusual, or malevolent activity.

Enhancement Supplemental Guidance: Related control: PE-6.

(7)   The organization specifies the permitted actions for each authorized information system process, role, and/or user in the audit and accountability policy.

Enhancement Supplemental Guidance: Permitted actions for information system processes, roles, and/or users associated with the review, analysis, and reporting of audit records include, for example, read, write, append, and delete.

(8)   The organization employs automated mechanisms to alert security personnel of the following inappropriate or unusual activities with security implications: [Assignment: organization-defined list of inappropriate or unusual activities that are to result in alerts].

(9)   The organization performs, in a physically dedicated information system, full-text analysis of privileged functions executed.

References: None.

Priority and Baseline Allocation:

P1	LOW AU-6	MOD AU-6	HIGH AU-6 (1)

AU-7   AUDIT REDUCTION AND REPORT GENERATION

Control: The information system provides an audit reduction and report generation capability.

Supplemental Guidance: An audit reduction and report generation capability provides support for near real-time audit review, analysis, and reporting requirements described in AU-6 and after-the-fact investigations of security incidents. Audit reduction and reporting tools do not alter original audit records. Related control: AU-6.

Control Enhancements:

(1)   The information system provides the capability to automatically process audit records for events of interest based on selectable event criteria.

References: None.

Priority and Baseline Allocation:

P2	**LOW** Not Selected	**MOD** AU-7 (1)	**HIGH** AU-7 (1)

AU-8   TIME STAMPS

Control: The information system uses internal system clocks to generate time stamps for audit records.

Supplemental Guidance: Time stamps generated by the information system include both date and time. The time may be expressed in Coordinated Universal Time (UTC), a modern continuation of Greenwich Mean Time (GMT), or local time with an offset from UTC. Related control: AU-3.

Control Enhancements:

(1)   The information system synchronizes internal information system clocks [*Assignment: organization-defined frequency*] with [*Assignment: organization-defined authoritative time source*].

References: None.

Priority and Baseline Allocation:

P1	**LOW** AU-8	**MOD** AU-8 (1)	**HIGH** AU-8 (1)

AU-9   PROTECTION OF AUDIT INFORMATION

Control: The information system protects audit information and audit tools from unauthorized access, modification, and deletion.

Supplemental Guidance: Audit information includes all information (e.g., audit records, audit settings, and audit reports) needed to successfully audit information system activity. Related controls: AC-3, AC-6.

Control Enhancements:

(1)   The information system produces audit records on hardware-enforced, write-once media.

(2)   The information system backs up audit records [*Assignment: organization-defined frequency*] onto a different system or media than the system being audited.

(3)   The information system uses cryptographic mechanisms to protect the integrity of audit information and audit tools.

Enhancement Supplemental Guidance: An example of a cryptographic mechanism for the protection of integrity is the computation and application of a cryptographic-signed hash using asymmetric cryptography, protecting the confidentiality of the key used to generate the hash, and using the public key to verify the hash information.

(4)   The organization:

(a)   Authorizes access to management of audit functionality to only a limited subset of privileged users; and

(b)   Protects the audit records of non-local accesses to privileged accounts and the execution of privileged functions.

Enhancement Supplemental Guidance: Auditing may not be reliable when performed by the information system to which the user being audited has privileged access. The privileged user may inhibit auditing or modify audit records. This control enhancement helps mitigate this risk by requiring that privileged access be further defined between audit-related privileges and other privileges, thus, limiting the users with audit-related privileges. Reducing the risk of audit compromises by privileged users can also be achieved, for example, by performing audit activity on a separate information system or by using storage media that cannot be modified (e.g., write-once recording devices).

References: None.

Priority and Baseline Allocation:

P1	**LOW** AU-9	**MOD** AU-9	**HIGH** AU-9

AU-10   NON-REPUDIATION

Control: The information system protects against an individual falsely denying having performed a particular action.

Supplemental Guidance: Examples of particular actions taken by individuals include creating information, sending a message, approving information (e.g., indicating concurrence or signing a contract), and receiving a message. Non-repudiation protects individuals against later claims by an author of not having authored a particular document, a sender of not having transmitted a message, a receiver of not having received a message, or a signatory of not having signed a document. Non-repudiation services can be used to determine if information originated from an individual, or if an individual took specific actions (e.g., sending an email, signing a contract, approving a procurement request) or received specific information. Non-repudiation services are obtained by employing various techniques or mechanisms (e.g., digital signatures, digital message receipts).

Control Enhancements:

(1)   **The information system associates the identity of the information producer with the information.**

Enhancement Supplemental Guidance: This control enhancement supports audit requirements that provide appropriate organizational officials the means to identify who produced specific information in the event of an information transfer. The nature and strength of the binding between the information producer and the information are determined and approved by the appropriate organizational officials based on the security categorization of the information and relevant risk factors.

(2)   **The information system validates the binding of the information producer's identity to the information.**

Enhancement Supplemental Guidance: This control enhancement is intended to mitigate the risk that information is modified between production and review. The validation of bindings can be achieved, for example, by the use of cryptographic checksums.

(3)   **The information system maintains reviewer/releaser identity and credentials within the established chain of custody for all information reviewed or released.**

Enhancement Supplemental Guidance: If the reviewer is a human or if the review function is automated but separate from the release/transfer function, the information system associates the identity of the reviewer of the information to be released with the information and the information label. In the case of human reviews, this control enhancement provides appropriate organizational officials the means to identify who reviewed and released the information. In the case of automated reviews, this control enhancement helps ensure that only approved review functions are employed.

(4)   **The information system validates the binding of the reviewer's identity to the information at the transfer/release point prior to release/transfer from one security domain to another security domain.**

Enhancement Supplemental Guidance: This control enhancement is intended to mitigate the risk that information is modified between review and transfer/release.

(5)   **The organization employs [*Selection: FIPS-validated; NSA-approved*] cryptography to implement digital signatures.**

Enhancement Supplemental Guidance: Related control: SC-13.

References: None.

Priority and Baseline Allocation:

P1	**LOW** Not Selected	**MOD** Not Selected	**HIGH** AU-10

AU-11   AUDIT RECORD RETENTION

Control: The organization retains audit records for [*Assignment: organization-defined time period consistent with records retention policy*] to provide support for after-the-fact investigations of security incidents and to meet regulatory and organizational information retention requirements.

Supplemental Guidance: The organization retains audit records until it is determined that they are no longer needed for administrative, legal, audit, or other operational purposes. This includes, for example, retention and availability of audit records relative to Freedom of Information Act (FOIA) requests, subpoena, and law enforcement actions. Standard categorizations of audit records relative to such types of actions and standard response processes for each type of action are developed and disseminated. The National Archives and Records Administration (NARA) General Records Schedules (GRS) provide federal policy on record retention.

Control Enhancements: None.

References: None.

Priority and Baseline Allocation:

P3	**LOW** AU-11	**MOD** AU-11	**HIGH** AU-11

AU-12   AUDIT GENERATION

Control: The information system:

a.   Provides audit record generation capability for the list of auditable events defined in AU-2 at [*Assignment: organization-defined information system components*];

b.   Allows designated organizational personnel to select which auditable events are to be audited by specific components of the system; and

c.   Generates audit records for the list of audited events defined in AU-2 with the content as defined in AU-3.

Supplemental Guidance: Audits records can be generated from various components within the information system. The list of audited events is the set of events for which audits are to be generated. This set of events is typically a subset of the list of all events for which the system is capable of generating audit records (i.e., auditable events). Related controls: AU-2, AU-3.

Control Enhancements:

(1)   **The information system compiles audit records from [*Assignment: organization-defined information system components*] into a system-wide (logical or physical) audit trail that is time-correlated to within [*Assignment: organization-defined level of tolerance for relationship between time stamps of individual records in the audit trail*].**

Enhancement Supplemental Guidance: The audit trail is time-correlated if the time stamp in the individual audit records can be reliably related to the time stamp in other audit records to achieve a time ordering of the records within the organization-defined tolerance.

(2)   **The information system produces a system-wide (logical or physical) audit trail composed of audit records in a standardized format.**

Enhancement Supplemental Guidance: Audit information normalized to a common standard promotes interoperability and exchange of such information between dissimilar devices and information systems. This facilitates an audit system that produces event information that can be more readily analyzed and correlated. System log records and audit records compliant with the Common Event Expression (CEE) are examples of standard formats for audit records. If individual logging mechanisms within the information system do not conform to a standardized format, the system may convert individual audit records into a standardized format when compiling the system-wide audit trail.

References: None.

Priority and Baseline Allocation:

P1	**LOW** AU-12	**MOD** AU-12	**HIGH** AC-12 (1)

AU-13   MONITORING FOR INFORMATION DISCLOSURE

Control: The organization monitors open source information for evidence of unauthorized exfiltration or disclosure of organizational information [*Assignment: organization-defined frequency*].

Supplemental Guidance: None.

Control Enhancements: None.

References: None.

Priority and Baseline Allocation:

P0	**LOW** Not Selected	**MOD** Not Selected	**HIGH** Not Selected

AU-14   SESSION AUDIT

Control: The information system provides the capability to:

a.   Capture/record and log all content related to a user session; and

b.   Remotely view/hear all content related to an established user session in real time.

Supplemental Guidance: Session auditing activities are developed, integrated, and used in consultation with legal counsel in accordance with applicable federal laws, Executive Orders, directives, policies, or regulations.

Control Enhancements:

(1)   **The information system initiates session audits at system start-up.**

References: None.

Priority and Baseline Allocation:

P0	**LOW** Not Selected	**MOD** Not Selected	**HIGH** Not Selected

FAMILY: SECURITY ASSESSMENT AND AUTHORIZATION   **CLASS:** MANAGEMENT

CA-1   **SECURITY ASSESSMENT AND AUTHORIZATION POLICIES AND PROCEDURES**

Control: The organization develops, disseminates, and reviews/updates [*Assignment: organization-defined frequency*]:

a. Formal, documented security assessment and authorization policies that address purpose, scope, roles, responsibilities, management commitment, coordination among organizational entities, and compliance; and

b. Formal, documented procedures to facilitate the implementation of the security assessment and authorization policies and associated security assessment and authorization controls.

Supplemental Guidance: This control is intended to produce the policy and procedures that are required for the effective implementation of selected security controls and control enhancements in the security assessment and authorization family. The policies and procedures are consistent with applicable federal laws, Executive Orders, directives, policies, regulations, standards, and guidance. Existing organizational policies and procedures may make the need for additional specific policies and procedures unnecessary. The security assessment/authorization policies can be included as part of the general information security policy for the organization. Security assessment/authorization procedures can be developed for the security program in general and for a particular information system, when required. The organizational risk management strategy is a key factor in the development of the security assessment and authorization policy. Related control: PM-9.

Control Enhancements: None.

References: NIST Special Publications 800-12, 800-37, 800-53A, 800-100.

Priority and Baseline Allocation:

P1	**LOW** CA-1	**MOD** CA-1	**HIGH** CA-1

CA-2   **SECURITY ASSESSMENTS**

Control: The organization:

a. Develops a security assessment plan that describes the scope of the assessment including:

  - Security controls and control enhancements under assessment;

  - Assessment procedures to be used to determine security control effectiveness; and

  - Assessment environment, assessment team, and assessment roles and responsibilities;

b. Assesses the security controls in the information system [*Assignment: organization-defined frequency*] to determine the extent to which the controls are implemented correctly, operating as intended, and producing the desired outcome with respect to meeting the security requirements for the system;

c. Produces a security assessment report that documents the results of the assessment; and

d. Provides the results of the security control assessment, in writing, to the authorizing official or authorizing official designated representative.

Supplemental Guidance: The organization assesses the security controls in an information system as part of: (i) security authorization or reauthorization; (ii) meeting the FISMA requirement for annual assessments; (iii) continuous monitoring; and (iv) testing/evaluation of the information system as part of the system development life cycle process. The assessment report documents the assessment results in sufficient detail as deemed necessary by the organization, to determine the accuracy and completeness of the report and whether the security controls are implemented correctly, operating as intended, and producing the desired outcome with respect to meeting the security requirements of the information system. The FISMA requirement for (at least) annual security control assessments should *not* be interpreted by organizations as adding additional assessment requirements to those requirements already in place in the security authorization process. To satisfy the FISMA annual assessment requirement, organizations can draw upon the security control assessment results from any of the following sources, including but not limited to: (i) assessments conducted as part of an information system authorization or reauthorization process; (ii) continuous monitoring (see CA-7); or (iii) testing and evaluation of an information system as part of the ongoing system development life cycle (provided that the testing and evaluation results are current and relevant to the determination of security control effectiveness). Existing security control assessment results are reused to the extent that they are still valid and are supplemented with additional assessments as needed.

Subsequent to the initial authorization of the information system and in accordance with OMB policy, the organization assesses a subset of the security controls annually during continuous monitoring. The organization establishes the security control selection criteria and subsequently selects a subset of the security controls within the information system and its environment of operation for assessment. Those security controls that are the most volatile (i.e., controls most affected by ongoing changes to the information system or its environment of operation) or deemed critical by the organization to protecting organizational operations and assets, individuals, other organizations, and the Nation are assessed more frequently in accordance with an organizational assessment of risk. All other controls are assessed at least once during the information system's three-year authorization cycle. The organization can use the current year's assessment results from any of the above sources to meet the FISMA annual assessment requirement provided that the results are current, valid, and relevant to determining security control effectiveness. External audits (e.g., audits conducted by external entities such as regulatory agencies) are outside the scope of this control. Related controls: CA-6, CA-7, PM-9, SA-11.

Control Enhancements:

(1) **The organization employs an independent assessor or assessment team to conduct an assessment of the security controls in the information system.**

Enhancement Supplemental Guidance: An independent assessor or assessment team is any individual or group capable of conducting an impartial assessment of an organizational information system. Impartiality implies that the assessors are free from any perceived or actual conflicts of interest with respect to the developmental, operational, and/or management chain associated with the information system or to the determination of security control effectiveness. Independent security assessment services can be obtained from other elements within the organization or can be contracted to a public or private sector entity outside of the organization. Contracted assessment services are considered independent if the information system owner is not directly involved in the contracting process or cannot unduly influence the impartiality of the assessor or assessment team conducting the assessment of the security controls in the information system. The authorizing official determines the required level of assessor independence based on the security categorization of the information system and/or the ultimate risk to organizational operations and assets, and to individuals. The authorizing official determines if the level of assessor independence is sufficient to provide confidence that the assessment results produced are sound and can be used to make a credible, risk-based decision. In special situations, for example when the organization that owns the information system is small or the organizational structure requires that the assessment be accomplished by individuals that are in the developmental, operational, and/or management chain of the system owner, independence in the assessment process can be achieved by ensuring that the assessment results are carefully reviewed and analyzed by an independent team of experts to validate the completeness, accuracy, integrity, and reliability of the results.

(2) **The organization includes as part of security control assessments, [*Assignment: organization-defined frequency*], [*Selection: announced; unannounced*], [*Selection: in-depth monitoring; malicious user testing; penetration testing; red team exercises; [Assignment: organization-defined other forms of security testing*]]].**

Enhancement Supplemental Guidance: Penetration testing exercises both physical and technical security controls. A standard method for penetration testing consists of: (i) pretest analysis based on full knowledge of the target system; (ii) pretest identification of potential vulnerabilities based on pretest analysis; and (iii) testing designed to determine exploitability of identified vulnerabilities. Detailed rules of engagement are agreed upon by all parties before the commencement of any penetration testing scenario. These rules of engagement are correlated with the tools, techniques, and procedures that are anticipated to be employed by threat-sources in carrying out attacks. An organizational assessment of risk guides the decision on the level of independence required for penetration agents or penetration teams conducting penetration testing. Red team exercises are conducted as a simulated adversarial attempt to compromise organizational missions and/or business processes to provide a comprehensive assessment of the security capability of the information system and organization. While penetration testing may be laboratory-based testing, red team exercises are intended to be more comprehensive in nature and reflect real-world conditions. Information system monitoring, malicious user testing, penetration testing, red-team exercises, and other forms of security testing (e.g., independent verification and validation) are conducted to improve the readiness of the organization by exercising organizational capabilities and indicating current performance levels as a means of focusing organizational actions to improve the security state of the system and organization. Testing is conducted in accordance with applicable federal laws, Executive Orders, directives, policies, regulations, and standards. Testing methods are approved by authorizing officials in coordination with the organization's Risk Executive Function. Vulnerabilities uncovered during red team exercises are incorporated into the vulnerability remediation process. Related controls: RA-5, SI-2.

References: FIPS Publication 199; NIST Special Publications 800-37, 800-53A, 800-115.

Priority and Baseline Allocation:

| P2 | LOW CA-2 | MOD CA-2 (1) | HIGH CA-2 (1) (2) |

CA-3   INFORMATION SYSTEM CONNECTIONS

Control: The organization:

a. Authorizes connections from the information system to other information systems outside of the authorization boundary through the use of Interconnection Security Agreements;

b. Documents, for each connection, the interface characteristics, security requirements, and the nature of the information communicated; and

c. Monitors the information system connections on an ongoing basis verifying enforcement of security requirements.

Supplemental Guidance: This control applies to dedicated connections between information systems and does not apply to transitory, user-controlled connections such as email and website browsing. The organization carefully considers the risks that may be introduced when information systems are connected to other systems with different security requirements and security controls, both within the organization and external to the organization. Authorizing officials determine the risk associated with each connection and the appropriate controls employed. If the interconnecting systems have the same authorizing official, an Interconnection Security Agreement is not required. Rather, the interface characteristics between the interconnecting information systems are described in the security plans for the respective systems. If the interconnecting systems have different authorizing officials but the authorizing officials are in the same organization, the organization determines whether an Interconnection Security Agreement is required, or alternatively, the interface characteristics between systems are described in the security plans of the respective systems. Instead of developing an Interconnection Security Agreement, organizations may choose to incorporate this information into a formal contract, especially if the interconnection is to be established between a federal agency and a nonfederal (private sector) organization. In every case, documenting the interface characteristics is required, yet the formality and approval process vary considerably even though all accomplish the same fundamental objective of managing the risk being incurred by the interconnection of the information systems. Risk considerations also include information systems sharing the same networks. Information systems may be identified and authenticated as devices in accordance with IA-3. Related controls: AC-4, IA-3, SC-7, SA-9.

Control Enhancements:

(1) **The organization prohibits the direct connection of an unclassified, national security system to an external network.**

Enhancement Supplemental Guidance: An external network is a network that is not controlled by the organization (e.g., the Internet). No direct connection means that an information system cannot connect to an external network without the use of an approved boundary protection device (e.g., firewall) that mediates the communication between the system and the network.

(2) **The organization prohibits the direct connection of a classified, national security system to an external network.**

Enhancement Supplemental Guidance: An external network is a network that is not controlled by the organization (e.g., the Internet). No direct connection means that an information system cannot connect to an external network without the use of an approved boundary protection device (e.g., firewall) that mediates the communication between the system and the network. In addition, the approved boundary protection device (typically a managed interface/cross-domain system), provides information flow enforcement from the information system to the external network consistent with AC-4.

References: FIPS Publication 199; NIST Special Publication 800-47.

Priority and Baseline Allocation:

P1	**LOW** CA-3	**MOD** CA-3	**HIGH** CA-3

CA-4   SECURITY CERTIFICATION

[Withdrawn: Incorporated into CA-2].

CA-5   PLAN OF ACTION AND MILESTONES

Control: The organization:

a. Develops a plan of action and milestones for the information system to document the organization's planned remedial actions to correct weaknesses or deficiencies noted during the assessment of the security controls and to reduce or eliminate known vulnerabilities in the system; and

b. Updates existing plan of action and milestones [*Assignment: organization-defined frequency*] based on the findings from security controls assessments, security impact analyses, and continuous monitoring activities.

Supplemental Guidance: The plan of action and milestones is a key document in the security authorization package and is subject to federal reporting requirements established by OMB. Related control: PM-4.

Control Enhancements:

(1) **The organization employs automated mechanisms to help ensure that the plan of action and milestones for the information system is accurate, up to date, and readily available.**

References: OMB Memorandum 02-01; NIST Special Publication 800-37.

Priority and Baseline Allocation:

P3	LOW CA-5	MOD CA-5	HIGH CA-5

CA-6   SECURITY AUTHORIZATION

Control: The organization:

a. Assigns a senior-level executive or manager to the role of authorizing official for the information system;

b. Ensures that the authorizing official authorizes the information system for processing before commencing operations; and

c. Updates the security authorization [*Assignment: organization-defined frequency*].

Supplemental Guidance: Security authorization is the official management decision given by a senior organizational official or executive (i.e., authorizing official) to authorize operation of an information system and to explicitly accept the risk to organizational operations and assets, individuals, other organizations, and the Nation based on the implementation of an agreed-upon set of security controls. Authorizing officials typically have budgetary oversight for information systems or are responsible for the mission or business operations supported by the systems. Security authorization is an inherently federal responsibility and therefore, authorizing officials must be federal employees. Through the security authorization process, authorizing officials are accountable for the security risks associated with information system operations. Accordingly, authorizing officials are in management positions with a level of authority commensurate with understanding and accepting such information system-related security risks. Through the employment of a comprehensive continuous monitoring process, the critical information contained in the authorization package (i.e., the security plan (including risk assessment), the security assessment report, and the plan of action and milestones) is updated on an ongoing basis, providing the authorizing official and the information system owner with an up-to-date status of the security state of the information system. To reduce the administrative cost of security reauthorization, the authorizing official uses the results of the continuous monitoring process to the maximum extent possible as the basis for rendering a reauthorization decision. OMB policy requires that federal information systems are reauthorized at least every three years or when there is a significant change to the system. The organization defines what constitutes a significant change to the information system. Related controls: CA-2, CA-7, PM-9, PM-10.

Control Enhancements: None.

References: OMB Circular A-130; NIST Special Publication 800-37.

Priority and Baseline Allocation:

P3	LOW CA-6	MOD CA-6	HIGH CA-6

CA-7   CONTINUOUS MONITORING

Control: The organization establishes a continuous monitoring strategy and implements a continuous monitoring program that includes:

a. A configuration management process for the information system and its constituent components;

b. A determination of the security impact of changes to the information system and environment of operation;

c. Ongoing security control assessments in accordance with the organizational continuous monitoring strategy; and

d. Reporting the security state of the information system to appropriate organizational officials [*Assignment: organization-defined frequency*].

Supplemental Guidance: A continuous monitoring program allows an organization to maintain the security authorization of an information system over time in a highly dynamic environment of operation with changing threats, vulnerabilities, technologies, and missions/business processes. Continuous monitoring of security controls using automated support tools facilitates near real-time risk management and promotes organizational situational awareness with regard to the security state of the information system. The implementation of a continuous monitoring program results in ongoing updates to the security plan, the security assessment report, and the plan of action and milestones, the three principal documents in the security authorization package. A rigorous and well executed continuous monitoring program significantly reduces the level of effort required for the reauthorization of the information system. Continuous monitoring activities are scaled in accordance with the impact level of the information system. Related controls: CA-2, CA-5, CA-6, CM-3, CM-4.

Control Enhancements:

(1) **The organization employs an independent assessor or assessment team to monitor the security controls in the information system on an ongoing basis.**

Enhancement Supplemental Guidance: The organization can extend and maximize the value of the ongoing assessment of security controls during the continuous monitoring process by requiring an independent assessor or team to assess all of the security controls during the information system's three-year authorization cycle. See supplemental guidance for CA-2, enhancement (1), for further information on assessor independence. Related controls: CA-2, CA-5, CA-6, CM-4.

(2) **The organization plans, schedules, and conducts assessments [*Assignment: organization-defined frequency*], [*Selection: announced; unannounced*], [*Selection: in-depth monitoring; malicious user testing; penetration testing; red team exercises; [Assignment: organization-defined other forms of security assessment*]] to ensure compliance with all vulnerability mitigation procedures.**

Enhancement Supplemental Guidance: Examples of vulnerability mitigation procedures are contained in Information Assurance Vulnerability Alerts. Testing is intended to ensure that the information system continues to provide adequate security against constantly evolving threats and vulnerabilities. Conformance testing also provides independent validation. See supplemental guidance for CA-2, enhancement (2) for further information on malicious user testing, penetration testing, red-team exercises, and other forms of security testing. Related control: CA-2.

References: NIST Special Publications 800-37, 800-53A; US-CERT Technical Cyber Security Alerts; DOD Information Assurance Vulnerability Alerts.

Priority and Baseline Allocation:

P3	LOW CA-7	MOD CA-7	HIGH CA-7

FAMILY: CONFIGURATION MANAGEMENT   **CLASS:** OPERATIONAL

CM-1   CONFIGURATION MANAGEMENT POLICY AND PROCEDURES

Control: The organization develops, disseminates, and reviews/updates [*Assignment: organization-defined frequency*]:

a. A formal, documented configuration management policy that addresses purpose, scope, roles, responsibilities, management commitment, coordination among organizational entities, and compliance; and

b. Formal, documented procedures to facilitate the implementation of the configuration management policy and associated configuration management controls.

Supplemental Guidance: This control is intended to produce the policy and procedures that are required for the effective implementation of selected security controls and control enhancements in the configuration management family. The policy and procedures are consistent with applicable federal laws, Executive Orders, directives, policies, regulations, standards, and guidance. Existing organizational policies and procedures may make the need for additional specific policies and procedures unnecessary. The configuration management policy can be included as part of the general information security policy for the organization. Configuration management procedures can be developed for the security program in general and for a particular information system, when required. The organizational risk management strategy is a key factor in the development of the configuration management policy. Related control: PM-9.

Control Enhancements: None.

References: NIST Special Publications 800-12, 800-100.

Priority and Baseline Allocation:

P1	**LOW** CM-1	**MOD** CM-1	**HIGH** CM-1

CM-2   BASELINE CONFIGURATION

Control: The organization develops, documents, and maintains under configuration control, a current baseline configuration of the information system.

Supplemental Guidance: This control establishes a baseline configuration for the information system and its constituent components including communications and connectivity-related aspects of the system. The baseline configuration provides information about the components of an information system (e.g., the standard software load for a workstation, server, network component, or mobile device including operating system/installed applications with current version numbers and patch information), network topology, and the logical placement of the component within the system architecture. The baseline configuration is a documented, up-to-date specification to which the information system is built. Maintaining the baseline configuration involves creating new baselines as the information system changes over time. The baseline configuration of the information system is consistent with the organization's enterprise architecture. Related controls: CM-3, CM-6, CM-8, CM-9.

Control Enhancements:

(1)   The organization reviews and updates the baseline configuration of the information

    system: (a)   [*Assignment: organization-defined frequency*];

    (b)   When required due to [*Assignment organization-defined circumstances*]; and

    (c)   As an integral part of information system component installations and upgrades.

(2)   The organization employs automated mechanisms to maintain an up-to-date, complete, accurate, and readily available baseline configuration of the information system.

Enhancement Supplemental Guidance: Software inventory tools are examples of automated mechanisms that help organizations maintain consistent baseline configurations for information systems. Software inventory tools can be deployed for each operating system in use within the organization (e.g., on workstations, servers, network components, mobile devices) and used to track operating system version numbers, applications and types of software installed on the operating systems, and current patch levels. Software inventory tools can also scan information systems for unauthorized software to validate organization-defined lists of authorized and unauthorized software programs.

(3) **The organization retains older versions of baseline configurations as deemed necessary to support rollback.**

(4) **The organization:**

    (a) **Develops and maintains [*Assignment: organization-defined list of software programs not authorized to execute on the information system*]; and**

    (b) **Employs an allow-all, deny-by-exception authorization policy to identify software allowed to execute on the information system.**

(5) **The organization:**

    (a) **Develops and maintains [*Assignment: organization-defined list of software programs authorized to execute on the information system*]; and**

    (b) **Employs a deny-all, permit-by-exception authorization policy to identify software allowed to execute on the information system.**

(6) **The organization maintains a baseline configuration for development and test environments that is managed separately from the operational baseline configuration.**

References: NIST Special Publication 800-128.

Priority and Baseline Allocation:

P1	**LOW** CM-2	**MOD** CM-2 (1) (3) (4)	**HIGH** CM-2 (1) (2) (3) (5) (6)

CM-3   CONFIGURATION CHANGE CONTROL

Control: The organization:

a. Determines the types of changes to the information system that are configuration controlled;

b. Approves configuration-controlled changes to the system with explicit consideration for security impact analyses;

c. Documents approved configuration-controlled changes to the system;

d. Retains and reviews records of configuration-controlled changes to the system;

e. Audits activities associated with configuration-controlled changes to the system; and

f. Coordinates and provides oversight for configuration change control activities through [*Assignment: organization-defined configuration change control element (e.g., committee, board*] that convenes [*Selection: (one or more)*: [*Assignment: organization-defined frequency*]; [*Assignment: organization-defined configuration change conditions*]].

Supplemental Guidance: The organization determines the types of changes to the information system that are configuration controlled. Configuration change control for the information system involves the systematic proposal, justification, implementation, test/evaluation, review, and disposition of changes to the system, including upgrades and modifications. Configuration change control includes changes to components of the information system, changes to the configuration settings for information technology products (e.g., operating systems, applications, firewalls, routers), emergency changes, and changes to remediate flaws. A typical organizational process for managing configuration changes to the information system includes, for example, a chartered

Configuration Control Board that approves proposed changes to the system. Auditing of changes refers to changes in activity before and after a change is made to the information system and the auditing activities required to implement the change. Related controls: CM-4, CM-5, CM-6, SI-2.

Control Enhancements:

(1) **The organization employs automated mechanisms to:**

   (a) **Document proposed changes to the information**

   system; (b) Notify designated approval authorities;

   (c) **Highlight approvals that have not been received by [*Assignment: organization-defined time period*];**

   (d) **Inhibit change until designated approvals are received; and**

   (e) **Document completed changes to the information system.**

(2) **The organization tests, validates, and documents changes to the information system before implementing the changes on the operational system.**

   Enhancement Supplemental Guidance: The organization ensures that testing does not interfere with information system operations. The individual/group conducting the tests understands the organizational information security policies and procedures, the information system security policies and procedures, and the specific health, safety, and environmental risks associated with a particular facility and/or process. An operational system may need to be taken off-line, or replicated to the extent feasible, before testing can be conducted. If an information system must be taken off-line for testing, the tests are scheduled to occur during planned system outages whenever possible. In situations where the organization cannot conduct testing of an operational system, the organization employs compensating controls (e.g., providing a replicated system to conduct testing) in accordance with the general tailoring guidance.

(3) **The organization employs automated mechanisms to implement changes to the current information system baseline and deploys the updated baseline across the installed base.**

   Enhancement Supplemental Guidance: Related controls: CM-2, CM-6.

(4) **The organization requires an information security representative to be a member of the [*Assignment: organization-defined configuration change control element (e.g., committee, board)*].**

   Enhancement Supplemental Guidance: Information security representatives can include, for example, information system security officers or information system security managers. The configuration change control element in this control enhancement is consistent with the change control element defined by the organization in CM-3.

References: NIST Special Publication 800-128.

Priority and Baseline Allocation:

P1	**LOW** Not Selected	**MOD** CM-3 (2)	**HIGH** CM-3 (1) (2)

CM-4   SECURITY IMPACT ANALYSIS

Control: The organization analyzes changes to the information system to determine potential security impacts prior to change implementation.

Supplemental Guidance: Security impact analyses are conducted by organizational personnel with information security responsibilities, including for example, Information System Administrators, Information System Security Officers, Information System Security Managers, and Information System Security Engineers. Individuals conducting security impact analyses have the appropriate skills and technical expertise to analyze the changes to information systems and the associated security ramifications. Security impact analysis may include, for example, reviewing information system documentation such as the security plan to understand how specific security controls are implemented within the system and how the changes might affect the controls. Security impact analysis may also include an assessment of risk to understand the impact of the changes and to determine if additional security controls are required. Security impact analysis is scaled in accordance with the impact level of the information system. Related controls: CA-2, CA-7, CM-3, CM-9, SI-2.

Control Enhancements:

(1) The organization analyzes new software in a separate test environment before installation in an operational environment, looking for security impacts due to flaws, weaknesses, incompatibility, or intentional malice.

(2) The organization, after the information system is changed, checks the security functions to verify that the functions are implemented correctly, operating as intended, and producing the desired outcome with regard to meeting the security requirements for the system.

Enhancement Supplemental Guidance: Changes include information system upgrades and modifications.

References: NIST Special Publication 800-128.

Priority and Baseline Allocation:

P2	LOW CM-4	MOD CM-4	HIGH CM-4 (1)

CM-5 ACCESS RESTRICTIONS FOR CHANGE

Control: The organization defines, documents, approves, and enforces physical and logical access restrictions associated with changes to the information system.

Supplemental Guidance: Any changes to the hardware, software, and/or firmware components of the information system can potentially have significant effects on the overall security of the system. Accordingly, only qualified and authorized individuals are allowed to obtain access to information system components for purposes of initiating changes, including upgrades and modifications. Additionally, maintaining records of access is essential for ensuring that configuration change control is being implemented as intended and for supporting after-the-fact actions should the organization become aware of an unauthorized change to the information system. Access restrictions for change also include software libraries. Examples of access restrictions include, for example, physical and logical access controls (see AC-3 and PE-3), workflow automation, media libraries, abstract layers (e.g., changes are implemented into a third-party interface rather than directly into the information system component), and change windows (e.g., changes occur only during specified times, making unauthorized changes outside the window easy to discover). Some or all of the enforcement mechanisms and processes necessary to implement this security control are included in other controls. For measures implemented in other controls, this control provides information to be used in the implementation of the other controls to cover specific needs related to enforcing authorizations to make changes to the information system, auditing changes, and retaining and review records of changes. Related controls: AC-3, AC-6, PE-3.

Control Enhancements:

(1) The organization employs automated mechanisms to enforce access restrictions and support auditing of the enforcement actions.

(2) The organization conducts audits of information system changes [Assignment: organization-defined frequency] and when indications so warrant to determine whether unauthorized changes have occurred.

(3) The information system prevents the installation of [Assignment: organization-defined critical software programs] that are not signed with a certificate that is recognized and approved by the organization.

Enhancement Supplemental Guidance: Critical software programs and/or modules include, for example, patches, service packs, and where applicable, device drivers.

(4)   The organization enforces a two-person rule for changes to [*Assignment: organization-defined information system components and system-level information*].

(5)   The organization:

   (a)   Limits information system developer/integrator privileges to change hardware, software, and firmware components and system information directly within a production environment; and

   (b)   Reviews and reevaluates information system developer/integrator privileges [*Assignment: organization-defined frequency*].

(6)   The organization limits privileges to change software resident within software libraries (including privileged programs).

(7)   The information system automatically implements [*Assignment: organization-defined safeguards and countermeasures*] if security functions (or mechanisms) are changed inappropriately.

   Enhancement Supplemental Guidance: The information system reacts automatically when inappropriate and/or unauthorized modifications have occurred to security functions or mechanisms. Automatic implementation of safeguards and countermeasures includes, for example, reversing the change, halting the information system or triggering an audit alert when an unauthorized modification to a critical security file occurs.

References: None.

Priority and Baseline Allocation:

P1	**LOW** Not Selected	**MOD** CM-5	**HIGH** CM-5 (1) (2) (3)

CM-6   CONFIGURATION SETTINGS

Control: The organization:

a.   Establishes and documents mandatory configuration settings for information technology products employed within the information system using [*Assignment: organization-defined security configuration checklists*] that reflect the most restrictive mode consistent with operational requirements;

b.   Implements the configuration settings;

c.   Identifies, documents, and approves exceptions from the mandatory configuration settings for individual components within the information system based on explicit operational requirements; and

d.   Monitors and controls changes to the configuration settings in accordance with organizational policies and procedures.

Supplemental Guidance: Configuration settings are the configurable security-related parameters of information technology products that are part of the information system. Security-related parameters are those parameters impacting the security state of the system including parameters related to meeting other security control requirements. Security-related parameters include, for example, registry settings; account, file, and directory settings (i.e., permissions); and settings for services, ports, protocols, and remote connections. Organizations establish organization-wide mandatory configuration settings from which the settings for a given information system are derived. A *security configuration checklist* (sometimes referred to as a lockdown guide, hardening guide, security guide, security technical implementation guide [STIG], or benchmark) is a series of instructions or procedures for configuring an information system component to meet operational requirements. Checklists can be developed by information technology developers and vendors, consortia, academia, industry, federal agencies (and other government organizations), and others in the public and private sectors. An example of a security configuration checklist is the Federal Desktop Core Configuration (FDCC) which potentially affects the implementation of CM-6 and other controls such as AC-19 and CM-7. The Security Content Automation Protocol (SCAP) and defined standards within the protocol (e.g., Common Configuration Enumeration) provide an effective method to uniquely identify, track, and control configuration settings. OMB establishes federal policy on configuration requirements for federal information systems. Related controls: CM-2, CM-3, SI-4.

Control Enhancements:

(1)   The organization employs automated mechanisms to centrally manage, apply, and verify configuration settings.

(2)   The organization employs automated mechanisms to respond to unauthorized changes to [*Assignment: organization-defined configuration settings*].

Enhancement Supplemental Guidance: Responses to unauthorized changes to configuration settings can include, for example, alerting designated organizational personnel, restoring mandatory/organization-defined configuration settings, or in the extreme case, halting affected information system processing.

(3)   The organization incorporates detection of unauthorized, security-relevant configuration changes into the organization's incident response capability to ensure that such detected events are tracked, monitored, corrected, and available for historical purposes.

Enhancement Supplemental Guidance: Related controls: IR-4, IR-5.

(4)   The information system (including modifications to the baseline configuration) demonstrates conformance to security configuration guidance (i.e., security checklists), prior to being introduced into a production environment.

References: OMB Memoranda 07-11, 07-18, 08-22; NIST Special Publications 800-70, 800-128; Web: NVD.NIST.GOV; WWW.NSA.GOV.

Priority and Baseline Allocation:

P1	**LOW** CM-6	**MOD** CM-6 (3)	**HIGH** CM-6 (1) (2) (3)

CM-7   LEAST FUNCTIONALITY

Control: The organization configures the information system to provide only essential capabilities and specifically prohibits or restricts the use of the following functions, ports, protocols, and/or services: [*Assignment: organization-defined list of prohibited or restricted functions, ports, protocols, and/or services*].

Supplemental Guidance: Information systems are capable of providing a wide variety of functions and services. Some of the functions and services, provided by default, may not be necessary to support essential organizational operations (e.g., key missions, functions). Additionally, it is sometimes convenient to provide multiple services from a single component of an information system, but doing so increases risk over limiting the services provided by any one component. Where feasible, organizations limit component functionality to a single function per device (e.g., email server or web server, not both). The functions and services provided by organizational information systems, or individual components of information systems, are carefully reviewed to determine which functions and services are candidates for elimination (e.g., Voice Over Internet Protocol, Instant Messaging, auto-execute, file sharing). Organizations consider disabling unused or unnecessary physical and logical ports and protocols (e.g., Universal Serial Bus [USB], File Transfer Protocol [FTP], Internet Protocol Version 6 [IPv6], Hyper Text Transfer Protocol [HTTP]) on information system components to prevent unauthorized connection of devices, unauthorized transfer of information, or unauthorized tunneling. Organizations can utilize network scanning tools, intrusion detection and prevention systems, and end-point protections such as firewalls and host-based intrusion detection systems to identify and prevent the use of prohibited functions, ports, protocols, and services. Related control: RA-5.

Control Enhancements:

(1)   The organization reviews the information system [*Assignment: organization-defined frequency*] to identify and eliminate unnecessary functions, ports, protocols, and/or services.

(2)   **The organization employs automated mechanisms to prevent program execution in accordance with [*Selection (one or more): list of authorized software programs; list of unauthorized software programs; rules authorizing the terms and conditions of software program usage*].**

Enhancement Supplemental Guidance: Related control: CM-2.

(3)   **The organization ensures compliance with [*Assignment: organization-defined registration requirements for ports, protocols, and services*].**

Enhancement Supplemental Guidance: Organizations use the registration process to manage, track, and provide oversight for information systems and implemented functionality.

References: None.

Priority and Baseline Allocation:

P1	LOW CM-7	MOD CM-7 (1)	HIGH CM-7 (1) (2)

CM-8   INFORMATION SYSTEM COMPONENT INVENTORY

Control: The organization develops, documents, and maintains an inventory of information system components that:

a.   Accurately reflects the current information system;

b.   Is consistent with the authorization boundary of the information system;

c.   Is at the level of granularity deemed necessary for tracking and reporting;

d.   Includes [*Assignment: organization-defined information deemed necessary to achieve effective property accountability*]; and

e.   Is available for review and audit by designated organizational officials.

Supplemental Guidance: Information deemed to be necessary by the organization to achieve effective property accountability can include, for example, hardware inventory specifications (manufacturer, type, model, serial number, physical location), software license information, information system/component owner, and for a networked component/device, the machine name and network address. Related controls: CM-2, CM-6.

Control Enhancements:

(1)   **The organization updates the inventory of information system components as an integral part of component installations, removals, and information system updates.**

(2)   **The organization employs automated mechanisms to help maintain an up-to-date, complete, accurate, and readily available inventory of information system components.**

Enhancement Supplemental Guidance: Organizations maintain the information system inventory to the extent feasible. Virtual machines, for example, can be difficult to monitor because they are not visible to the network when not in use. In such cases, the intent of this control enhancement is to maintain as up-to-date, complete, and accurate an inventory as is reasonable.

(3)   **The organization:**

(a)   **Employs automated mechanisms [*Assignment: organization-defined frequency*] to detect the addition of unauthorized components/devices into the information system; and**

(b)   **Disables network access by such components/devices or notifies designated organizational officials.**

Enhancement Supplemental Guidance: This control enhancement is applied in addition to the monitoring for unauthorized remote connections in AC-17 and for unauthorized mobile devices in AC-19. The monitoring for unauthorized components/devices on information system networks may be accomplished on an ongoing basis or by the periodic scanning of organizational networks for that purpose. Automated mechanisms can be implemented within the information system and/or in another separate information system or device. Related controls: AC-17, AC-19.

(4)   The organization includes in property accountability information for information system components, a means for identifying by [*Selection (one or more): name; position; role*] individuals responsible for administering those components.

(5)   The organization verifies that all components within the authorization boundary of the information system are either inventoried as a part of the system or recognized by another system as a component within that system.

(6)   The organization includes assessed component configurations and any approved deviations to current deployed configurations in the information system component inventory.

Enhancement Supplemental Guidance: This control enhancement focuses on the configuration settings established by the organization for its information system components, the specific information system components that have been assessed to determine compliance with the required configuration settings, and any approved deviations from established configuration settings in the deployed information system components. Related controls: CM-2, CM-6.

References: NIST Special Publication 800-128.

Priority and Baseline Allocation:

P1	LOW CM-8	MOD CM-8 (1) (5)	HIGH CM-8 (1) (2) (3) (4) (5)

CM-9   CONFIGURATION MANAGEMENT PLAN

Control: The organization develops, documents, and implements a configuration management plan for the information system that:

a.   Addresses roles, responsibilities, and configuration management processes and procedures;

b.   Defines the configuration items for the information system and when in the system development life cycle the configuration items are placed under configuration management; and

c.   Establishes the means for identifying configuration items throughout the system development life cycle and a process for managing the configuration of the configuration items.

Supplemental Guidance: Configuration items are the information system items (hardware, software, firmware, and documentation) to be configuration managed. The configuration management plan satisfies the requirements in the organization's configuration management policy while being tailored to the individual information system. The configuration management plan defines detailed processes and procedures for how configuration management is used to support system development life cycle activities at the information system level. The plan describes how to move a change through the change management process, how configuration settings and configuration baselines are updated, how the information system component inventory is maintained, how development, test, and operational environments are controlled, and finally, how documents are developed, released, and updated. The configuration management approval process includes designation of key management stakeholders that are responsible for reviewing and approving proposed changes to the information system, and security personnel that would conduct an impact analysis prior to the implementation of any changes to the system. Related control: SA-10.

Control Enhancements:

(1)   The organization assigns responsibility for developing the configuration management process to organizational personnel that are not directly involved in system development.

Enhancement Supplemental Guidance: In the absence of a dedicated configuration management team, the system integrator may be tasked with developing the configuration management process.

References: NIST Special Publication 800-128.

Priority and Baseline Allocation:

P1	LOW Not Selected	MOD CM-9	HIGH CM-9

FAMILY: CONTINGENCY PLANNING   **CLASS:** OPERATIONAL

CP-1   **CONTINGENCY PLANNING POLICY AND PROCEDURES**

Control: The organization develops, disseminates, and reviews/updates [*Assignment: organization-defined frequency*]:

a. A formal, documented contingency planning policy that addresses purpose, scope, roles, responsibilities, management commitment, coordination among organizational entities, and compliance; and

b. Formal, documented procedures to facilitate the implementation of the contingency planning policy and associated contingency planning controls.

Supplemental Guidance: This control is intended to produce the policy and procedures that are required for the effective implementation of selected security controls and control enhancements in the contingency planning family. The policy and procedures are consistent with applicable federal laws, Executive Orders, directives, policies, regulations, standards, and guidance. Existing organizational policies and procedures may make the need for additional specific policies and procedures unnecessary. The contingency planning policy can be included as part of the general information security policy for the organization. Contingency planning procedures can be developed for the security program in general and for a particular information system, when required. The organizational risk management strategy is a key factor in the development of the contingency planning policy. Related control: PM-9.

Control Enhancements: None.

References: Federal Continuity Directive 1; NIST Special Publications 800-12, 800-34, 800-100.

Priority and Baseline Allocation:

P1	**LOW** CP-1	**MOD** CP-1	**HIGH** CP-1

CP-2   **CONTINGENCY PLAN**

Control: The organization:

a. Develops a contingency plan for the information system that:

  - Identifies essential missions and business functions and associated contingency requirements;

  - Provides recovery objectives, restoration priorities, and metrics;

  - Addresses contingency roles, responsibilities, assigned individuals with contact information;

  - Addresses maintaining essential missions and business functions despite an information system disruption, compromise, or failure;

  - Addresses eventual, full information system restoration without deterioration of the security measures originally planned and implemented; and

  - Is reviewed and approved by designated officials within the organization;

b. Distributes copies of the contingency plan to [*Assignment: organization-defined list of key contingency personnel (identified by name and/or by role) and organizational elements*];

c. Coordinates contingency planning activities with incident handling activities;

d. Reviews the contingency plan for the information system [*Assignment: organization-defined frequency*];

e. Revises the contingency plan to address changes to the organization, information system, or environment of operation and problems encountered during contingency plan implementation, execution, or testing; and

f. Communicates contingency plan changes to [*Assignment: organization-defined list of key contingency personnel (identified by name and/or by role) and organizational elements*].

Supplemental Guidance: Contingency planning for information systems is part of an overall organizational program for achieving continuity of operations for mission/business operations. Contingency planning addresses both information system restoration and implementation of alternative mission/business processes when systems are compromised. Information system recovery objectives are consistent with applicable laws, Executive Orders, directives, policies, standards, or regulations. In addition to information system availability, contingency plans also address other security-related events resulting in a reduction in mission/business effectiveness, such as malicious attacks compromising the confidentiality or integrity of the information system. Examples of actions to call out in contingency plans include, for example, graceful degradation, information system shutdown, fall back to a manual mode, alternate information flows, or operating in a mode that is reserved solely for when the system is under attack. Related controls: AC-14, CP-6, CP-7, CP-8, IR-4, PM-8, PM-11.

Control Enhancements:

(1) The organization coordinates contingency plan development with organizational elements responsible for related plans.

Enhancement Supplemental Guidance: Examples of related plans include Business Continuity Plan, Disaster Recovery Plan, Continuity of Operations Plan, Crisis Communications Plan, Critical Infrastructure Plan, Cyber Incident Response Plan, and Occupant Emergency Plan.

(2) The organization conducts capacity planning so that necessary capacity for information processing, telecommunications, and environmental support exists during contingency operations.

(3) The organization plans for the resumption of essential missions and business functions within [*Assignment: organization-defined time period*] of contingency plan activation.

(4) The organization plans for the full resumption of missions and business functions within [*Assignment: organization-defined time period*] of contingency plan activation.

(5) The organization plans for the continuance of essential missions and business functions with little or no loss of operational continuity and sustains that continuity until full information system restoration at primary processing and/or storage sites.

(6) The organization provides for the transfer of all essential missions and business functions to alternate processing and/or storage sites with little or no loss of operational continuity and sustains that continuity through restoration to primary processing and/or storage sites.

References: Federal Continuity Directive 1; NIST Special Publication 800-34.

Priority and Baseline Allocation:

P1	LOW CP-2	MOD CP-2 (1)	HIGH CP-2 (1) (2) (3)

CP-3 CONTINGENCY TRAINING

Control: The organization trains personnel in their contingency roles and responsibilities with respect to the information system and provides refresher training [*Assignment: organization-defined frequency*].

Supplemental Guidance: None.

Control Enhancements:

(1) The organization incorporates simulated events into contingency training to facilitate effective response by personnel in crisis situations.

(2)   The organization employs automated mechanisms to provide a more thorough and realistic training environment.

References: NIST Special Publications 800-16, 800-50.

Priority and Baseline Allocation:

P2	**LOW** CP-3	**MOD** CP-3	**HIGH** CP-3 (1)

CP-4   CONTINGENCY PLAN TESTING AND EXERCISES

Control: The organization:

a.   Tests and/or exercises the contingency plan for the information system [*Assignment: organization-defined frequency*] using [*Assignment: organization-defined tests and/or exercises*] to determine the plan's effectiveness and the organization's readiness to execute the plan; and

b.   Reviews the contingency plan test/exercise results and initiates corrective actions.

Supplemental Guidance: There are several methods for testing and/or exercising contingency plans to identify potential weaknesses (e.g., checklist, walk-through/tabletop, simulation: parallel, full interrupt). Contingency plan testing and/or exercises include a determination of the effects on organizational operations and assets (e.g., reduction in mission capability) and individuals arising due to contingency operations in accordance with the plan.

Control Enhancements:

(1)   The organization coordinates contingency plan testing and/or exercises with organizational elements responsible for related plans.

Enhancement Supplemental Guidance: Examples of related plans include Business Continuity Plan, Disaster Recovery Plan, Continuity of Operations Plan, Crisis Communications Plan, Critical Infrastructure Plan, Cyber Incident Response Plan, and Occupant Emergency Plan.

(2)   The organization tests/exercises the contingency plan at the alternate processing site to familiarize contingency personnel with the facility and available resources and to evaluate the site's capabilities to support contingency operations.

(3)   The organization employs automated mechanisms to more thoroughly and effectively test/exercise the contingency plan by providing more complete coverage of contingency issues, selecting more realistic test/exercise scenarios and environments, and more effectively stressing the information system and supported missions.

(4)   The organization includes a full recovery and reconstitution of the information system to a known state as part of contingency plan testing.

Enhancement Supplemental Guidance: Related controls: CP-10, SC-24.

References: FIPS Publication 199; NIST Special Publications 800-34, 800-84.

Priority and Baseline Allocation:

P2	**LOW** CP-4	**MOD** CP-4 (1)	**HIGH** CP-4 (1) (2) (4)

CP-5   CONTINGENCY PLAN UPDATE

[Withdrawn: Incorporated into CP-2].

CP-6   ALTERNATE STORAGE SITE

Control: The organization establishes an alternate storage site including necessary agreements to permit the storage and recovery of information system backup information.

Supplemental Guidance: Related controls: CP-2, CP-9, MP-4.

Control Enhancements:

(1)   **The organization identifies an alternate storage site that is separated from the primary storage site so as not to be susceptible to the same hazards.**

   Enhancement Supplemental Guidance: Hazards of concern to the organization are typically defined in an organizational assessment of risk.

(2)   **The organization configures the alternate storage site to facilitate recovery operations in accordance with recovery time and recovery point objectives.**

(3)   **The organization identifies potential accessibility problems to the alternate storage site in the event of an area-wide disruption or disaster and outlines explicit mitigation actions.**

   Enhancement Supplemental Guidance: Explicit mitigation actions include, for example, duplicating backup information at another alternate storage site if access to the first alternate site is hindered; or, if electronic accessibility to the alternate site is disrupted, planning for physical access to retrieve backup information.

References: NIST Special Publication 800-34.

Priority and Baseline Allocation:

P1	**LOW** Not Selected	**MOD** CP-6 (1) (3)	**HIGH** CP-6 (1) (2) (3)

CP-7   ALTERNATE PROCESSING SITE

Control: The organization:

a.   Establishes an alternate processing site including necessary agreements to permit the resumption of information system operations for essential missions and business functions within [*Assignment: organization-defined time period consistent with recovery time objectives*] when the primary processing capabilities are unavailable; and

b.   Ensures that equipment and supplies required to resume operations are available at the alternate site or contracts are in place to support delivery to the site in time to support the organization-defined time period for resumption.

Supplemental Guidance: Related control: CP-2.

Control Enhancements:

(1)   **The organization identifies an alternate processing site that is separated from the primary processing site so as not to be susceptible to the same hazards.**

   Enhancement Supplemental Guidance: Hazards that might affect the information system are typically defined in the risk assessment.

(2)   **The organization identifies potential accessibility problems to the alternate processing site in the event of an area-wide disruption or disaster and outlines explicit mitigation actions.**

(3)   **The organization develops alternate processing site agreements that contain priority-of-service provisions in accordance with the organization's availability requirements.**

(4)   **The organization configures the alternate processing site so that it is ready to be used as the operational site supporting essential missions and business functions.**

(5)   **The organization ensures that the alternate processing site provides information security measures equivalent to that of the primary site.**

References: NIST Special Publication 800-34.

Priority and Baseline Allocation:

P1	LOW Not Selected	MOD CP-7 (1) (2) (3) (5)	HIGH CP-7 (1) (2) (3) (4) (5)

CP-8   TELECOMMUNICATIONS SERVICES

Control: The organization establishes alternate telecommunications services including necessary agreements to permit the resumption of information system operations for essential missions and business functions within [*Assignment: organization-defined time period*] when the primary telecommunications capabilities are unavailable.

Supplemental Guidance: Related control: CP-2.

Control Enhancements:

(1)   **The organization:**

   (a)   **Develops primary and alternate telecommunications service agreements that contain priority- of-service provisions in accordance with the organization's availability requirements; and**

   (b)   **Requests Telecommunications Service Priority for all telecommunications services used for national security emergency preparedness in the event that the primary and/or alternate telecommunications services are provided by a common carrier.**

(2)   **The organization obtains alternate telecommunications services with consideration for reducing the likelihood of sharing a single point of failure with primary telecommunications services.**

(3)   **The organization obtains alternate telecommunications service providers that are separated from primary service providers so as not to be susceptible to the same hazards.**

(4)   **The organization requires primary and alternate telecommunications service providers to have contingency plans.**

References: NIST Special Publication 800-34; Web: TSP.NCS.GOV.

Priority and Baseline Allocation:

P1	LOW Not Selected	MOD CP-8 (1) (2)	HIGH CP-8 (1) (2) (3) (4)

CP-9   INFORMATION SYSTEM BACKUP

Control: The organization:

a.   Conducts backups of user-level information contained in the information system [*Assignment: organization-defined frequency consistent with recovery time and recovery point objectives*];

b.   Conducts backups of system-level information contained in the information system [*Assignment: organization-defined frequency consistent with recovery time and recovery point objectives*];

c.   Conducts backups of information system documentation including security-related documentation [*Assignment: organization-defined frequency consistent with recovery time and recovery point objectives*]; and

d.   Protects the confidentiality and integrity of backup information at the storage location.

Supplemental Guidance: System-level information includes, for example, system-state information, operating system and application software, and licenses. Digital signatures and cryptographic hashes are examples of mechanisms that can be employed by organizations to protect the integrity of information system backups. An organizational assessment of risk guides the use of encryption for protecting backup information. The protection of system backup information while in transit is beyond the scope of this control. Related controls: CP-6, MP-4.

Control Enhancements:

(1)   The organization tests backup information [*Assignment: organization-defined frequency*] to verify media reliability and information integrity.

(2)   The organization uses a sample of backup information in the restoration of selected information system functions as part of contingency plan testing.

(3)   The organization stores backup copies of the operating system and other critical information system software, as well as copies of the information system inventory (including hardware, software, and firmware components) in a separate facility or in a fire-rated container that is not colocated with the operational system.

(4)   [Withdrawn: Incorporated into CP-9].

(5)   The organization transfers information system backup information to the alternate storage site [*Assignment: organization-defined time period and transfer rate consistent with the recovery time and recovery point objectives*].

(6)   The organization accomplishes information system backup by maintaining a redundant secondary system, not collocated, that can be activated without loss of information or disruption to the operation.

References: NIST Special Publication 800-34.

Priority and Baseline Allocation:

P1	LOW CP-9	MOD CP-9 (1)	HIGH CP-9 (1) (2) (3)

CP-10   INFORMATION SYSTEM RECOVERY AND RECONSTITUTION

Control: The organization provides for the recovery and reconstitution of the information system to a known state after a disruption, compromise, or failure.

Supplemental Guidance: Recovery is executing information system contingency plan activities to restore essential missions and business functions. Reconstitution takes place following recovery and includes activities for returning the information system to its original functional state before contingency plan activation. Recovery and reconstitution procedures are based on organizational priorities, established recovery point/time and reconstitution objectives, and appropriate metrics. Reconstitution includes the deactivation of any interim information system capability that may have been needed during recovery operations. Reconstitution also includes an assessment of the fully restored information system capability, a potential system reauthorization and the necessary activities to prepare the system against another disruption, compromise, or failure. Recovery and reconstitution capabilities employed by the organization can be a combination of automated mechanisms and manual procedures. Related controls: CA-2, CA-6, CA-7, SC-24.

Control Enhancements:

(1)   [Withdrawn: Incorporated into CP-4].

(2)   The information system implements transaction recovery for systems that are transaction-based.

      Enhancement Supplemental Guidance: Database management systems and transaction processing systems are examples of information systems that are transaction-based. Transaction rollback and transaction journaling are examples of mechanisms supporting transaction recovery.

(3)   The organization provides compensating security controls for [*Assignment: organization-defined circumstances that can inhibit recovery and reconstitution to a known state*].

(4)   The organization provides the capability to reimage information system components within [*Assignment: organization-defined restoration time-periods*] from configuration-controlled and integrity-protected disk images representing a secure, operational state for the components.

(5)   The organization provides [*Selection: real-time; near-real-time*] [*Assignment: organization-defined failover capability for the information system*].

      Enhancement Supplemental Guidance: Examples of failover capability are incorporating mirrored information system operations at an alternate processing site or periodic data mirroring at regular intervals during a time period defined by the organization's recovery time period.

(6)   The organization protects backup and restoration hardware, firmware, and software.

Enhancement Supplemental Guidance: Protection of backup and restoration hardware, firmware, and software includes both physical and technical measures. Router tables, compilers, and other security-relevant system software are examples of backup and restoration software.

References: NIST Special Publication 800-34.

Priority and Baseline Allocation:

P1	LOW CP-10	MOD CP-10 (2) (3)	HIGH CP-10 (2) (3) (4)

FAMILY: IDENTIFICATION AND AUTHENTICATION   **CLASS:** TECHNICAL

IA-1   **IDENTIFICATION AND AUTHENTICATION POLICY AND PROCEDURES**

Control: The organization develops, disseminates, and reviews/updates [*Assignment: organization-defined frequency*]:

a. A formal, documented identification and authentication policy that addresses purpose, scope, roles, responsibilities, management commitment, coordination among organizational entities, and compliance; and

b. Formal, documented procedures to facilitate the implementation of the identification and authentication policy and associated identification and authentication controls.

Supplemental Guidance: This control is intended to produce the policy and procedures that are required for the effective implementation of selected security controls and control enhancements in the identification and authentication family. The policy and procedures are consistent with applicable federal laws, Executive Orders, directives, policies, regulations, standards, and guidance. Existing organizational policies and procedures may make the need for additional specific policies and procedures unnecessary. The identification and authentication policy can be included as part of the general information security policy for the organization. Identification and authentication procedures can be developed for the security program in general and for a particular information system, when required. The organizational risk management strategy is a key factor in the development of the identification and authentication policy. Related control: PM-9.

Control Enhancements: None.

References: FIPS Publication 201; NIST Special Publications 800-12, 800-63, 800-73, 800-76, 800-78, 800-100.

Priority and Baseline Allocation:

P1	**LOW** IA-1	**MOD** IA-1	**HIGH** IA-1

IA-2   **IDENTIFICATION AND AUTHENTICATION (ORGANIZATIONAL USERS)**

Control: The information system uniquely identifies and authenticates organizational users (or processes acting on behalf of organizational users).

Supplemental Guidance: Organizational users include organizational employees or individuals the organization deems to have equivalent status of employees (e.g., contractors, guest researchers, individuals from allied nations). Users are uniquely identified and authenticated for all accesses other than those accesses explicitly identified and documented by the organization in AC-14. Unique identification of individuals in group accounts (e.g., shared privilege accounts) may need to be considered for detailed accountability of activity. Authentication of user identities is accomplished through the use of passwords, tokens, biometrics, or in the case of multifactor authentication, some combination thereof. Access to organizational information systems is defined as either local or network. Local access is any access to an organizational information system by a user (or process acting on behalf of a user) where such access is obtained by direct connection without the use of a network. Network access is any access to an organizational information system by a user (or process acting on behalf of a user) where such access is obtained through a network connection. Remote access is a type of network access which involves communication through an external network (e.g., the Internet). Internal networks include local area networks, wide area networks, and virtual private networks that are under the control of the organization. For a virtual private network (VPN), the VPN is considered an internal network if the organization establishes the VPN connection between organization-controlled endpoints in a manner that does not require the organization to depend on any external networks across which the VPN transits to protect the confidentiality and integrity of information transmitted. Identification and authentication requirements for information system access by other than organizational users are described in IA-8.

The identification and authentication requirements in this control are satisfied by complying with Homeland Security Presidential Directive 12 consistent with organization-specific implementation plans provided to OMB. In addition to identifying and authenticating users at the information-system level (i.e., at logon), identification and authentication mechanisms are employed at the application level, when necessary, to provide increased information security for the organization. Related controls: AC-14, AC-17, AC-18, IA-4, IA-5.

Control Enhancements:

(1)   The information system uses multifactor authentication for network access to privileged accounts. (2)   The information system uses multifactor authentication for network access to non-privileged
     accounts.

(3)   The information system uses multifactor authentication for local access to privileged accounts. (4)   The information system uses multifactor authentication for local access to non-privileged
     accounts.

(5)   The organization:

   (a)   Allows the use of group authenticators only when used in conjunction with an individual/unique authenticator; and

   (b)   Requires individuals to be authenticated with an individual authenticator prior to using a group authenticator.

(6)   The information system uses multifactor authentication for network access to privileged accounts where one of the factors is provided by a device separate from the information system being accessed.

(7)   The information system uses multifactor authentication for network access to non-privileged accounts where one of the factors is provided by a device separate from the information system being accessed.

(8)   The information system uses [Assignment: organization-defined replay-resistant authentication mechanisms] for network access to privileged accounts.

   Enhancement Supplemental Guidance: An authentication process resists replay attacks if it is impractical to achieve a successful authentication by recording and replaying a previous authentication message. Techniques used to address this include protocols that use nonces or challenges (e.g., TLS), and time synchronous or challenge-response one-time authenticators.

(9)   The information system uses [Assignment: organization-defined replay-resistant authentication mechanisms] for network access to non-privileged accounts.

   Enhancement Supplemental Guidance: An authentication process resists replay attacks if it is impractical to achieve a successful authentication by recording and replaying a previous authentication message. Techniques used to address this include protocols that use nonces or challenges (e.g., TLS), and time synchronous or challenge-response one-time authenticators.

References: HSPD 12; OMB Memorandum 04-04; FIPS Publication 201; NIST Special Publications 800-63, 800-73, 800-76, 800-78.

Priority and Baseline Allocation:

P1	LOW IA-2 (1)	MOD IA-2 (1) (2) (3) (8)	HIGH IA-2 (1) (2) (3) (4) (8) (9)

IA-3   DEVICE IDENTIFICATION AND AUTHENTICATION

Control: The information system uniquely identifies and authenticates [Assignment: organization-defined list of specific and/or types of devices] before establishing a connection.

Supplemental Guidance: The devices requiring unique identification and authentication may be defined by type, by specific device, or by a combination of type and device as deemed appropriate by the organization. The information system typically uses either shared known information (e.g., Media Access Control [MAC] or Transmission Control Protocol/Internet Protocol [TCP/IP] addresses) for identification or an organizational authentication solution (e.g., IEEE 802.1x and Extensible Authentication Protocol [EAP], Radius server with EAP-Transport Layer Security [TLS] authentication, Kerberos) to identify and authenticate devices on local and/or wide area networks. The required strength of the device authentication mechanism is determined by the security categorization of the information system.

Control Enhancements:

(1) **The information system authenticates devices before establishing remote and wireless network connections using bidirectional authentication between devices that is cryptographically based.**

Enhancement Supplemental Guidance: Remote network connection is any connection with a device communicating through an external network (e.g., the Internet). Related controls: AC-17, AC-18.

(2) **The information system authenticates devices before establishing network connections using bidirectional authentication between devices that is cryptographically based.**

(3) **The organization standardizes, with regard to dynamic address allocation, Dynamic Host Control Protocol (DHCP) lease information and the time assigned to devices, and audits lease information when assigned to a device.**

Enhancement Supplemental Guidance: With regard to dynamic address allocation for devices, DHCP-enabled clients typically obtain *leases* for IP addresses from DHCP servers.

References: None.

Priority and Baseline Allocation:

P1	**LOW** Not Selected	**MOD** IA-3	**HIGH** IA-3

IA-4   IDENTIFIER MANAGEMENT

Control: The organization manages information system identifiers for users and devices by:

a. Receiving authorization from a designated organizational official to assign a user or device identifier;

b. Selecting an identifier that uniquely identifies an individual or device;

c. Assigning the user identifier to the intended party or the device identifier to the intended device;

d. Preventing reuse of user or device identifiers for [*Assignment: organization-defined time period*]; and

e. Disabling the user identifier after [*Assignment: organization-defined time period of inactivity*].

Supplemental Guidance: Common device identifiers include media access control (MAC) or Internet protocol (IP) addresses, or device-unique token identifiers. Management of user identifiers is not applicable to shared information system accounts (e.g., guest and anonymous accounts). It is commonly the case that a user identifier is the name of an information system account associated with an individual. In such instances, identifier management is largely addressed by the account management activities of AC-2. IA-4 also covers user identifiers not necessarily associated with an information system account (e.g., the identifier used in a physical security control database accessed by a badge reader system for access to the information system). Related control: AC-2, IA-2.

Control Enhancements:

(1)   The organization prohibits the use of information system account identifiers as public identifiers for user electronic mail accounts (i.e., user identifier portion of the electronic mail address).

Enhancement Supplemental Guidance: The organization implements this control enhancement to the extent that the information system allows.

(2)   The organization requires that registration to receive a user ID and password include authorization by a supervisor, and be done in person before a designated registration authority.

(3)   The organization requires multiple forms of certification of individual identification such as documentary evidence or a combination of documents and biometrics be presented to the registration authority.

(4)   The organization manages user identifiers by uniquely identifying the user as [*Assignment: organization-defined characteristic identifying user status*].

Enhancement Supplemental Guidance: Characteristics identifying user status include, for example, contractors and foreign nationals.

(5)   The information system dynamically manages identifiers, attributes, and associated access authorizations.

Enhancement Supplemental Guidance: In contrast to conventional approaches to identification and authentication which employ static information system accounts for preregistered users, many service-oriented architecture implementations rely on establishing identities at run time for entities that were previously unknown. Dynamic establishment of identities and association of attributes and privileges with these identities is anticipated and provisioned. Pre-established trust relationships and mechanisms with appropriate authorities to validate identities and related credentials are essential.

References: FIPS Publication 201; NIST Special Publications 800-73, 800-76, 800-78.

Priority and Baseline Allocation:

P1	LOW IA-4	MOD IA-4	HIGH IA-4

IA-5   AUTHENTICATOR MANAGEMENT

Control: The organization manages information system authenticators for users and devices by:

a.   Verifying, as part of the initial authenticator distribution, the identity of the individual and/or device receiving the authenticator;

b.   Establishing initial authenticator content for authenticators defined by the organization;

c.   Ensuring that authenticators have sufficient strength of mechanism for their intended use;

d.   Establishing and implementing administrative procedures for initial authenticator distribution, for lost/compromised or damaged authenticators, and for revoking authenticators;

e.   Changing default content of authenticators upon information system installation;

f.   Establishing minimum and maximum lifetime restrictions and reuse conditions for authenticators (if appropriate);

g.   Changing/refreshing authenticators [*Assignment: organization-defined time period by authenticator type*];

h.   Protecting authenticator content from unauthorized disclosure and modification; and

i.   Requiring users to take, and having devices implement, specific measures to safeguard authenticators.

Supplemental Guidance: User authenticators include, for example, passwords, tokens, biometrics, PKI certificates, and key cards. Initial authenticator content is the actual content (e.g., the initial password) as opposed to requirements about authenticator content (e.g., minimum password length). Many information system components are shipped with factory default authentication credentials to allow for initial installation and configuration. Default authentication credentials are often well known, easily discoverable, present a significant security risk, and therefore, are changed upon installation. The requirement to protect user authenticators may be implemented via control PL-4 or PS-6 for authenticators in the possession of users and by controls AC-3, AC-6, and SC-28 for authenticators stored within the information system (e.g., passwords stored in a hashed or encrypted format, files containing encrypted or hashed passwords accessible only with super user privileges). The information system supports user authenticator management by organization-defined settings and restrictions for various authenticator characteristics including, for example, minimum password length, password composition, validation time window for time synchronous one time tokens, and number of allowed rejections during verification stage of biometric authentication. Measures to safeguard user authenticators include, for example, maintaining possession of individual authenticators, not loaning or sharing authenticators with others, and reporting lost or compromised authenticators immediately. Authenticator management includes issuing and revoking, when no longer needed, authenticators for temporary access such as that required for remote maintenance. Device authenticators include, for example, certificates and passwords. Related controls: AC-2, IA-2, PL-4, PS-6.

Control Enhancements:

(1) The information system, for password-based authentication:

   (a) Enforces minimum password complexity of [*Assignment: organization-defined requirements for case sensitivity, number of characters, mix of upper-case letters, lower-case letters, numbers, and special characters, including minimum requirements for each type*];

   (b) Enforces at least a [*Assignment: organization-defined number of changed characters*] when new passwords are created;

   (c) Encrypts passwords in storage and in transmission;

   (d) Enforces password minimum and maximum lifetime restrictions of [Assignment: organization- defined numbers for lifetime minimum, lifetime maximum]; and

   (e) Prohibits password reuse for [Assignment: organization-defined number] generations.

   Enhancement Supplemental Guidance: This control enhancement is intended primarily for environments where passwords are used as a single factor to authenticate users, or in a similar manner along with one or more additional authenticators. The enhancement generally does *not* apply to situations where passwords are used to unlock hardware authenticators. The implementation of such password mechanisms may not meet all of the requirements in the enhancement.

(2) The information system, for PKI-based authentication:

   (a) Validates certificates by constructing a certification path with status information to an accepted trust anchor;

   (b) Enforces authorized access to the corresponding private key; and

   (c) Maps the authenticated identity to the user account.

   Enhancement Supplemental Guidance: Status information for certification paths includes, for example, certificate revocation lists or online certificate status protocol responses.

(3) The organization requires that the registration process to receive [*Assignment: organization-defined types of and/or specific authenticators*] be carried out in person before a designated registration authority with authorization by a designated organizational official (e.g., a supervisor).

(4) The organization employs automated tools to determine if authenticators are sufficiently strong to resist attacks intended to discover or otherwise compromise the authenticators.

(5) The organization requires vendors and/or manufacturers of information system components to provide unique authenticators or change default authenticators prior to delivery.

Enhancement Supplemental Guidance: This control enhancement extends the requirement for organizations to change default authenticators upon information system installation, by requiring vendors and/or manufacturers of information system components to provide unique authenticators or change default authenticators for those components prior to delivery to the organization. Unique authenticators are assigned by vendors and/or manufacturers to specific information system components (i.e., delivered information technology products) with distinct serial numbers. This requirement is included in acquisition documents prepared by the organization when procuring information systems and/or information system components.

(6)   **The organization protects authenticators commensurate with the classification or sensitivity of the information accessed.**

(7)   **The organization ensures that unencrypted static authenticators are not embedded in applications or access scripts or stored on function keys.**

Enhancement Supplemental Guidance: Organizations exercise caution in determining whether an embedded or stored authenticator is in encrypted or unencrypted form. If the authenticator in its stored representation, is used in the manner stored, then that representation is considered an unencrypted authenticator. This is irrespective of whether that representation is perhaps an encrypted version of something else (e.g., a password).

(8)   **The organization takes [*Assignment: organization-defined measures*] to manage the risk of compromise due to individuals having accounts on multiple information systems.**

Enhancement Supplemental Guidance: When an individual has accounts on multiple information systems, there is the risk that if one account is compromised and the individual is using the same user identifier and authenticator, other accounts will be compromised as well. Possible alternatives include, but are not limited to: (i) having the same user identifier but different authenticators on all systems; (ii) having different user identifiers and authenticators on each system; (iii) employing some form of single sign-on mechanism; or (iv) including some form of one-time passwords on all systems.

References: OMB Memorandum 04-04; FIPS Publication 201; NIST Special Publications 800-73, 800-63, 800-76, 800-78.

Priority and Baseline Allocation:

P1	**LOW** IA-5 (1)	**MOD** IA-5 (1) (2) (3)	**HIGH** IA-5 (1) (2) (3)

IA-6   AUTHENTICATOR FEEDBACK

Control: The information system obscures feedback of authentication information during the authentication process to protect the information from possible exploitation/use by unauthorized individuals.

Supplemental Guidance: The feedback from the information system does not provide information that would allow an unauthorized user to compromise the authentication mechanism. Displaying asterisks when a user types in a password, is an example of obscuring feedback of authentication information.

Control Enhancements: None.

References: None.

P1	LOW IA-6	MOD IA-6	HIGH IA-6

IA-7   CRYPTOGRAPHIC MODULE AUTHENTICATION

Control: The information system uses mechanisms for authentication to a cryptographic module that meet the requirements of applicable federal laws, Executive Orders, directives, policies, regulations, standards, and guidance for such authentication.

Supplemental Guidance: None.

Control Enhancements: None.

References: FIPS Publication 140-2; Web: CSRC.NIST.GOV/CRYPTVAL.

Priority and Baseline Allocation:

P1	LOW IA-7	MOD IA-7	HIGH IA-7

IA-8   IDENTIFICATION AND AUTHENTICATION (NON-ORGANIZATIONAL USERS)

Control: The information system uniquely identifies and authenticates non-organizational users (or processes acting on behalf of non-organizational users).

Supplemental Guidance: Non-organizational users include all information system users other than organizational users explicitly covered by IA-2. Users are uniquely identified and authenticated for all accesses other than those accesses explicitly identified and documented by the organization in accordance with AC-14. In accordance with the E-Authentication E-Government initiative, authentication of non-organizational users accessing federal information systems may be required to protect federal, proprietary, or privacy-related information (with exceptions noted for national security systems). Accordingly, a risk assessment is used in determining the authentication needs of the organization. Scalability, practicality, and security are simultaneously considered in balancing the need to ensure ease of use for access to federal information and information systems with the need to protect and adequately mitigate risk to organizational operations, organizational assets, individuals, other organizations, and the Nation. Identification and authentication requirements for information system access by organizational users are described in IA-2. Related controls: AC-14, AC-17, AC-18, MA-4.

Control Enhancements: None.

References: OMB Memorandum 04-04; Web: WWW.CIO.GOV/EAUTHENTICATION; NIST Special Publication 800-63.

Priority and Baseline Allocation:

P1	LOW IA-8	MOD IA-8	HIGH IA-8

FAMILY: INCIDENT RESPONSE   **CLASS:** OPERATIONAL

IR-1   **INCIDENT RESPONSE POLICY AND PROCEDURES**

Control: The organization develops, disseminates, and reviews/updates [*Assignment: organization-defined frequency*]:

a.   A formal, documented incident response policy that addresses purpose, scope, roles, responsibilities, management commitment, coordination among organizational entities, and compliance; and

b.   Formal, documented procedures to facilitate the implementation of the incident response policy and associated incident response controls.

Supplemental Guidance: This control is intended to produce the policy and procedures that are required for the effective implementation of selected security controls and control enhancements in the incident response family. The policy and procedures are consistent with applicable federal laws, Executive Orders, directives, policies, regulations, standards, and guidance. Existing organizational policies and procedures may make the need for additional specific policies and procedures unnecessary. The incident response policy can be included as part of the general information security policy for the organization. Incident response procedures can be developed for the security program in general and for a particular information system, when required. The organizational risk management strategy is a key factor in the development of the incident response policy. Related control: PM-9.

Control Enhancements: None.

References: NIST Special Publications 800-12, 800-61, 800-83, 800-100.

Priority and Baseline Allocation:

P1	**LOW** IR-1	**MOD** IR-1	**HIGH** IR-1

IR-2   **INCIDENT RESPONSE TRAINING**

Control: The organization:

a.   Trains personnel in their incident response roles and responsibilities with respect to the information system; and

b.   Provides refresher training [*Assignment: organization-defined frequency*].

Supplemental Guidance: Incident response training includes user training in the identification and reporting of suspicious activities, both from external and internal sources. Related control: AT-3.

Control Enhancements:

(1)   **The organization incorporates simulated events into incident response training to facilitate effective response by personnel in crisis situations.**

(2)   **The organization employs automated mechanisms to provide a more thorough and realistic training environment.**

References: NIST Special Publications 800-16, 800-50.

Priority and Baseline Allocation:

P2	**LOW** IR-2	**MOD** IR-2	**HIGH** IR-2 (1) (2)

IR-3   INCIDENT RESPONSE TESTING AND EXERCISES

Control: The organization tests and/or exercises the incident response capability for the information system [*Assignment: organization-defined frequency*] using [*Assignment: organization-defined tests and/or exercises*] to determine the incident response effectiveness and documents the results.

Supplemental Guidance: None.

Control Enhancements:

(1)   The organization employs automated mechanisms to more thoroughly and effectively test/exercise the incident response capability.

Enhancement Supplemental Guidance: Automated mechanisms can provide the ability to more thoroughly and effectively test or exercise the incident response capability by providing more complete coverage of incident response issues, selecting more realistic test/exercise scenarios and environments, and more effectively stressing the response capability. Related control: AT-2.

References: NIST Special Publications 800-84, 800-115.

Priority and Baseline Allocation:

P2	**LOW** Not Selected	**MOD** IR-3	**HIGH** IR-3 (1)

IR-4   INCIDENT HANDLING

Control: The organization:

a.   Implements an incident handling capability for security incidents that includes preparation, detection and analysis, containment, eradication, and recovery;

b.   Coordinates incident handling activities with contingency planning activities; and

c.   Incorporates lessons learned from ongoing incident handling activities into incident response procedures, training, and testing/exercises, and implements the resulting changes accordingly.

Supplemental Guidance: Incident-related information can be obtained from a variety of sources including, but not limited to, audit monitoring, network monitoring, physical access monitoring, and user/administrator reports. Related controls: AU-6, CP-2, IR-2, IR-3, PE-6, SC-5, SC-7, SI-3, SI-4, SI-7.

Control Enhancements:

(1)   The organization employs automated mechanisms to support the incident handling process.

Enhancement Supplemental Guidance: An online incident management system is an example of an automated mechanism.

(2)   The organization includes dynamic reconfiguration of the information system as part of the incident response capability.

Enhancement Supplemental Guidance: Dynamic reconfiguration includes, for example, changes to router rules, access control lists, intrusion detection/prevention system parameters, and filter rules for firewalls and gateways.

(3)   The organization identifies classes of incidents and defines appropriate actions to take in response to ensure continuation of organizational missions and business functions.

Enhancement Supplemental Guidance: Classes of incidents include, for example, malfunctions due to design/implementation errors and omissions, targeted malicious attacks, and untargeted malicious attacks. Incident response actions that may be appropriate include, for example, graceful degradation, information system shutdown, fall back to manual mode or alternative technology whereby the system operates differently, employing deceptive measures (e.g., false data flows, false status measures), alternate information flows, or operating in a mode that is reserved solely for when a system is under attack.

(4)   The organization correlates incident information and individual incident responses to achieve an organization-wide perspective on incident awareness and response.

(5)   The organization implements a configurable capability to automatically disable the information system if any of the following security violations are detected: [*Assignment: organization-defined list of security violations*].

References: NIST Special Publication 800-61.

Priority and Baseline Allocation:

P1	LOW IR-4	MOD IR-4 (1)	HIGH IR-4 (1)

IR-5   INCIDENT MONITORING

Control: The organization tracks and documents information system security incidents.

Supplemental Guidance: Documenting information system security incidents includes, for example, maintaining records about each incident, the status of the incident, and other pertinent information necessary for forensics, evaluating incident details, trends, and handling. Incident information can be obtained from a variety of sources including, for example, incident reports, incident response teams, audit monitoring, network monitoring, physical access monitoring, and user/administrator reports.

Control Enhancements:

(1)   The organization employs automated mechanisms to assist in the tracking of security incidents and in the collection and analysis of incident information.

Enhancement Supplemental Guidance: Automated mechanisms for tracking security incidents and collecting/analyzing incident information include, for example, the Einstein network monitoring device and monitoring online Computer Incident Response Centers (CIRCs) or other electronic databases of incidents. Related controls: AU-6, AU-7, SI-4.

References: NIST Special Publication 800-61.

Priority and Baseline Allocation:

P1	LOW IR-5	MOD IR-5	HIGH IR-5 (1)

IR-6   INCIDENT REPORTING

Control: The organization:

a.   Requires personnel to report suspected security incidents to the organizational incident response capability within [*Assignment: organization-defined time-period*]; and

b.   Reports security incident information to designated authorities.

Supplemental Guidance: The intent of this control is to address both specific incident reporting requirements within an organization and the formal incident reporting requirements for federal agencies and their subordinate organizations. The types of security incidents reported, the content and timeliness of the reports, and the list of designated reporting authorities are consistent with applicable federal laws, Executive Orders, directives, policies, regulations, standards, and guidance. Current federal policy requires that all federal agencies (unless specifically exempted from such requirements) report security incidents to the United States Computer Emergency Readiness Team (US-CERT) within specified time frames designated in the US-CERT Concept of Operations for Federal Cyber Security Incident Handling. Related controls: IR-4, IR-5.

Control Enhancements:

(1)   The organization employs automated mechanisms to assist in the reporting of security incidents.

(2)   The organization reports information system weaknesses, deficiencies, and/or vulnerabilities associated with reported security incidents to appropriate organizational officials.

References: NIST Special Publication 800-61: Web: WWW.US-CERT.GOV.

Priority and Baseline Allocation:

P1	**LOW** IR-6	**MOD** IR-6 (1)	**HIGH** IR-6 (1)

IR-7   INCIDENT RESPONSE ASSISTANCE

Control: The organization provides an incident response support resource, integral to the organizational incident response capability, that offers advice and assistance to users of the information system for the handling and reporting of security incidents.

Supplemental Guidance: Possible implementations of incident response support resources in an organization include a help desk or an assistance group and access to forensics services, when required. Related controls: IR-4, IR-6.

Control Enhancements:

(1)   The organization employs automated mechanisms to increase the availability of incident response- related information and support.

Enhancement Supplemental Guidance: Automated mechanisms can provide a push and/or pull capability for users to obtain incident response assistance. For example, individuals might have access to a website to query the assistance capability, or conversely, the assistance capability may have the ability to proactively send information to users (general distribution or targeted) as part of increasing understanding of current response capabilities and support.

(2)   The organization:

(a)   Establishes a direct, cooperative relationship between its incident response capability and external providers of information system protection capability; and

(b)   Identifies organizational incident response team members to the external providers.

Enhancement Supplemental Guidance: External providers of information system protection capability include, for example, the Computer Network Defense program within the U.S. Department of Defense. External providers help to protect, monitor, analyze, detect, and respond to unauthorized activity within organizational information systems and networks.

References: None.

Priority and Baseline Allocation:

P3	**LOW** IR-7	**MOD** IR-7 (1)	**HIGH** IR-7 (1)

IR-8   INCIDENT RESPONSE PLAN

Control: The organization:

a.   Develops an incident response plan that:

-   Provides the organization with a roadmap for implementing its incident response capability;

-   Describes the structure and organization of the incident response capability;

- Provides a high-level approach for how the incident response capability fits into the overall organization;

- Meets the unique requirements of the organization, which relate to mission, size, structure, and functions;

- Defines reportable incidents;

- Provides metrics for measuring the incident response capability within the organization.

- Defines the resources and management support needed to effectively maintain and mature an incident response capability; and

- Is reviewed and approved by designated officials within the organization;

b. Distributes copies of the incident response plan to [*Assignment: organization-defined list of incident response personnel (identified by name and/or by role) and organizational elements*];

c. Reviews the incident response plan [*Assignment: organization-defined frequency*];

d. Revises the incident response plan to address system/organizational changes or problems encountered during plan implementation, execution, or testing; and

e. Communicates incident response plan changes to [*Assignment: organization-defined list of incident response personnel (identified by name and/or by role) and organizational elements*].

Supplemental Guidance: It is important that organizations have a formal, focused, and coordinated approach to responding to incidents. The organization's mission, strategies, and goals for incident response help determine the structure of its incident response capability.

Control Enhancements: None.

References: NIST Special Publication 800-61.

Priority and Baseline Allocation:

P1	LOW IR-8	MOD IR-8	HIGH IR-8

FAMILY: MAINTENANCE   **CLASS:** OPERATIONAL

MA-1   **SYSTEM MAINTENANCE POLICY AND PROCEDURES**

Control: The organization develops, disseminates, and reviews/updates [*Assignment: organization-defined frequency*]:

a. A formal, documented information system maintenance policy that addresses purpose, scope, roles, responsibilities, management commitment, coordination among organizational entities, and compliance; and

b. Formal, documented procedures to facilitate the implementation of the information system maintenance policy and associated system maintenance controls.

Supplemental Guidance: This control is intended to produce the policy and procedures that are required for the effective implementation of selected security controls and control enhancements in the system maintenance family. The policy and procedures are consistent with applicable federal laws, Executive Orders, directives, policies, regulations, standards, and guidance. Existing organizational policies and procedures may make the need for additional specific policies and procedures unnecessary. The information system maintenance policy can be included as part of the general information security policy for the organization. System maintenance procedures can be developed for the security program in general and for a particular information system, when required. The organizational risk management strategy is a key factor in the development of the system maintenance policy. Related control: PM-9.

Control Enhancements: None.

References: NIST Special Publications 800-12, 800-100.

Priority and Baseline Allocation:

P1	**LOW** MA-1	**MOD** MA-1	**HIGH** MA-1

MA-2   **CONTROLLED MAINTENANCE**

Control: The organization:

a. Schedules, performs, documents, and reviews records of maintenance and repairs on information system components in accordance with manufacturer or vendor specifications and/or organizational requirements;

b. Controls all maintenance activities, whether performed on site or remotely and whether the equipment is serviced on site or removed to another location;

c. Requires that a designated official explicitly approve the removal of the information system or system components from organizational facilities for off-site maintenance or repairs;

d. Sanitizes equipment to remove all information from associated media prior to removal from organizational facilities for off-site maintenance or repairs; and

e. Checks all potentially impacted security controls to verify that the controls are still functioning properly following maintenance or repair actions.

Supplemental Guidance: The control is intended to address the information security aspects of the organization's information system maintenance program. Related controls: MP-6, SI-2.

Control Enhancements:

(1) The organization maintains maintenance records for the information system that

   include: (a) Date and time of maintenance;

   (b) Name of the individual performing the maintenance;

(c)   **Name of escort, if necessary;**

(d)   **A description of the maintenance performed; and**

(e)   **A list of equipment removed or replaced (including identification numbers, if**
applicable). **(2)   The organization employs automated mechanisms to schedule, conduct, and**
document
maintenance and repairs as required, producing up-to date, accurate, complete, and available
records of all maintenance and repair actions, needed, in process, and completed.

References: None.

Priority and Baseline Allocation:

P2	**LOW** MA-2	**MOD** MA-2 (1)	**HIGH** MA-2 (1) (2)

MA-3   MAINTENANCE TOOLS

Control: The organization approves, controls, monitors the use of, and maintains on an ongoing basis, information system maintenance tools.

Supplemental Guidance: The intent of this control is to address the security-related issues arising from the hardware and software brought into the information system specifically for diagnostic and repair actions (e.g., a hardware or software packet sniffer that is introduced for the purpose of a particular maintenance activity). Hardware and/or software components that may support information system maintenance, yet are a part of the system (e.g., the software implementing "ping," "ls," "ipconfig," or the hardware and software implementing the monitoring port of an Ethernet switch) are not covered by this control. Related control: MP-6.

Control Enhancements:

(1)   **The organization inspects all maintenance tools carried into a facility by maintenance personnel for obvious improper modifications.**

Enhancement Supplemental Guidance: Maintenance tools include, for example, diagnostic and test equipment used to conduct maintenance on the information system.

(2)   **The organization checks all media containing diagnostic and test programs for malicious code before the media are used in the information system.**

(3)   **The organization prevents the unauthorized removal of maintenance equipment by one of the following: (i) verifying that there is no organizational information contained on the equipment; (ii) sanitizing or destroying the equipment; (iii) retaining the equipment within the facility; or (iv) obtaining an exemption from a designated organization official explicitly authorizing removal of the equipment from the facility.**

(4)   **The organization employs automated mechanisms to restrict the use of maintenance tools to authorized personnel only.**

References: NIST Special Publication 800-88.

Priority and Baseline Allocation:

P2	**LOW** Not Selected	**MOD** MA-3 (1) (2)	**HIGH** MA-3 (1) (2) (3)

MA-4   NON-LOCAL MAINTENANCE

Control: The organization:

a.   Authorizes, monitors, and controls non-local maintenance and diagnostic activities;

b.   Allows the use of non-local maintenance and diagnostic tools only as consistent with organizational policy and documented in the security plan for the information system;

c.   Employs strong identification and authentication techniques in the establishment of non-local maintenance and diagnostic sessions;

d.   Maintains records for non-local maintenance and diagnostic activities; and

e.   Terminates all sessions and network connections when non-local maintenance is completed.

Supplemental Guidance: Non-local maintenance and diagnostic activities are those activities conducted by individuals communicating through a network; either an external network (e.g., the Internet) or an internal network. Local maintenance and diagnostic activities are those activities carried out by individuals physically present at the information system or information system component and not communicating across a network connection. Identification and authentication techniques used in the establishment of non-local maintenance and diagnostic sessions are consistent with the network access requirements in IA-2. Strong authenticators include, for example, PKI where certificates are stored on a token protected by a password, passphrase, or biometric. Enforcing requirements in MA-4 is accomplished in part, by other controls. Related controls: AC-2, AC-3, AC-6, AC-17, AU-2, AU-3, IA-2, IA-8, MA-5, MP-6, SC-7.

Control Enhancements:

(1)   The organization audits non-local maintenance and diagnostic sessions and designated organizational personnel review the maintenance records of the sessions.

(2)   The organization documents, in the security plan for the information system, the installation and use of non-local maintenance and diagnostic connections.

(3)   The organization:

   (a)   Requires that non-local maintenance and diagnostic services be performed from an information system that implements a level of security at least as high as that implemented on the system being serviced; or

   (b)   Removes the component to be serviced from the information system and prior to non-local maintenance or diagnostic services, sanitizes the component (with regard to organizational information) before removal from organizational facilities, and after the service is performed, inspects and sanitizes the component (with regard to potentially malicious software and surreptitious implants) before reconnecting the component to the information system.

(4)   The organization protects non-local maintenance sessions through the use of a strong authenticator tightly bound to the user and by separating the maintenance session from other network sessions with the information system by either:

   (a)   Physically separated communications paths; or

   (b)   Logically separated communications paths based upon encryption.

   Enhancement Supplemental Guidance: Related control: SC-13.

(5)   The organization requires that:

   (a)   Maintenance personnel notify [*Assignment: organization-defined personnel*] when non-local maintenance is planned (i.e., date/time); and

   (b)   A designated organizational official with specific information security/information system knowledge approves the non-local maintenance.

(6)   The organization employs cryptographic mechanisms to protect the integrity and confidentiality of non-local maintenance and diagnostic communications.

(7)   The organization employs remote disconnect verification at the termination of non-local maintenance and diagnostic sessions.

References: FIPS Publications 140-2, 197, 201; NIST Special Publications 800-63, 800-88; CNSS Policy 15.

Priority and Baseline Allocation:

P1	LOW MA-4	MOD MA-4 (1) (2)	HIGH MA-4 (1) (2) (3)

MA-5   MAINTENANCE PERSONNEL

Control: The organization:

a. Establishes a process for maintenance personnel authorization and maintains a current list of authorized maintenance organizations or personnel; and

b. Ensures that personnel performing maintenance on the information system have required access authorizations or designates organizational personnel with required access authorizations and technical competence deemed necessary to supervise information system maintenance when maintenance personnel do not possess the required access authorizations.

Supplemental Guidance: Individuals not previously identified in the information system, such as vendor personnel and consultants, may legitimately require privileged access to the system, for example, when required to conduct maintenance or diagnostic activities with little or no notice. Based on a prior assessment of risk, the organization may issue temporary credentials to these individuals. Temporary credentials may be for one-time use or for a very limited time period. Related controls: IA-8, MA-5.

Control Enhancements:

(1) The organization maintains procedures for the use of maintenance personnel that lack appropriate security clearances or are not U.S. citizens, that include the following requirements:

   (a) Maintenance personnel who do not have needed access authorizations, clearances, or formal access approvals are escorted and supervised during the performance of maintenance and diagnostic activities on the information system by approved organizational personnel who are fully cleared, have appropriate access authorizations, and are technically qualified;

   (b) Prior to initiating maintenance or diagnostic activities by personnel who do not have needed access authorizations, clearances or formal access approvals, all volatile information storage components within the information system are sanitized and all nonvolatile storage media are removed or physically disconnected from the system and secured; and

   (c) In the event an information system component cannot be sanitized, the procedures contained in the security plan for the system are enforced.

   Enhancement Supplemental Guidance: The intent of this control enhancement is to deny individuals who lack appropriate security clearances (i.e., individuals who do not possess security clearances or possess security clearances at a lower level than required) or who are not U.S. citizens, visual and electronic access to any classified information, Controlled Unclassified Information (CUI), or any other sensitive information contained on the information system. Procedures for the use of maintenance personnel can be documented in the security plan for the information system.

(2) The organization ensures that personnel performing maintenance and diagnostic activities on an information system processing, storing, or transmitting classified information are cleared (i.e., possess appropriate security clearances) for the highest level of information on the system.

(3) The organization ensures that personnel performing maintenance and diagnostic activities on an information system processing, storing, or transmitting classified information are U.S. citizens.

(4) The organization ensures that:

   (a) Cleared foreign nationals (i.e., foreign nationals with appropriate security clearances), are used to conduct maintenance and diagnostic activities on an information system only when the system is jointly owned and operated by the United States and foreign allied governments, or owned and operated solely by foreign allied governments; and

   (b) Approvals, consents, and detailed operational conditions regarding the use of foreign nationals to conduct maintenance and diagnostic activities on an information system are fully documented within a Memorandum of Agreement.

References: None.

Priority and Baseline Allocation:

P1	LOW MA-5	MOD MA-5	HIGH MA-5

MA-6   **TIMELY MAINTENANCE**

Control: The organization obtains maintenance support and/or spare parts for [*Assignment: organization-defined list of security-critical information system components and/or key information technology components*] within [*Assignment: organization-defined time period*] of failure.

Supplemental Guidance: The organization specifies those information system components that, when not operational, result in increased risk to organizations, individuals, or the Nation because the security functionality intended by that component is not being provided. Security-critical components include, for example, firewalls, guards, gateways, intrusion detection systems, audit repositories, authentication servers, and intrusion prevention systems. Related control: CP-2.

Control Enhancements: None.

References: None.

Priority and Baseline Allocation:

P1	**LOW** Not Selected	**MOD** MA-6	**HIGH** MA-6

FAMILY: MEDIA PROTECTION   **CLASS:** OPERATIONAL

MP-1   **MEDIA PROTECTION POLICY AND PROCEDURES**

Control: The organization develops, disseminates, and reviews/updates [*Assignment: organization-defined frequency*]:

a.   A formal, documented media protection policy that addresses purpose, scope, roles, responsibilities, management commitment, coordination among organizational entities, and compliance; and

b.   Formal, documented procedures to facilitate the implementation of the media protection policy and associated media protection controls.

Supplemental Guidance: This control is intended to produce the policy and procedures that are required for the effective implementation of selected security controls and control enhancements in the media protection family. The policy and procedures are consistent with applicable federal laws, Executive Orders, directives, policies, regulations, standards, and guidance. Existing organizational policies and procedures may make the need for additional specific policies and procedures unnecessary. The media protection policy can be included as part of the general information security policy for the organization. Media protection procedures can be developed for the security program in general and for a particular information system, when required. The organizational risk management strategy is a key factor in the development of the media protection policy. Related control: PM-9.

Control Enhancements: None.

References: NIST Special Publications 800-12, 800-100.

Priority and Baseline Allocation:

P1	**LOW** MP-1	**MOD** MP-1	**HIGH** MP-1

MP-2   **MEDIA ACCESS**

Control: The organization restricts access to [*Assignment: organization-defined types of digital and non-digital media*] to [*Assignment: organization-defined list of authorized individuals*] using [*Assignment: organization-defined security measures*].

Supplemental Guidance: Information system media includes both digital media (e.g., diskettes, magnetic tapes, external/removable hard drives, flash/thumb drives, compact disks, digital video disks) and non-digital media (e.g., paper, microfilm). This control also applies to mobile computing and communications devices with information storage capability (e.g., notebook/laptop computers, personal digital assistants, cellular telephones, digital cameras, and audio recording devices). An organizational assessment of risk guides the selection of media and associated information contained on that media requiring restricted access. Organizations document in policy and procedures, the media requiring restricted access, individuals authorized to access the media, and the specific measures taken to restrict access. Fewer protection measures are needed for media containing information determined by the organization to be in the public domain, to be publicly releasable, or to have limited or no adverse impact if accessed by other than authorized personnel. In these situations, it is assumed that the physical access controls where the media resides provide adequate protection. Related controls: MP-4, PE-3.

Control Enhancements:

(1)   **The organization employs automated mechanisms to restrict access to media storage areas and to audit access attempts and access granted.**

Enhancement Supplemental Guidance: This control enhancement is primarily applicable to media storage areas within an organization where a significant volume of media is stored and is not applicable to every location where some media is stored (e.g., in individual offices).

(2)   The information system uses cryptographic mechanisms to protect and restrict access to information on portable digital media.

References: FIPS Publication 199; NIST Special Publication 800-111.

Priority and Baseline Allocation:

P1	**LOW** MP-2	**MOD** MP-2 (1)	**HIGH** MP-2 (1)

MP-3   MEDIA MARKING

Control: The organization:

a. Marks, in accordance with organizational policies and procedures, removable information system media and information system output indicating the distribution limitations, handling caveats, and applicable security markings (if any) of the information; and

b. Exempts [*Assignment: organization-defined list of removable media types*] from marking as long as the exempted items remain within [*Assignment: organization-defined controlled areas*].

Supplemental Guidance: The term marking is used when referring to the application or use of human-readable security attributes. The term labeling is used when referring to the application or use of security attributes with regard to internal data structures within the information system (see AC-16, Security Attributes). Removable information system media includes both digital media (e.g., diskettes, magnetic tapes, external/removable hard drives, flash/thumb drives, compact disks, digital video disks) and non-digital media (e.g., paper, microfilm). An organizational assessment of risk guides the selection of media requiring marking. Marking is generally not required for media containing information determined by the organization to be in the public domain or to be publicly releasable. Some organizations, however, may require markings for public information indicating that the information is publicly releasable. Organizations may extend the scope of this control to include information system output devices containing organizational information, including, for example, monitors and printers. Marking of removable media and information system output is consistent with applicable federal laws, Executive Orders, directives, policies, regulations, standards, and guidance.

Control Enhancements: None.

References: FIPS Publication 199.

Priority and Baseline Allocation:

P1	**LOW** Not Selected	**MOD** MP-3	**HIGH** MP-3

MP-4   MEDIA STORAGE

Control: The organization:

a. Physically controls and securely stores [*Assignment: organization-defined types of digital and non-digital media*] within [*Assignment: organization-defined controlled areas*] using [*Assignment: organization-defined security measures*];

b. Protects information system media until the media are destroyed or sanitized using approved equipment, techniques, and procedures.

Supplemental Guidance: Information system media includes both digital media (e.g., diskettes, magnetic tapes, external/removable hard drives, flash/thumb drives, compact disks, digital video disks) and non-digital media (e.g., paper, microfilm). This control also applies to mobile computing and communications devices with information storage capability (e.g., notebook/laptop computers, personal digital assistants, cellular telephones, digital cameras, and audio recording devices). Telephone systems are also considered information systems and may have the capability to store information on internal media (e.g., on voicemail systems). Since telephone systems do not have, in most cases, the identification, authentication, and access control mechanisms typically employed in other information systems, organizational personnel use extreme caution in the types of information stored on telephone voicemail systems. A controlled area is any area or space for which the organization has confidence that the physical and procedural protections are sufficient to meet the requirements established for protecting the information and/or information system.

An organizational assessment of risk guides the selection of media and associated information contained on that media requiring physical protection. Fewer protection measures are needed for media containing information determined by the organization to be in the public domain, to be publicly releasable, or to have limited or no adverse impact on the organization or individuals if accessed by other than authorized personnel. In these situations, it is assumed that the physical access controls to the facility where the media resides provide adequate protection.

As part of a defense-in-depth strategy, the organization considers routinely encrypting information at rest on selected secondary storage devices. The employment of cryptography is at the discretion of the information owner/steward. The selection of the cryptographic mechanisms used is based upon maintaining the confidentiality and integrity of the information. The strength of mechanisms is commensurate with the classification and sensitivity of the information. Related controls: AC-3, AC-19, CP-6, CP-9, MP-2, PE-3.

Control Enhancements:

(1)   The organization employs cryptographic mechanisms to protect information in storage.

Enhancement Supplemental Guidance: Related control: SC-13.

References: FIPS Publication 199; NIST Special Publications 800-56, 800-57, 800-111.

Priority and Baseline Allocation:

P1	**LOW** Not Selected	**MOD** MP-4	**HIGH** MP-4

MP-5   MEDIA TRANSPORT

Control: The organization:

a. Protects and controls [*Assignment: organization-defined types of digital and non-digital media*] during transport outside of controlled areas using [*Assignment: organization-defined security measures*];

b. Maintains accountability for information system media during transport outside of controlled areas; and

c. Restricts the activities associated with transport of such media to authorized personnel.

Supplemental Guidance: Information system media includes both digital media (e.g., diskettes, magnetic tapes, removable hard drives, flash/thumb drives, compact disks, digital video disks) and non-digital media (e.g., paper, microfilm). This control also applies to mobile computing and communications devices with information storage capability (e.g., notebook/laptop computers, personal digital assistants, cellular telephones, digital cameras, and audio recording devices) that are transported outside of controlled areas. Telephone systems are also considered information systems and may have the capability to store information on internal media (e.g., on voicemail systems). Since telephone systems do not have, in most cases, the identification, authentication, and access control mechanisms typically employed in other information systems, organizational personnel use caution in the types of information stored on telephone voicemail systems that are transported outside of controlled areas. A controlled area is any area or space for which the organization has confidence that the physical and procedural protections provided are sufficient to meet the requirements established for protecting the information and/or information system.

Physical and technical security measures for the protection of digital and non-digital media are commensurate with the classification or sensitivity of the information residing on the media, and consistent with applicable federal laws, Executive Orders, directives, policies, regulations, standards, and guidance. Locked containers and cryptography are examples of security measures available to protect digital and non-digital media during transport. Cryptographic mechanisms can provide confidentiality and/or integrity protections depending upon the mechanisms used. An organizational assessment of risk guides: (i) the selection of media and associated information contained on that media requiring protection during transport; and (ii) the selection and use of storage containers for transporting non-digital media. Authorized transport and courier personnel may include individuals from outside the organization (e.g., U.S. Postal Service or a commercial transport or delivery service). Related controls: AC-19, CP-9.

Control Enhancements:

(1)   [Withdrawn: Incorporated into MP-5].

(2)   **The organization documents activities associated with the transport of information system media.**

Enhancement Supplemental Guidance: Organizations establish documentation requirements for activities associated with the transport of information system media in accordance with the organizational assessment of risk to include the flexibility to define different record-keeping methods for different types of media transport as part of an overall system of transport-related records.

(3)   **The organization employs an identified custodian throughout the transport of information system media.**

Enhancement Supplemental Guidance: Custodial responsibilities can be transferred from one individual to another as long as an unambiguous custodian is identified at all times.

(4)   **The organization employs cryptographic mechanisms to protect the confidentiality and integrity of information stored on digital media during transport outside of controlled areas.**

Enhancement Supplemental Guidance: This control enhancement also applies to mobile devices. Mobile devices include portable storage media (e.g., USB memory sticks, external hard disk drives) and portable computing and communications devices with storage capability (e.g., notebook/laptop computers, personal digital assistants, cellular telephones). Related control: MP-4. Related controls: MP-2; SC-13.

References: FIPS Publication 199; NIST Special Publication 800-60.

Priority and Baseline Allocation:

P1	**LOW** Not Selected	**MOD** MP-5 (2) (4)	**HIGH** MP-5 (2) (3) (4)

MP-6   MEDIA SANITIZATION

Control: The organization sanitizes information system media, both digital and non-digital, prior to disposal, release out of organizational control, or release for reuse.

Supplemental Guidance: This control applies to all media subject to disposal or reuse, whether or not considered removable. Sanitization is the process used to remove information from information system media such that there is reasonable assurance that the information cannot be retrieved or reconstructed. Sanitization techniques, including clearing, purging, and destroying media information, prevent the disclosure of organizational information to unauthorized individuals when such media is reused or released for disposal. The organization employs sanitization mechanisms with strength and integrity commensurate with the classification or sensitivity of the information. The organization uses its discretion on the employment of sanitization techniques and procedures for media containing information deemed to be in the public domain or publicly releasable, or deemed to have no adverse impact on the organization or individuals if released for reuse or disposal.

Control Enhancements:

(1)   The organization tracks, documents, and verifies media sanitization and disposal actions.

(2)   The organization tests sanitization equipment and procedures to verify correct performance [*Assignment: organization-defined frequency*].

(3)   The organization sanitizes portable, removable storage devices prior to connecting such devices to the information system under the following circumstances: [*Assignment: organization-defined list of circumstances requiring sanitization of portable, removable storage devices*].

Enhancement Supplemental Guidance: Portable, removable storage devices (e.g., thumb drives, flash drives, external storage devices) can be the source of malicious code insertions into organizational information systems. Many of these devices are obtained from unknown sources and may contain various types of malicious code that can be readily transferred to the information system through USB ports or other entry portals. While scanning such devices is always recommended, sanitization provides additional assurance that the device is free of all malicious code to include code capable of initiating zero-day attacks. Organizations consider sanitization of portable, removable storage devices, for example, when such devices are first purchased from the manufacturer or vendor prior to initial use or when the organization loses a positive chain of custody for the device. An organizational assessment of risk guides the specific circumstances for employing the sanitization process. Related control: SI-3.

(4)   The organization sanitizes information system media containing Controlled Unclassified Information (CUI) or other sensitive information in accordance with applicable organizational and/or federal standards and policies.

(5)   The organization sanitizes information system media containing classified information in accordance with NSA standards and policies.

(6)   The organization destroys information system media that cannot be sanitized.

References: FIPS Publication 199; NIST Special Publications 800-60, 800-88; Web: WWW.NSA.GOV/IA/GUIDANCE/MEDIA_DESTRUCTION_GUIDANCE/INDEX.SHTML.

Priority and Baseline Allocation:

P1	**LOW** MP-6	**MOD** MP-6	**HIGH** MP-6 (1) (2) (3)

FAMILY: PHYSICAL AND ENVIRONMENTAL PROTECTION   **CLASS:** OPERATIONAL

PE-1   **PHYSICAL AND ENVIRONMENTAL PROTECTION POLICY AND PROCEDURES**

Control: The organization develops, disseminates, and reviews/updates [*Assignment: organization-defined frequency*]:

a.   A formal, documented physical and environmental protection policy that addresses purpose, scope, roles, responsibilities, management commitment, coordination among organizational entities, and compliance; and

b.   Formal, documented procedures to facilitate the implementation of the physical and environmental protection policy and associated physical and environmental protection controls.

Supplemental Guidance: This control is intended to produce the policy and procedures that are required for the effective implementation of selected security controls and control enhancements in the physical and environmental protection family. The policy and procedures are consistent with applicable federal laws, Executive Orders, directives, policies, regulations, standards, and guidance. Existing organizational policies and procedures may make the need for additional specific policies and procedures unnecessary. The physical and environmental protection policy can be included as part of the general information security policy for the organization. Physical and environmental protection procedures can be developed for the security program in general and for a particular information system, when required. The organizational risk management strategy is a key factor in the development of the physical and environmental protection policy. Related control: PM-9.

Control Enhancements: None.

References: NIST Special Publications 800-12, 800-100.

Priority and Baseline Allocation:

P1	**LOW** PE-1	**MOD** PE-1	**HIGH** PE-1

PE-2   **PHYSICAL ACCESS AUTHORIZATIONS**

Control: The organization:

a.   Develops and keeps current a list of personnel with authorized access to the facility where the information system resides (except for those areas within the facility officially designated as publicly accessible);

b.   Issues authorization credentials;

c.   Reviews and approves the access list and authorization credentials [*Assignment: organization-defined frequency*], removing from the access list personnel no longer requiring access.

Supplemental Guidance: Authorization credentials include, for example, badges, identification cards, and smart cards. Related control: PE-3, PE-4.

Control Enhancements:

(1)   **The organization authorizes physical access to the facility where the information system resides based on position or role.**

(2)   **The organization requires two forms of identification to gain access to the facility where the information system resides.**

Enhancement Supplemental Guidance: Examples of forms of identification are identification badge, key card, cipher PIN, and biometrics.

(3)   **The organization restricts physical access to the facility containing an information system that processes classified information to authorized personnel with appropriate clearances and access authorizations.**

References: None.

Priority and Baseline Allocation:

P1	LOW PE-2	MOD PE-2	HIGH PE-2

PE-3   PHYSICAL ACCESS CONTROL

Control: The organization:

a.   Enforces physical access authorizations for all physical access points (including designated entry/exit points) to the facility where the information system resides (excluding those areas within the facility officially designated as publicly accessible);

b.   Verifies individual access authorizations before granting access to the facility;

c.   Controls entry to the facility containing the information system using physical access devices and/or guards;

d.   Controls access to areas officially designated as publicly accessible in accordance with the organization's assessment of risk;

e.   Secures keys, combinations, and other physical access devices;

f.   Inventories physical access devices [*Assignment: organization-defined frequency*]; and

g.   Changes combinations and keys [*Assignment: organization-defined frequency*] and when keys are lost, combinations are compromised, or individuals are transferred or terminated.

Supplemental Guidance: The organization determines the types of guards needed, for example, professional physical security staff or other personnel such as administrative staff or information system users, as deemed appropriate. Physical access devices include, for example, keys, locks, combinations, and card readers. Workstations and associated peripherals connected to (and part of) an organizational information system may be located in areas designated as publicly accessible with access to such devices being safeguarded. Related controls: MP-2, MP-4, PE-2.

Control Enhancements:

(1)   **The organization enforces physical access authorizations to the information system independent of the physical access controls for the facility.**

Enhancement Supplemental Guidance: This control enhancement applies to server rooms, media storage areas, communications centers, or any other areas within an organizational facility containing large concentrations of information system components. The intent is to provide additional physical security for those areas where the organization may be more vulnerable due to the concentration of information system components. Security requirements for facilities containing organizational information systems that process, store, or transmit Sensitive Compartmented Information (SCI) are consistent with applicable federal laws, Executive Orders, directives, policies, regulations, standards, and guidance. See also PS-3, security requirements for personnel access to SCI.

(2)   **The organization performs security checks at the physical boundary of the facility or information system for unauthorized exfiltration of information or information system components.**

Enhancement Supplemental Guidance: The extent/frequency or randomness of the checks is as deemed necessary by the organization to adequately mitigate risk associated with exfiltration.

(3)   **The organization guards, alarms, and monitors every physical access point to the facility where the information system resides 24 hours per day, 7 days per week.**

    (4)   **The organization uses lockable physical casings to protect [*Assignment: organization-defined information system components*] from unauthorized physical access.**

    (5)   **The information system detects/prevents physical tampering or alteration of hardware components within the system.**

    (6)   **The organization employs a penetration testing process that includes [*Assignment: organization- defined frequency*], unannounced attempts to bypass or circumvent security controls associated with physical access points to the facility.**

    Enhancement Supplemental Guidance: Related control: CA-2.

References: FIPS Publication 201; NIST Special Publications 800-73, 800-76, 800-78; ICD 704; DCID 6/9.

Priority and Baseline Allocation:

P1	LOW PE-3	MOD PE-3	HIGH PE-3 (1)

PE-4   ACCESS CONTROL FOR TRANSMISSION MEDIUM

Control: The organization controls physical access to information system distribution and transmission lines within organizational facilities.

Supplemental Guidance: Physical protections applied to information system distribution and transmission lines help prevent accidental damage, disruption, and physical tampering. Additionally, physical protections are necessary to help prevent eavesdropping or in transit modification of unencrypted transmissions. Protective measures to control physical access to information system distribution and transmission lines include: (i) locked wiring closets; (ii) disconnected or locked spare jacks; and/or (iii) protection of cabling by conduit or cable trays. Related control: PE-2.

Control Enhancements: None.

References: NSTISSI No. 7003.

Priority and Baseline Allocation:

P1	LOW Not Selected	MOD PE-4	HIGH PE-4

PE-5   ACCESS CONTROL FOR OUTPUT DEVICES

Control: The organization controls physical access to information system output devices to prevent unauthorized individuals from obtaining the output.

Supplemental Guidance: Monitors, printers, and audio devices are examples of information system output devices.

Control Enhancements: None.

References: None.

Priority and Baseline Allocation:

P1	LOW Not Selected	MOD PE-5	HIGH PE-5

PE-6   **MONITORING PHYSICAL ACCESS**

Control: The organization:

a. Monitors physical access to the information system to detect and respond to physical security incidents;

b. Reviews physical access logs [*Assignment: organization-defined frequency*]; and

c. Coordinates results of reviews and investigations with the organization's incident response capability.

Supplemental Guidance: Investigation of and response to detected physical security incidents, including apparent security violations or suspicious physical access activities, are part of the organization's incident response capability.

Control Enhancements:

(1)   The organization monitors real-time physical intrusion alarms and surveillance equipment.

(2)   The organization employs automated mechanisms to recognize potential intrusions and initiate designated response actions.

References: None.

Priority and Baseline Allocation:

P1	**LOW** PE-6	**MOD** PE-6 (1)	**HIGH** PE-6 (1) (2)

PE-7   **VISITOR CONTROL**

Control: The organization controls physical access to the information system by authenticating visitors before authorizing access to the facility where the information system resides other than areas designated as publicly accessible.

Supplemental Guidance: Individuals (to include organizational employees, contract personnel, and others) with permanent authorization credentials for the facility are not considered visitors.

Control Enhancements:

(1)   The organization escorts visitors and monitors visitor activity, when required.

(2)   The organization requires two forms of identification for visitor access to the facility.

References: None.

Priority and Baseline Allocation:

P1	**LOW** PE-7	**MOD** PE-7 (1)	**HIGH** PE-7 (1)

PE-8   **ACCESS RECORDS**

Control: The organization:

a. Maintains visitor access records to the facility where the information system resides (except for those areas within the facility officially designated as publicly accessible); and

b. Reviews visitor access records [*Assignment: organization-defined frequency*].

Supplemental Guidance: Visitor access records include, for example, name/organization of the person visiting, signature of the visitor, form(s) of identification, date of access, time of entry and departure, purpose of visit, and name/organization of person visited.

Control Enhancements:

(1)   The organization employs automated mechanisms to facilitate the maintenance and review of access records.

(2)   The organization maintains a record of all physical access, both visitor and authorized individuals.

References: None.

Priority and Baseline Allocation:

P3	**LOW** PE-8	**MOD** PE-8	**HIGH** PE-8 (1) (2)

PE-9   POWER EQUIPMENT AND POWER CABLING

Control: The organization protects power equipment and power cabling for the information system from damage and destruction.

Supplemental Guidance: This control, to include any enhancements specified, may be satisfied by similar requirements fulfilled by another organizational entity other than the information security program. Organizations avoid duplicating actions already covered.

Control Enhancements:

(1)   The organization employs redundant and parallel power cabling paths.

(2)   The organization employs automatic voltage controls for [*Assignment: organization-defined list of critical information system components*].

References: None.

Priority and Baseline Allocation:

P1	**LOW** Not Selected	**MOD** PE-9	**HIGH** PE-9

PE-10   EMERGENCY SHUTOFF

Control: The organization:

a.   Provides the capability of shutting off power to the information system or individual system components in emergency situations;

b.   Places emergency shutoff switches or devices in [*Assignment: organization-defined location by information system or system component*] to facilitate safe and easy access for personnel; and

c.   Protects emergency power shutoff capability from unauthorized activation.

Supplemental Guidance: This control applies to facilities containing concentrations of information system resources, for example, data centers, server rooms, and mainframe computer rooms.

Control Enhancements:

(1)   [Withdrawn: Incorporated into PE-

10]. References: None.

Priority and Baseline Allocation:

P1	**LOW** Not Selected	**MOD** PE-10	**HIGH** PE-10

PE-11   EMERGENCY POWER

Control: The organization provides a short-term uninterruptible power supply to facilitate an orderly shutdown of the information system in the event of a primary power source loss.

Supplemental Guidance: This control, to include any enhancements specified, may be satisfied by similar requirements fulfilled by another organizational entity other than the information security program. Organizations avoid duplicating actions already covered.

Control Enhancements:

(1)   The organization provides a long-term alternate power supply for the information system that is capable of maintaining minimally required operational capability in the event of an extended loss of the primary power source.

(2)   The organization provides a long-term alternate power supply for the information system that is self-contained and not reliant on external power generation.

   Enhancement Supplemental Guidance: Long-term alternate power supplies for the information system are either manually or automatically activated.

References: None.

Priority and Baseline Allocation:

P1	LOW Not Selected	MOD PE-11	HIGH PE-11 (1)

PE-12   EMERGENCY LIGHTING

Control: The organization employs and maintains automatic emergency lighting for the information system that activates in the event of a power outage or disruption and that covers emergency exits and evacuation routes within the facility.

Supplemental Guidance: This control, to include any enhancements specified, may be satisfied by similar requirements fulfilled by another organizational entity other than the information security program. Organizations avoid duplicating actions already covered.

Control Enhancements:

(1)   The organization provides emergency lighting for all areas within the facility supporting essential missions and business functions.

References: None.

Priority and Baseline Allocation:

P1	LOW PE-12	MOD PE-12	HIGH PE-12

PE-13   FIRE PROTECTION

Control: The organization employs and maintains fire suppression and detection devices/systems for the information system that are supported by an independent energy source.

Supplemental Guidance: Fire suppression and detection devices/systems include, for example, sprinkler systems, handheld fire extinguishers, fixed fire hoses, and smoke detectors. This control, to include any enhancements specified, may be satisfied by similar requirements fulfilled by another organizational entity other than the information security program. Organizations avoid duplicating actions already covered.

Control Enhancements:

(1)   The organization employs fire detection devices/systems for the information system that activate automatically and notify the organization and emergency responders in the event of a fire.

(2)   The organization employs fire suppression devices/systems for the information system that provide automatic notification of any activation to the organization and emergency responders.

(3)   The organization employs an automatic fire suppression capability for the information system when the facility is not staffed on a continuous basis.

(4)   The organization ensures that the facility undergoes [*Assignment: organization-defined frequency*] fire marshal inspections and promptly resolves identified deficiencies.

References: None.

Priority and Baseline Allocation:

P1	LOW PE-13	MOD PE-13 (1) (2) (3)	HIGH PE-13 (1) (2) (3)

PE-14   TEMPERATURE AND HUMIDITY CONTROLS

Control: The organization:

a.   Maintains temperature and humidity levels within the facility where the information system resides at [*Assignment: organization-defined acceptable levels*]; and

b.   Monitors temperature and humidity levels [*Assignment: organization-defined frequency*].

Supplemental Guidance: This control, to include any enhancements specified, may be satisfied by similar requirements fulfilled by another organizational entity other than the information security program. Organizations avoid duplicating actions already covered.

Control Enhancements:

(1)   The organization employs automatic temperature and humidity controls in the facility to prevent fluctuations potentially harmful to the information system.

(2)   The organization employs temperature and humidity monitoring that provides an alarm or notification of changes potentially harmful to personnel or equipment.

References: None.

Priority and Baseline Allocation:

P1	LOW PE-14	MOD PE-14	HIGH PE-14

PE-15   WATER DAMAGE PROTECTION

Control: The organization protects the information system from damage resulting from water leakage by providing master shutoff valves that are accessible, working properly, and known to key personnel.

Supplemental Guidance: This control, to include any enhancements specified, may be satisfied by similar requirements fulfilled by another organizational entity other than the information security program. Organizations avoid duplicating actions already covered.

Control Enhancements:

(1)   The organization employs mechanisms that, without the need for manual intervention, protect the information system from water damage in the event of a water leak.

References: None.

Priority and Baseline Allocation:

P1	LOW PE-15	MOD PE-15	HIGH PE-15 (1)

PE-16   DELIVERY AND REMOVAL

Control: The organization authorizes, monitors, and controls [*Assignment: organization-defined types of information system components*] entering and exiting the facility and maintains records of those items.

Supplemental Guidance: Effectively enforcing authorizations for entry and exit of information system components may require restricting access to delivery areas and possibly isolating the areas from the information system and media libraries.

Control Enhancements: None.

References: None.

Priority and Baseline Allocation:

P1	**LOW** PE-16	**MOD** PE-16	**HIGH** PE-16

PE-17   ALTERNATE WORK SITE

Control: The organization:

a. Employs [*Assignment: organization-defined management, operational, and technical information system security controls*] at alternate work sites;

b. Assesses as feasible, the effectiveness of security controls at alternate work sites; and

c. Provides a means for employees to communicate with information security personnel in case of security incidents or problems.

Supplemental Guidance: Alternate work sites may include, for example, government facilities or private residences of employees. The organization may define different sets of security controls for specific alternate work sites or types of sites.

Control Enhancements: None.

References: NIST Special Publication 800-46.

Priority and Baseline Allocation:

P1	**LOW** Not Selected	**MOD** PE-17	**HIGH** PE-17

PE-18   LOCATION OF INFORMATION SYSTEM COMPONENTS

Control: The organization positions information system components within the facility to minimize potential damage from physical and environmental hazards and to minimize the opportunity for unauthorized access.

Supplemental Guidance: Physical and environmental hazards include, for example, flooding, fire, tornados, earthquakes, hurricanes, acts of terrorism, vandalism, electromagnetic pulse, electrical interference, and electromagnetic radiation. Whenever possible, the organization also considers the location or site of the facility with regard to physical and environmental hazards. In addition, the organization considers the location of physical entry points where unauthorized individuals, while not being granted access, might nonetheless be in close proximity to the information system and therefore, increase the potential for unauthorized access to organizational communications (e.g., through the use of wireless sniffers or microphones). This control, to include any enhancements specified, may be satisfied by similar requirements fulfilled by another organizational entity other than the information security program. Organizations avoid duplicating actions already covered.

Control Enhancements:

(1)   **The organization plans the location or site of the facility where the information system resides with regard to physical and environmental hazards and for existing facilities, considers the physical and environmental hazards in its risk mitigation strategy.**

References: None.

Priority and Baseline Allocation:

P2	**LOW** Not Selected	**MOD** PE-18	**HIGH** PE-18 (1)

PE-19   INFORMATION LEAKAGE

Control: The organization protects the information system from information leakage due to electromagnetic signals emanations.

Supplemental Guidance: The security categorization of the information system (with respect to confidentiality) and organizational security policy guides the application of safeguards and countermeasures employed to protect the information system against information leakage due to electromagnetic signals emanations.

Control Enhancements:

(1)   **The organization ensures that information system components, associated data communications, and networks are protected in accordance with: (i) national emissions and TEMPEST policies and procedures; and (ii) the sensitivity of the information being transmitted.**

References: FIPS Publication 199.

Priority and Baseline Allocation:

P0	**LOW** Not Selected	**MOD** Not Selected	**HIGH** Not Selected

___

FAMILY: PLANNING   **CLASS:** MANAGEMENT

PL-1   **SECURITY PLANNING POLICY AND PROCEDURES**

Control: The organization develops, disseminates, and reviews/updates [*Assignment: organization-defined frequency*]:

a.   A formal, documented security planning policy that addresses purpose, scope, roles, responsibilities, management commitment, coordination among organizational entities, and compliance; and

b.   Formal, documented procedures to facilitate the implementation of the security planning policy and associated security planning controls.

Supplemental Guidance: This control is intended to produce the policy and procedures that are required for the effective implementation of selected security controls and control enhancements in the security planning family. The policy and procedures are consistent with applicable federal laws, Executive Orders, directives, policies, regulations, standards, and guidance. Existing organizational policies and procedures may make the need for additional specific policies and procedures unnecessary. The security planning policy addresses the overall policy requirements for confidentiality, integrity, and availability and can be included as part of the general information security policy for the organization. Security planning procedures can be developed for the security program in general and for a particular information system, when required. The organizational risk management strategy is a key factor in the development of the security planning policy. Related control: PM-9.

Control Enhancements: None.

References: NIST Special Publications 800-12, 800-18, 800-100.

Priority and Baseline Allocation:

P1	**LOW** PL-1	**MOD** PL-1	**HIGH** PL-1

PL-2   **SYSTEM SECURITY PLAN**

Control: The organization:

a.   Develops a security plan for the information system that:

- Is consistent with the organization's enterprise architecture;

- Explicitly defines the authorization boundary for the system;

- Describes the operational context of the information system in terms of missions and business processes;

- Provides the security category and impact level of the information system including supporting rationale;

- Describes the operational environment for the information system;

- Describes relationships with or connections to other information systems;

- Provides an overview of the security requirements for the system;

- Describes the security controls in place or planned for meeting those requirements including a rationale for the tailoring and supplementation decisions; and

- Is reviewed and approved by the authorizing official or designated representative prior to plan implementation;

b. Reviews the security plan for the information system [*Assignment: organization-defined frequency*]; and

c. Updates the plan to address changes to the information system/environment of operation or problems identified during plan implementation or security control assessments.

Supplemental Guidance: The security plan contains sufficient information (including specification of parameters for assignment and selection statements in security controls either explicitly or by reference) to enable an implementation that is unambiguously compliant with the intent of the plan and a subsequent determination of risk to organizational operations and assets, individuals, other organizations, and the Nation if the plan is implemented as intended. Related controls: PM-1, PM-7, PM-8, PM-9, PM-11.

Control Enhancements:

(1) **The organization:**

(a) **Develops a security Concept of Operations (CONOPS) for the information system containing, at a minimum: (i) the purpose of the system; (ii) a description of the system architecture; (iii) the security authorization schedule; and (iv) the security categorization and associated factors considered in determining the categorization; and**

(b) **Reviews and updates the CONOPS [*Assignment: organization-defined frequency*].**

Enhancement Supplemental Guidance: The security CONOPS may be included in the security plan for the information system.

(2) **The organization develops a functional architecture for the information system that identifies and maintains:**

(a) **External interfaces, the information being exchanged across the interfaces, and the protection mechanisms associated with each interface;**

(b) **User roles and the access privileges assigned to each**

role; (c) **Unique security requirements;**

(d) **Types of information processed, stored, or transmitted by the information system and any specific protection needs in accordance with applicable federal laws, Executive Orders, directives, policies, regulations, standards, and guidance; and**

(e) **Restoration priority of information or information system services.**

Enhancement Supplemental Guidance: Unique security requirements for the information system include, for example, encryption of key data elements at rest. Specific protection needs for the information system include, for example, the Privacy Act and Health Insurance Portability and Accountability Act.

References: NIST Special Publication 800-18.

Priority and Baseline Allocation:

P1	LOW PL-2	MOD PL-2	HIGH PL-2

PL-3   SYSTEM SECURITY PLAN UPDATE

[Withdrawn: Incorporated into PL-2].

PL-4   RULES OF BEHAVIOR

Control: The organization:

a. Establishes and makes readily available to all information system users, the rules that describe their responsibilities and expected behavior with regard to information and information system usage; and

b. Receives signed acknowledgment from users indicating that they have read, understand, and agree to abide by the rules of behavior, before authorizing access to information and the information system.

Supplemental Guidance: The organization considers different sets of rules based on user roles and responsibilities, for example, differentiating between the rules that apply to privileged users and rules that apply to general users. Electronic signatures are acceptable for use in acknowledging rules of behavior. Related control: PS-6.

Control Enhancements:

(1)   The organization includes in the rules of behavior, explicit restrictions on the use of social networking sites, posting information on commercial websites, and sharing information system account information.

References: NIST Publication 800-18.

Priority and Baseline Allocation:

P1	LOW PL-4	MOD PL-4	HIGH PL-4

PL-5   PRIVACY IMPACT ASSESSMENT

Control: The organization conducts a privacy impact assessment on the information system in accordance with OMB policy.

Supplemental Guidance: None.

Control Enhancements: None.

References: OMB Memorandum 03-22.

Priority and Baseline Allocation:

P1	LOW PL-5	MOD PL-5	HIGH PL-5

PL-6   SECURITY-RELATED ACTIVITY PLANNING

Control: The organization plans and coordinates security-related activities affecting the information system before conducting such activities in order to reduce the impact on organizational operations (i.e., mission, functions, image, and reputation), organizational assets, and individuals.

Supplemental Guidance: Security-related activities include, for example, security assessments, audits, system hardware and software maintenance, and contingency plan testing/exercises. Organizational advance planning and coordination includes both emergency and nonemergency (i.e., planned or nonurgent unplanned) situations.

Control Enhancements: None.

References: None.

Priority and Baseline Allocation:

P3	LOW Not Selected	MOD PL-6	HIGH PL-6

FAMILY: PERSONNEL SECURITY   **CLASS:** OPERATIONAL

PS-1   **PERSONNEL SECURITY POLICY AND PROCEDURES**

Control: The organization develops, disseminates, and reviews/updates [*Assignment: organization-defined frequency*]:

a.   A formal, documented personnel security policy that addresses purpose, scope, roles, responsibilities, management commitment, coordination among organizational entities, and compliance; and

b.   Formal, documented procedures to facilitate the implementation of the personnel security policy and associated personnel security controls.

Supplemental Guidance: This control is intended to produce the policy and procedures that are required for the effective implementation of selected security controls and control enhancements in the personnel security family. The policy and procedures are consistent with applicable federal laws, Executive Orders, directives, policies, regulations, standards, and guidance. Existing organizational policies and procedures may make the need for additional specific policies and procedures unnecessary. The personnel security policy can be included as part of the general information security policy for the organization. Personnel security procedures can be developed for the security program in general and for a particular information system, when required. The organizational risk management strategy is a key factor in the development of the personnel security policy. Related control: PM-9.

Control Enhancements: None.

References: NIST Special Publications 800-12, 800-100.

Priority and Baseline Allocation:

P1	**LOW** PS-1	**MOD** PS-1	**HIGH** PS-1

PS-2   **POSITION CATEGORIZATION**

Control: The organization:

a.   Assigns a risk designation to all positions;

b.   Establishes screening criteria for individuals filling those positions; and

c.   Reviews and revises position risk designations [*Assignment: organization-defined frequency*].

Supplemental Guidance: Position risk designations are consistent with Office of Personnel Management policy and guidance. The screening criteria include explicit information security role appointment requirements (e.g., training, security clearance).

Control Enhancements: None.

References: 5 CFR 731.106(a).

Priority and Baseline Allocation:

P1	**LOW** PS-2	**MOD** PS-2	**HIGH** PS-2

PS-3   **PERSONNEL SCREENING**

Control: The organization:

a.   Screens individuals prior to authorizing access to the information system; and

b. Rescreens individuals according to [*Assignment: organization-defined list of conditions requiring rescreening and, where re-screening is so indicated, the frequency of such rescreening*].

Supplemental Guidance: Screening and rescreening are consistent with applicable federal laws, Executive Orders, directives, policies, regulations, standards, guidance, and the criteria established for the risk designation of the assigned position. The organization may define different rescreening conditions and frequencies for personnel accessing the information system based on the type of information processed, stored, or transmitted by the system.

Control Enhancements:

(1) **The organization ensures that every user accessing an information system processing, storing, or transmitting classified information is cleared and indoctrinated to the highest classification level of the information on the system.**

(2) **The organization ensures that every user accessing an information system processing, storing, or transmitting types of classified information which require formal indoctrination, is formally indoctrinated for all of the relevant types of information on the system.**

Enhancement Supplemental Guidance: Types of information requiring formal indoctrination include, for example, Special Access Program (SAP), Restricted Data (RD), and Sensitive Compartment Information (SCI).

References: 5 CFR 731.106; FIPS Publications 199, 201; NIST Special Publications 800-73, 800-76, 800-78; ICD 704.

Priority and Baseline Allocation:

P1	**LOW** PS-3	**MOD** PS-3	**HIGH** PS-3

PS-4   PERSONNEL TERMINATION

Control: The organization, upon termination of individual employment:

a. Terminates information system access;

b. Conducts exit interviews;

c. Retrieves all security-related organizational information system-related property; and

d. Retains access to organizational information and information systems formerly controlled by terminated individual.

Supplemental Guidance: Information system-related property includes, for example, hardware authentication tokens, system administration technical manuals, keys, identification cards, and building passes. Exit interviews ensure that individuals understand any security constraints imposed by being former employees and that proper accountability is achieved for all information system-related property. Exit interviews may not be possible for some employees (e.g., in the case of job abandonment, some illnesses, and nonavailability of supervisors). Exit interviews are important for individuals with security clearances. Timely execution of this control is particularly essential for employees or contractors terminated for cause.

Control Enhancements: None.

References: None.

Priority and Baseline Allocation:

P2	**LOW** PS-4	**MOD** PS-4	**HIGH** PS-4

PS-5   PERSONNEL TRANSFER

Control: The organization reviews logical and physical access authorizations to information systems/facilities when personnel are reassigned or transferred to other positions within the organization and initiates [*Assignment: organization-defined transfer or reassignment actions*] within [*Assignment: organization-defined time period following the formal transfer action*].

Supplemental Guidance: This control applies when the reassignment or transfer of an employee is permanent or of such an extended duration as to make the actions warranted. In addition the organization defines the actions appropriate for the type of reassignment or transfer; whether permanent or temporary. Actions that may be required when personnel are transferred or reassigned to other positions within the organization include, for example: (i) returning old and issuing new keys, identification cards, and building passes; (ii) closing previous information system accounts and establishing new accounts; (iii) changing information system access authorizations; and (iv) providing for access to official records to which the employee had access at the previous work location and in the previous information system accounts.

Control Enhancements: None.

References: None.

Priority and Baseline Allocation:

P2	LOW PS-5	MOD PS-5	HIGH PS-5

PS-6   ACCESS AGREEMENTS

Control: The organization:

a.   Ensures that individuals requiring access to organizational information and information systems sign appropriate access agreements prior to being granted access; and

b.   Reviews/updates the access agreements [*Assignment: organization-defined frequency*].

Supplemental Guidance: Access agreements include, for example, nondisclosure agreements, acceptable use agreements, rules of behavior, and conflict-of-interest agreements. Signed access agreements include an acknowledgement that individuals have read, understand, and agree to abide by the constraints associated with the information system to which access is authorized. Electronic signatures are acceptable for use in acknowledging access agreements unless specifically prohibited by organizational policy. Related control: PL-4.

Control Enhancements:

(1)   The organization ensures that access to information with special protection measures is granted only to individuals who:

   (a)   Have a valid access authorization that is demonstrated by assigned official government duties; and

   (b)   Satisfy associated personnel security criteria.

Enhancement Supplemental Guidance: Information with special protection measures includes, for example, privacy information, proprietary information, and Sources and Methods Information (SAMI). Personnel security criteria include, for example, position sensitivity background screening requirements.

(2)   The organization ensures that access to classified information with special protection measures is granted only to individuals who:

   (a)   Have a valid access authorization that is demonstrated by assigned official government duties;

   (b)   Satisfy associated personnel security criteria consistent with applicable federal laws, Executive Orders, directives, policies, regulations, standards, and guidance; and

    (c) Have read, understand, and signed a nondisclosure agreement.

Enhancement Supplemental Guidance: Examples of special protection measures include, for example, collateral, Special Access Program (SAP) and Sensitive Compartmented Information (SCI).

References: None.

Priority and Baseline Allocation:

P3	LOW PS-6	MOD PS-6	HIGH PS-6

PS-7   THIRD-PARTY PERSONNEL SECURITY

Control: The organization:

a. Establishes personnel security requirements including security roles and responsibilities for third-party providers;

b. Documents personnel security requirements; and

c. Monitors provider compliance.

Supplemental Guidance: Third-party providers include, for example, service bureaus, contractors, and other organizations providing information system development, information technology services, outsourced applications, and network and security management. The organization explicitly includes personnel security requirements in acquisition-related documents.

Control Enhancements: None.

References: NIST Special Publication 800-35.

Priority and Baseline Allocation:

P1	LOW PS-7	MOD PS-7	HIGH PS-7

PS-8   PERSONNEL SANCTIONS

Control: The organization employs a formal sanctions process for personnel failing to comply with established information security policies and procedures.

Supplemental Guidance: The sanctions process is consistent with applicable federal laws, Executive Orders, directives, policies, regulations, standards, and guidance. The process is described in access agreements and can be included as part of the general personnel policies and procedures for the organization. Related controls: PL-4, PS-6.

Control Enhancements: None.

References: None.

Priority and Baseline Allocation:

P3	LOW PS-8	MOD PS-8	HIGH PS-8

FAMILY: RISK ASSESSMENT   **CLASS:** MANAGEMENT

RA-1   **RISK ASSESSMENT POLICY AND PROCEDURES**

Control: The organization develops, disseminates, and reviews/updates [*Assignment: organization-defined frequency*]:

a.   A formal, documented risk assessment policy that addresses purpose, scope, roles, responsibilities, management commitment, coordination among organizational entities, and compliance; and

b.   Formal, documented procedures to facilitate the implementation of the risk assessment policy and associated risk assessment controls.

Supplemental Guidance: This control is intended to produce the policy and procedures that are required for the effective implementation of selected security controls and control enhancements in the risk assessment family. The policy and procedures are consistent with applicable federal laws, Executive Orders, directives, policies, regulations, standards, and guidance. Existing organizational policies and procedures may make the need for additional specific policies and procedures unnecessary. The risk assessment policy can be included as part of the general information security policy for the organization. Risk assessment procedures can be developed for the security program in general and for a particular information system, when required. The organizational risk management strategy is a key factor in the development of the risk assessment policy. Related control: PM-9.

Control Enhancements: None.

References: NIST Special Publications 800-12, 800-30,800-100.

Priority and Baseline Allocation:

P1	**LOW** RA-1	**MOD** RA-1	**HIGH** RA-1

RA-2   **SECURITY CATEGORIZATION**

Control: The organization:

a.   Categorizes information and the information system in accordance with applicable federal laws, Executive Orders, directives, policies, regulations, standards, and guidance;

b.   Documents the security categorization results (including supporting rationale) in the security plan for the information system; and

c.   Ensures the security categorization decision is reviewed and approved by the authorizing official or authorizing official designated representative.

Supplemental Guidance: A clearly defined authorization boundary is a prerequisite for an effective security categorization. Security categorization describes the potential adverse impacts to organizational operations, organizational assets, and individuals should the information and information system be comprised through a loss of confidentiality, integrity, or availability. The organization conducts the security categorization process as an organization-wide activity with the involvement of the chief information officer, senior information security officer, information system owner, mission owners, and information owners/stewards. The organization also considers potential adverse impacts to other organizations and, in accordance with the USA PATRIOT Act of 2001 and Homeland Security Presidential Directives, potential national-level adverse impacts in categorizing the information system. The security categorization process facilitates the creation of an *inventory* of information assets, and in conjunction with CM-8, a mapping to the information system components where the information is processed, stored, and transmitted. Related controls: CM-8, MP-4, SC-7.

Control Enhancements: None.

References: FIPS Publication 199; NIST Special Publications 800-30, 800-39, 800-60.

Priority and Baseline Allocation:

P1	LOW RA-2	MOD RA-2	HIGH RA-2

RA-3   RISK ASSESSMENT

Control: The organization:

a. Conducts an assessment of risk, including the likelihood and magnitude of harm, from the unauthorized access, use, disclosure, disruption, modification, or destruction of the information system and the information it processes, stores, or transmits;

b. Documents risk assessment results in [*Selection: security plan; risk assessment report;* [*Assignment: organization-defined document*]];

c. Reviews risk assessment results [*Assignment: organization-defined frequency*]; and

d. Updates the risk assessment [*Assignment: organization-defined frequency*] or whenever there are significant changes to the information system or environment of operation (including the identification of new threats and vulnerabilities), or other conditions that may impact the security state of the system.

Supplemental Guidance: A clearly defined authorization boundary is a prerequisite for an effective risk assessment. Risk assessments take into account vulnerabilities, threat sources, and security controls planned or in place to determine the level of residual risk posed to organizational operations and assets, individuals, other organizations, and the Nation based on the operation of the information system. Risk assessments also take into account risk posed to organizational operations, organizational assets, or individuals from external parties (e.g., service providers, contractors operating information systems on behalf of the organization, individuals accessing organizational information systems, outsourcing entities). In accordance with OMB policy and related E-authentication initiatives, authentication of public users accessing federal information systems may also be required to protect nonpublic or privacy-related information. As such, organizational assessments of risk also address public access to federal information systems. The General Services Administration provides tools supporting that portion of the risk assessment dealing with public access to federal information systems.

Risk assessments (either formal or informal) can be conducted by organizations at various steps in the Risk Management Framework including: information system categorization; security control selection; security control implementation; security control assessment; information system authorization; and security control monitoring. RA-3 is a noteworthy security control in that the control must be partially *implemented* prior to the implementation of other controls in order to complete the first two steps in the Risk Management Framework. Risk assessments can play an important role in the security control selection process during the application of tailoring guidance for security control baselines and when considering supplementing the tailored baselines with additional security controls or control enhancements.

Control Enhancements: None.

References: NIST Special Publication 800-30.

Priority and Baseline Allocation:

P1	LOW RA-3	MOD RA-3	HIGH RA-3

RA-4   RISK ASSESSMENT UPDATE

[Withdrawn: Incorporated into RA-3].

RA-5   VULNERABILITY SCANNING

Control: The organization:

a.   Scans for vulnerabilities in the information system and hosted applications [*Assignment: organization-defined frequency and/or randomly in accordance with organization-defined process*] and when new vulnerabilities potentially affecting the system/applications are identified and reported;

b.   Employs vulnerability scanning tools and techniques that promote interoperability among tools and automate parts of the vulnerability management process by using standards for:

   - Enumerating platforms, software flaws, and improper configurations;

   - Formatting and making transparent, checklists and test procedures; and

   - Measuring vulnerability impact;

c.   Analyzes vulnerability scan reports and results from security control assessments;

d.   Remediates legitimate vulnerabilities [*Assignment: organization-defined response times*] in accordance with an organizational assessment of risk; and

e.   Shares information obtained from the vulnerability scanning process and security control assessments with designated personnel throughout the organization to help eliminate similar vulnerabilities in other information systems (i.e., systemic weaknesses or deficiencies).

Supplemental Guidance: The security categorization of the information system guides the frequency and comprehensiveness of the vulnerability scans. Vulnerability analysis for custom software and applications may require additional, more specialized techniques and approaches (e.g., web-based application scanners, source code reviews, source code analyzers). Vulnerability scanning includes scanning for specific functions, ports, protocols, and services that should not be accessible to users or devices and for improperly configured or incorrectly operating information flow mechanisms. The organization considers using tools that express vulnerabilities in the Common Vulnerabilities and Exposures (CVE) naming convention and that use the Open Vulnerability Assessment Language (OVAL) to test for the presence of vulnerabilities. The Common Weakness Enumeration (CWE) and the National Vulnerability Database (NVD) are also excellent sources for vulnerability information. In addition, security control assessments such as red team exercises are another source of potential vulnerabilities for which to scan. Related controls: CA-2, CM-6, RA-3, SI-2.

Control Enhancements:

(1)   The organization employs vulnerability scanning tools that include the capability to readily update the list of information system vulnerabilities scanned.

(2)   The organization updates the list of information system vulnerabilities scanned [*Assignment: organization-defined frequency*] or when new vulnerabilities are identified and reported.

(3)   The organization employs vulnerability scanning procedures that can demonstrate the breadth and depth of coverage (i.e., information system components scanned and vulnerabilities checked).

(4)   The organization attempts to discern what information about the information system is discoverable by adversaries.

(5)   The organization includes privileged access authorization to [*Assignment: organization-identified information system components*] for selected vulnerability scanning activities to facilitate more thorough scanning.

(6)   The organization employs automated mechanisms to compare the results of vulnerability scans over time to determine trends in information system vulnerabilities.

(7)   The organization employs automated mechanisms [*Assignment: organization-defined frequency*] to detect the presence of unauthorized software on organizational information systems and notify designated organizational officials.

(8)   The organization reviews historic audit logs to determine if a vulnerability identified in the information system has been previously exploited.

(9)   The organization employs an independent penetration agent or penetration team

    to: (a)   Conduct a vulnerability analysis on the information system; and

    (b)   Perform penetration testing on the information system based on the vulnerability analysis to determine the exploitability of identified vulnerabilities.

Enhancement Supplemental Guidance: A standard method for penetration testing includes: (i) pre-test analysis based on full knowledge of the target information system; (ii) pre-test identification of potential vulnerabilities based on pre-test analysis; and (iii) testing designed to determine exploitability of identified vulnerabilities. Detailed rules of engagement are agreed upon by all parties before the commencement of any penetration testing scenario.

References: NIST Special Publications 800-40, 800-70, 800-115; Web: CWE.MITRE.ORG; NVD.NIST.GOV.

Priority and Baseline Allocation:

P1	LOW RA-5	MOD RA-5 (1)	HIGH RA-5 (1) (2) (3) (4) (5) (7)

FAMILY: SYSTEM AND SERVICES ACQUISITION   **CLASS:** MANAGEMENT

SA-1   SYSTEM AND SERVICES ACQUISITION POLICY AND PROCEDURES

Control: The organization develops, disseminates, and reviews/updates [*Assignment: organization-defined frequency*]:

a. A formal, documented system and services acquisition policy that includes information security considerations and that addresses purpose, scope, roles, responsibilities, management commitment, coordination among organizational entities, and compliance; and

b. Formal, documented procedures to facilitate the implementation of the system and services acquisition policy and associated system and services acquisition controls.

Supplemental Guidance: This control is intended to produce the policy and procedures that are required for the effective implementation of selected security controls and control enhancements in the system and services acquisition family. The policy and procedures are consistent with applicable federal laws, Executive Orders, directives, policies, regulations, standards, and guidance. Existing organizational policies and procedures may make the need for additional specific policies and procedures unnecessary. The system and services acquisition policy can be included as part of the general information security policy for the organization. System and services acquisition procedures can be developed for the security program in general and for a particular information system, when required. The organizational risk management strategy is a key factor in the development of the system and services acquisition policy. Related control: PM-9.

Control Enhancements: None.

References: NIST Special Publications 800-12, 800-100.

Priority and Baseline Allocation:

P1	**LOW** SA-1	**MOD** SA-1	**HIGH** SA-1

SA-2   ALLOCATION OF RESOURCES

Control: The organization:

a. Includes a determination of information security requirements for the information system in mission/business process planning;

b. Determines, documents, and allocates the resources required to protect the information system as part of its capital planning and investment control process; and

c. Establishes a discrete line item for information security in organizational programming and budgeting documentation.

Supplemental Guidance: Related controls: PM-3, PM-11.

Control Enhancements: None.

References: NIST Special Publication 800-65.

Priority and Baseline Allocation:

P1	**LOW** SA-2	**MOD** SA-2	**HIGH** SA-2

SA-3   **LIFE CYCLE SUPPORT**

Control: The organization:

a. Manages the information system using a system development life cycle methodology that includes information security considerations;

b. Defines and documents information system security roles and responsibilities throughout the system development life cycle; and

c. Identifies individuals having information system security roles and responsibilities.

Supplemental Guidance: Related control: PM-7.

Control Enhancements: None.

References: NIST Special Publication 800-64.

Priority and Baseline Allocation:

P1	**LOW** SA-3	**MOD** SA-3	**HIGH** SA-3

SA-4   **ACQUISITIONS**

Control: The organization includes the following requirements and/or specifications, explicitly or by reference, in information system acquisition contracts based on an assessment of risk and in accordance with applicable federal laws, Executive Orders, directives, policies, regulations, and standards:

a. Security functional requirements/specifications;

b. Security-related documentation requirements; and

c. Developmental and evaluation-related assurance requirements.

Supplemental Guidance: The acquisition documents for information systems, information system components, and information system services include, either explicitly or by reference, security requirements that describe: (i) required security capabilities (i.e., security needs and, as necessary, specific security controls and other specific FISMA requirements); (ii) required design and development processes; (iii) required test and evaluation procedures; and (iv) required documentation. The requirements in the acquisition documents permit updating security controls as new threats/vulnerabilities are identified and as new technologies are implemented. Acquisition documents also include requirements for appropriate information system documentation. The documentation addresses user and system administrator guidance and information regarding the implementation of the security controls in the information system. The level of detail required in the documentation is based on the security categorization for the information system. In addition, the required documentation includes security configuration settings and security implementation guidance. FISMA reporting instructions provide guidance on configuration requirements for federal information systems.

Control Enhancements:

(1) The organization requires in acquisition documents that vendors/contractors provide information describing the functional properties of the security controls to be employed within the information system, information system components, or information system services in sufficient detail to permit analysis and testing of the controls.

(2) The organization requires in acquisition documents that vendors/contractors provide information describing the design and implementation details of the security controls to be employed within the information system, information system components, or information system services (including functional interfaces among control components) in sufficient detail to permit analysis and testing of the controls.

(3)   The organization requires software vendors/manufacturers to demonstrate that their software development processes employ state-of-the-practice software and security engineering methods, quality control processes, and validation techniques to minimize flawed or malformed software.

(4)   The organization ensures that each information system component acquired is explicitly assigned to an information system, and that the owner of the system acknowledges this assignment.

(5)   The organization requires in acquisition documents, that information system components are delivered in a secure, documented configuration, and that the secure configuration is the default configuration for any software reinstalls or upgrades.

(6)   The organization:

(a)   Employs only government off-the-shelf (GOTS) or commercial off-the-shelf (COTS) information assurance (IA) and IA-enabled information technology products that composes an NSA-approved solution to protect classified information when the networks used to transmit the information are at a lower classification level than the information being transmitted; and

(b)   Ensures that these products have been evaluated and/or validated by the NSA or in accordance with NSA-approved procedures.

Enhancement Supplemental Guidance: COTS IA or IA-enabled information technology products used to protect classified information by cryptographic means, may be required to use NSA-approved key management.

(7)   The organization:

(a)   Limits the use of commercially provided information technology products to those products that have been successfully evaluated against a validated U.S. Government Protection Profile for a specific technology type, if such a profile exists; and

(b)   Requires, if no U.S. Government Protection Profile exists for a specific technology type but a commercially provided information technology product relies on cryptographic functionality to enforce its security policy, then the cryptographic module is FIPS-validated.

References: ISO/IEC 15408; FIPS 140-2; NIST Special Publications 800-23, 800-35, 800-36, 800-64, 800-70; Web: WWW.NIAP-CCEVS.ORG.

Priority and Baseline Allocation:

P1	LOW SA-4	MOD SA-4 (1) (4)	HIGH SA-4 (1) (2) (4)

SA-5   INFORMATION SYSTEM DOCUMENTATION

Control: The organization:

a.   Obtains, protects as required, and makes available to authorized personnel, administrator documentation for the information system that describes:

-   Secure configuration, installation, and operation of the information system;

-   Effective use and maintenance of security features/functions; and

-   Known vulnerabilities regarding configuration and use of administrative (i.e., privileged) functions; and

b.   Obtains, protects as required, and makes available to authorized personnel, user documentation for the information system that describes:

-   User-accessible security features/functions and how to effectively use those security features/functions;

-   Methods for user interaction with the information system, which enables individuals to use the system in a more secure manner; and

-   User responsibilities in maintaining the security of the information and information system; and

c.   Documents attempts to obtain information system documentation when such documentation is either unavailable or nonexistent.

Supplemental Guidance: The inability of the organization to obtain necessary information system documentation may occur, for example, due to the age of the system and/or lack of support from the vendor/contractor. In those situations, organizations may need to recreate selected information system documentation if such documentation is essential to the effective implementation and/or operation of security controls.

Control Enhancements:

(1)   The organization obtains, protects as required, and makes available to authorized personnel, vendor/manufacturer documentation that describes the functional properties of the security controls employed within the information system with sufficient detail to permit analysis and testing.

(2)   The organization obtains, protects as required, and makes available to authorized personnel, vendor/manufacturer documentation that describes the security-relevant external interfaces to the information system with sufficient detail to permit analysis and testing.

(3)   The organization obtains, protects as required, and makes available to authorized personnel, vendor/manufacturer documentation that describes the high-level design of the information system in terms of subsystems and implementation details of the security controls employed within the system with sufficient detail to permit analysis and testing.

Enhancement Supplemental Guidance: An information system can be partitioned into multiple subsystems.

(4)   The organization obtains, protects as required, and makes available to authorized personnel, vendor/manufacturer documentation that describes the low-level design of the information system in terms of modules and implementation details of the security controls employed within the system with sufficient detail to permit analysis and testing.

Enhancement Supplemental Guidance: Each subsystem within an information system can contain one or more modules.

(5)   The organization obtains, protects as required, and makes available to authorized personnel, the source code for the information system to permit analysis and testing.

References: None.

Priority and Baseline Allocation:

P2	LOW SA-5	MOD SA-5 (1) (3)	HIGH SA-5 (1) (2) (3)

SA-6   SOFTWARE USAGE RESTRICTIONS

Control: The organization:

a.   Uses software and associated documentation in accordance with contract agreements and copyright laws;

b.   Employs tracking systems for software and associated documentation protected by quantity licenses to control copying and distribution; and

c.   Controls and documents the use of peer-to-peer file sharing technology to ensure that this capability is not used for the unauthorized distribution, display, performance, or reproduction of copyrighted work.

Supplemental Guidance: Tracking systems can include, for example, simple spreadsheets or fully automated, specialized applications depending on the needs of the organization.

Control Enhancements:

(1)   The organization:

    (a)   **Prohibits the use of binary or machine executable code from sources with limited or no warranty without accompanying source code; and**

    (b)   **Provides exceptions to the source code requirement only for compelling mission/operational requirements when no alternative solutions are available and with the express written consent of the authorizing official.**

Enhancement Supplemental Guidance: Software products without accompanying source code from sources with limited or no warranty are assessed for potential security impacts. The assessment addresses the fact that these types of software products are difficult or impossible to review, repair, or extend, given that the organization does not have access to the original source code and there is no owner who could make such repairs on behalf of the organization.

References: None.

Priority and Baseline Allocation:

P1	LOW SA-6	MOD SA-6	HIGH SA-6

SA-7   USER-INSTALLED SOFTWARE

Control: The organization enforces explicit rules governing the installation of software by users.

Supplemental Guidance: If provided the necessary privileges, users have the ability to install software. The organization identifies what types of software installations are permitted (e.g., updates and security patches to existing software) and what types of installations are prohibited (e.g., software whose pedigree with regard to being potentially malicious is unknown or suspect). Related control: CM-2.

Control Enhancements: None.

References: None.

Priority and Baseline Allocation:

P1	LOW SA-7	MOD SA-7	HIGH SA-7

SA-8   SECURITY ENGINEERING PRINCIPLES

Control: The organization applies information system security engineering principles in the specification, design, development, implementation, and modification of the information system.

Supplemental Guidance: The application of security engineering principles is primarily targeted at new development information systems or systems undergoing major upgrades and is integrated into the system development life cycle. For legacy information systems, the organization applies security engineering principles to system upgrades and modifications to the extent feasible, given the current state of the hardware, software, and firmware within the system. Examples of security engineering principles include, for example: (i) developing layered protections; (ii) establishing sound security policy, architecture, and controls as the foundation for design; (iii) incorporating security into the system development life cycle; (iv) delineating physical and logical security boundaries; (v) ensuring system developers and integrators are trained on how to develop secure software; (vi) tailoring security controls to meet organizational and operational needs; and (vii) reducing risk to acceptable levels, thus enabling informed risk management decisions.

Control Enhancements: None.

References: NIST Special Publication 800-27.

Priority and Baseline Allocation:

P1	**LOW** Not Selected	**MOD** SA-8	**HIGH** SA-8

SA-9   EXTERNAL INFORMATION SYSTEM SERVICES

Control: The organization:

a. Requires that providers of external information system services comply with organizational information security requirements and employ appropriate security controls in accordance with applicable federal laws, Executive Orders, directives, policies, regulations, standards, and guidance;

b. Defines and documents government oversight and user roles and responsibilities with regard to external information system services; and

c. Monitors security control compliance by external service providers.

Supplemental Guidance: An external information system service is a service that is implemented outside of the authorization boundary of the organizational information system (i.e., a service that is used by, but not a part of, the organizational information system). Relationships with external service providers are established in a variety of ways, for example, through joint ventures, business partnerships, outsourcing arrangements (i.e., contracts, interagency agreements, lines of business arrangements), licensing agreements, and/or supply chain exchanges. The responsibility for adequately mitigating risks arising from the use of external information system services remains with the authorizing official. Authorizing officials require that an appropriate chain of trust be established with external service providers when dealing with the many issues associated with information security. For services external to the organization, a chain of trust requires that the organization establish and retain a level of confidence that each participating provider in the potentially complex consumer-provider relationship provides adequate protection for the services rendered to the organization. The extent and nature of this chain of trust varies based on the relationship between the organization and the external provider. Where a sufficient level of trust cannot be established in the external services and/or service providers, the organization employs compensating security controls or accepts the greater degree of risk. The external information system services documentation includes government, service provider, and end user security roles and responsibilities, and any service-level agreements. Service-level agreements define the expectations of performance for each required security control, describe measurable outcomes, and identify remedies and response requirements for any identified instance of noncompliance.

Control Enhancements:

(1) The organization:

  (a) Conducts an organizational assessment of risk prior to the acquisition or outsourcing of dedicated information security services; and

  (b) Ensures that the acquisition or outsourcing of dedicated information security services is approved by [*Assignment: organization-defined senior organizational official*].

  Enhancement Supplemental Guidance: Dedicated information security services include, for example, incident monitoring, analysis and response, operation of information security-related devices such as firewalls, or key management services.

References: NIST Special Publication 800-35.

Priority and Baseline Allocation:

P1	**LOW** SA-9	**MOD** SA-9	**HIGH** SA-9

SA-10   DEVELOPER CONFIGURATION MANAGEMENT

Control: The organization requires that information system developers/integrators:

a.   Perform configuration management during information system design, development, implementation, and operation;

b.   Manage and control changes to the information system;

c.   Implement only organization-approved changes;

d.   Document approved changes to the information system; and

e.   Track security flaws and flaw resolution.

Supplemental Guidance: Related controls: CM-3, CM-4, CM-9.

Control Enhancements:

(1)   **The organization requires that information system developers/integrators provide an integrity check of software to facilitate organizational verification of software integrity after delivery.**

(2)   **The organization provides an alternative configuration management process with organizational personnel in the absence of dedicated developer/integrator configuration management team.**

Enhancement Supplemental Guidance: The configuration management process includes key organizational personnel that are responsible for reviewing and approving proposed changes to the information system, and security personnel that conduct impact analyses prior to the implementation of any changes to the system.

References: None.

Priority and Baseline Allocation:

P1	**LOW** Not Selected	**MOD** SA-10	**HIGH** SA-10

SA-11   DEVELOPER SECURITY TESTING

Control: The organization requires that information system developers/integrators, in consultation with associated security personnel (including security engineers):

a.   Create and implement a security test and evaluation plan;

b.   Implement a verifiable flaw remediation process to correct weaknesses and deficiencies identified during the security testing and evaluation process; and

c.   Document the results of the security testing/evaluation and flaw remediation processes.

Supplemental Guidance: Developmental security test results are used to the greatest extent feasible after verification of the results and recognizing that these results are impacted whenever there have been security-relevant modifications to the information system subsequent to developer testing. Test results may be used in support of the security authorization process for the delivered information system. Related control: CA-2, SI-2.

Control Enhancements:

(1)   **The organization requires that information system developers/integrators employ code analysis tools to examine software for common flaws and document the results of the analysis.**

(2)   **The organization requires that information system developers/integrators perform a vulnerability analysis to document vulnerabilities, exploitation potential, and risk mitigations.**

(3)   **The organization requires that information system developers/integrators create a security test and evaluation plan and implement the plan under the witness of an independent verification and validation agent.**

References: None.

Priority and Baseline Allocation:

P2	LOW Not Selected	MOD SA-11	HIGH SA-11

SA-12   SUPPLY CHAIN PROTECTION

Control: The organization protects against supply chain threats by employing: [*Assignment: organization-defined list of measures to protect against supply chain threats*] as part of a comprehensive, defense-in-breadth information security strategy.

Supplemental Guidance: A defense-in-breadth approach helps to protect information systems (including the information technology products that compose those systems) throughout the system development life cycle (i.e., during design and development, manufacturing, packaging, assembly, distribution, system integration, operations, maintenance, and retirement). This is accomplished by the identification, management, and elimination of vulnerabilities at each phase of the life cycle and the use of complementary, mutually reinforcing strategies to mitigate risk.

Control Enhancements:

(1)   The organization purchases all anticipated information system components and spares in the initial acquisition.

   Enhancement Supplemental Guidance: Stockpiling information system components and spares avoids the need to use less trustworthy secondary or resale markets in future years.

(2)   The organization conducts a due diligence review of suppliers prior to entering into contractual agreements to acquire information system hardware, software, firmware, or services.

   Enhancement Supplemental Guidance: The organization reviews supplier claims with regard to the use of appropriate security processes in the development and manufacture of information system components or products.

(3)   The organization uses trusted shipping and warehousing for information systems, information system components, and information technology products.

   Enhancement Supplemental Guidance: Trusted shipping and warehousing reduces opportunities for subversive activities or interception during transit. Examples of supporting techniques include the use of a geographically aware beacon to detect shipment diversions or delays. Related control: PE-16.

(4)   The organization employs a diverse set of suppliers for information systems, information system components, information technology products, and information system services.

   Enhancement Supplemental Guidance: Diversification of suppliers is intended to limit the potential harm from a given supplier in a supply chain, increasing the work factor for an adversary.

(5)   The organization employs standard configurations for information systems, information system components, and information technology products.

   Enhancement Supplemental Guidance: By avoiding the purchase of custom configurations for information systems, information system components, and information technology products, the organization limits the possibility of acquiring systems and products that have been corrupted via the supply chain actions targeted at the organization.

(6)   The organization minimizes the time between purchase decisions and delivery of information systems, information system components, and information technology products.

   Enhancement Supplemental Guidance: By minimizing the time between purchase decisions and required delivery of information systems, information system components, and information technology products, the organization limits the opportunity for an adversary to corrupt the purchased system, component, or product.

(7)   The organization employs independent analysis and penetration testing against delivered information systems, information system components, and information technology products.

References: None.

Priority and Baseline Allocation:

P1	**LOW** Not Selected	**MOD** Not Selected	**HIGH** SA-12

SA-13   TRUSTWORTHINESS

Control: The organization requires that the information system meets [*Assignment: organization-defined level of trustworthiness*].

Supplemental Guidance: The intent of this control is to ensure that organizations recognize the importance of trustworthiness and making explicit trustworthiness decisions when designing, developing, and implementing organizational information systems. Trustworthiness is a characteristic or property of an information system that expresses the degree to which the system can be expected to preserve the confidentiality, integrity, and availability of the information being processed, stored, or transmitted by the system. Trustworthy information systems are systems that are capable of being trusted to operate within defined levels of *risk* despite the environmental disruptions, human errors, and purposeful attacks that are expected to occur in the specified environments of operation. Two factors affecting the trustworthiness of an information system include: (i) *security functionality* (i.e., the security features or functions employed within the system); and (ii) *security assurance* (i.e., the grounds for confidence that the security functionality is effective in its application).

Appropriate security functionality for the information system can be obtained by using the Risk Management Framework (Steps 1, 2, and 3) to select and implement the necessary management, operational, and technical security controls necessary to mitigate risk to organizational operations and assets, individuals, other organizations, and the Nation. Appropriate security assurance can be obtained by: (i) the actions taken by developers and implementers of security controls with regard to the design, development, implementation, and operation of those controls; and (ii) the actions taken by assessors to determine the extent to which the controls are implemented correctly, operating as intended, and producing the desired outcome with respect to meeting the security requirements for the information system.

Developers and implementers can increase the assurance in security controls by employing well-defined security policy models, structured, disciplined, and rigorous hardware and software development techniques, and sound system/security engineering principles. Assurance is also based on the assessment of evidence produced during the initiation, acquisition/development, implementation, and operations/maintenance phases of the system development life cycle. For example, developmental evidence may include the techniques and methods used to design and develop security functionality. Operational evidence may include flaw reporting and remediation, the results of security incident reporting, and the results of the ongoing monitoring of security controls. Independent assessments by qualified assessors may include analyses of the evidence as well as testing, inspections, and audits. Minimum assurance requirements are described in Appendix E.

Explicit trustworthiness decisions highlight situations where achieving the information system resilience and security capability necessary to withstand cyber attacks from adversaries with certain threat capabilities may require adjusting the risk management strategy, the design of mission/business processes with regard to automation, the selection and implementation rigor of management and operational protections, or the selection of information technology components with higher levels of trustworthiness. Trustworthiness may be defined on a component-by-component, subsystem-by-subsystem, or function-by-function basis. It is noted, however, that typically functions, subsystems, and components are highly interrelated, making separation by trustworthiness perhaps problematic and at a minimum, something that likely requires careful attention in order to achieve practically useful results. Related controls: RA-2, SA-4, SA-8, SC-3.

Control Enhancements: None.

References: FIPS Publications 199, 200; NIST Special Publications 800-53, 800-53A, 800-60, 800-64.

Priority and Baseline Allocation:

P1	**LOW** Not Selected	**MOD** Not Selected	**HIGH** SA-13

SA-14   CRITICAL INFORMATION SYSTEM COMPONENTS

Control: The organization:

a.   Determines [*Assignment: organization-defined list of critical information system components that require re-implementation*]; and

b.   Re-implements or custom develops such information system components.

Supplemental Guidance: The underlying assumption is that the list of information technology products defined by the organization cannot be trusted due to threats from the supply chain that the organization finds unacceptable. The organization re-implements or custom develops such components to satisfy requirements for high assurance. Related controls: SA-12, SA-13.

Control Enhancements:

(1)   The organization:

   (a)   Identifies information system components for which alternative sourcing is not viable; and

   (b)   Employs [*Assignment: organization-defined measures*] to ensure that critical security controls for the information system components are not compromised.

   Enhancement Supplemental Guidance: Measures that the organization considers implementing include, for example, enhanced auditing, restrictions on source code and system utility access, and protection from deletion of system and application files.

References: None.

Priority and Baseline Allocation:

P0	**LOW** Not Selected	**MOD** Not Selected	**HIGH** Not Selected

FAMILY: SYSTEM AND COMMUNICATIONS PROTECTION   **CLASS:** TECHNICAL

SC-1   **SYSTEM AND COMMUNICATIONS PROTECTION POLICY AND PROCEDURES**

Control: The organization develops, disseminates, and reviews/updates [*Assignment: organization-defined frequency*]:

a. A formal, documented system and communications protection policy that addresses purpose, scope, roles, responsibilities, management commitment, coordination among organizational entities, and compliance; and

b. Formal, documented procedures to facilitate the implementation of the system and communications protection policy and associated system and communications protection controls.

Supplemental Guidance: This control is intended to produce the policy and procedures that are required for the effective implementation of selected security controls and control enhancements in the system and communications protection family. The policy and procedures are consistent with applicable federal laws, Executive Orders, directives, policies, regulations, standards, and guidance. Existing organizational policies and procedures may make the need for additional specific policies and procedures unnecessary. The system and communications protection policy can be included as part of the general information security policy for the organization. System and communications protection procedures can be developed for the security program in general and for a particular information system, when required. The organizational risk management strategy is a key factor in the development of the system and communications protection policy. Related control: PM-9.

Control Enhancements: None.

References: NIST Special Publications 800-12, 800-100.

Priority and Baseline Allocation:

P1	**LOW** SC-1	**MOD** SC-1	**HIGH** SC-1

SC-2   **APPLICATION PARTITIONING**

Control: The information system separates user functionality (including user interface services) from information system management functionality.

Supplemental Guidance: Information system management functionality includes, for example, functions necessary to administer databases, network components, workstations, or servers, and typically requires privileged user access. The separation of user functionality from information system management functionality is either physical or logical and is accomplished by using different computers, different central processing units, different instances of the operating system, different network addresses, combinations of these methods, or other methods as appropriate. An example of this type of separation is observed in web administrative interfaces that use separate authentication methods for users of any other information system resources. This may include isolating the administrative interface on a different domain and with additional access controls.

Control Enhancements:

(1) **The information system prevents the presentation of information system management-related functionality at an interface for general (i.e., non-privileged) users.**

Enhancement Supplemental Guidance: The intent of this control enhancement is to ensure that administration options are not available to general users (including prohibiting the use of the grey-out option commonly used to eliminate accessibility to such information). For example, administration options are not presented until the user has appropriately established a session with administrator privileges.

References: None.

Priority and Baseline Allocation:

P1	LOW Not Selected	MOD SC-2	HIGH SC-2

SC-3   SECURITY FUNCTION ISOLATION

Control: The information system isolates security functions from nonsecurity functions.

Supplemental Guidance: The information system isolates security functions from nonsecurity functions by means of an isolation boundary (implemented via partitions and domains) that controls access to and protects the integrity of, the hardware, software, and firmware that perform those security functions. The information system maintains a separate execution domain (e.g., address space) for each executing process. Related control: SA-13.

Control Enhancements:

(1)   The information system implements underlying hardware separation mechanisms to facilitate security function isolation.

(2)   The information system isolates security functions enforcing access and information flow control from both nonsecurity functions and from other security functions.

(3)   The organization implements an information system isolation boundary to minimize the number of nonsecurity functions included within the boundary containing security functions.

   Enhancement Supplemental Guidance: Nonsecurity functions contained within the isolation boundary are considered security-relevant.

(4)   The organization implements security functions as largely independent modules that avoid unnecessary interactions between modules.

(5)   The organization implements security functions as a layered structure minimizing interactions between layers of the design and avoiding any dependence by lower layers on the functionality or correctness of higher layers.

References: None.

Priority and Baseline Allocation:

P1	LOW Not Selected	MOD Not Selected	HIGH SC-3

SC-4   INFORMATION IN SHARED RESOURCES

Control: The information system prevents unauthorized and unintended information transfer via shared system resources.

Supplemental Guidance: The purpose of this control is to prevent information, including encrypted representations of information, produced by the actions of a prior user/role (or the actions of a process acting on behalf of a prior user/role) from being available to any current user/role (or current process) that obtains access to a shared system resource (e.g., registers, main memory, secondary storage) after that resource has been released back to the information system. Control of information in shared resources is also referred to as object reuse. This control does not address: (i) information remanence which refers to residual representation of data that has been in some way nominally erased or removed; (ii) covert channels where shared resources are manipulated to achieve a violation of information flow restrictions; or (iii) components in the information system for which there is only a single user/role.

Control Enhancements:

(1)   The information system does not share resources that are used to interface with systems operating at different security levels.

Enhancement Supplemental Guidance: Shared resources include, for example, memory, input/output queues, and network interface cards.

References: None.

Priority and Baseline Allocation:

P1	**LOW** Not Selected	**MOD** SC-4	**HIGH** SC-4

SC-5   DENIAL OF SERVICE PROTECTION

Control: The information system protects against or limits the effects of the following types of denial of service attacks: [*Assignment: organization-defined list of types of denial of service attacks or reference to source for current list*].

Supplemental Guidance: A variety of technologies exist to limit, or in some cases, eliminate the effects of denial of service attacks. For example, boundary protection devices can filter certain types of packets to protect devices on an organization's internal network from being directly affected by denial of service attacks. Employing increased capacity and bandwidth combined with service redundancy may reduce the susceptibility to some denial of service attacks. Related control: SC-7.

Control Enhancements:

(1) The information system restricts the ability of users to launch denial of service attacks against other information systems or networks.

(2) The information system manages excess capacity, bandwidth, or other redundancy to limit the effects of information flooding types of denial of service attacks.

References: None.

Priority and Baseline Allocation:

P1	**LOW** SC-5	**MOD** SC-5	**HIGH** SC-5

SC-6   RESOURCE PRIORITY

Control: The information system limits the use of resources by priority.

Supplemental Guidance: Priority protection helps prevent a lower-priority process from delaying or interfering with the information system servicing any higher-priority process. This control does not apply to components in the information system for which there is only a single user/role.

Control Enhancements: None.

References: None.

Priority and Baseline Allocation:

P0	**LOW** Not Selected	**MOD** Not Selected	**HIGH** Not Selected

SC-7   BOUNDARY PROTECTION

Control: The information system:

a. Monitors and controls communications at the external boundary of the system and at key internal boundaries within the system; and

b.   Connects to external networks or information systems only through managed interfaces consisting of boundary protection devices arranged in accordance with an organizational security architecture.

Supplemental Guidance: Restricting external web traffic only to organizational web servers within managed interfaces and prohibiting external traffic that appears to be spoofing an internal address as the source are examples of restricting and prohibiting communications. Managed interfaces employing boundary protection devices include, for example, proxies, gateways, routers, firewalls, guards, or encrypted tunnels arranged in an effective security architecture (e.g., routers protecting firewalls and application gateways residing on a protected subnetwork commonly referred to as a demilitarized zone or DMZ).

The organization considers the intrinsically shared nature of commercial telecommunications services in the implementation of security controls associated with the use of such services. Commercial telecommunications services are commonly based on network components and consolidated management systems shared by all attached commercial customers, and may include third-party provided access lines and other service elements. Consequently, such interconnecting transmission services may represent sources of increased risk despite contract security provisions. Therefore, when this situation occurs, the organization either implements appropriate compensating security controls or explicitly accepts the additional risk. Related controls: AC-4, IR-4, SC-5.

Control Enhancements:

(1)   The organization physically allocates publicly accessible information system components to separate subnetworks with separate physical network interfaces.

    Enhancement Supplemental Guidance: Publicly accessible information system components include, for example, public web servers.

(2)   The information system prevents public access into the organization's internal networks except as appropriately mediated by managed interfaces employing boundary protection devices.

(3)   The organization limits the number of access points to the information system to allow for more comprehensive monitoring of inbound and outbound communications and network traffic.

    Enhancement Supplemental Guidance: The Trusted Internet Connection (TIC) initiative is an example of limiting the number of managed network access points.

(4)   The organization:

    (a)   Implements a managed interface for each external telecommunication

    service; (b)   Establishes a traffic flow policy for each managed interface;

    (c)   Employs security controls as needed to protect the confidentiality and integrity of the information being transmitted;

    (d)   Documents each exception to the traffic flow policy with a supporting mission/business need and duration of that need;

    (e)   Reviews exceptions to the traffic flow policy [*Assignment: organization-defined frequency*]; and

    (f)   Removes traffic flow policy exceptions that are no longer supported by an explicit mission/business need.

(5)   The information system at managed interfaces, denies network traffic by default and allows network traffic by exception (i.e., deny all, permit by exception).

(6)   The organization prevents the unauthorized release of information outside of the information system boundary or any unauthorized communication through the information system boundary when there is an operational failure of the boundary protection mechanisms.

(7)   The information system prevents remote devices that have established a non-remote connection with the system from communicating outside of that communications path with resources in external networks.

    Enhancement Supplemental Guidance: This control enhancement is implemented within the remote device (e.g., notebook/laptop computer) via configuration settings that are not configurable by the user of that device. An example of a non-remote communications path from a remote device is a virtual private network. When a non-remote connection is established using a virtual private network, the configuration settings prevent *split-tunneling*. Split tunneling might otherwise be used by remote users to communicate with the information system as an extension of that system and to communicate with local resources such as a printer or file server. Since the remote device, when connected by a non-remote connection, becomes an extension of the information system, allowing dual communications paths such as split-tunneling would be, in effect, allowing unauthorized external connections into the system.

(8)   **The information system routes [*Assignment: organization-defined internal communications traffic*] to [*Assignment: organization-defined external networks*] through authenticated proxy servers within the managed interfaces of boundary protection devices.**

Enhancement Supplemental Guidance: External networks are networks outside the control of the organization. Proxy servers support logging individual Transmission Control Protocol (TCP) sessions and blocking specific Uniform Resource Locators (URLs), domain names, and Internet Protocol (IP) addresses. Proxy servers are also configurable with organization-defined lists of authorized and unauthorized websites.

(9)   **The information system, at managed interfaces, denies network traffic and audits internal users (or malicious code) posing a threat to external information systems.**

Enhancement Supplemental Guidance: Detecting internal actions that may pose a security threat to external information systems is sometimes termed extrusion detection. Extrusion detection at the information system boundary includes the analysis of network traffic (incoming as well as outgoing) looking for indications of an internal threat to the security of external systems.

(10)   **The organization prevents the unauthorized exfiltration of information across managed interfaces.**

Enhancement Supplemental Guidance: Measures to prevent unauthorized exfiltration of information from the information system include, for example: (i) strict adherence to protocol formats; (ii) monitoring for indications of beaconing from the information system; (iii) monitoring for use of steganography; (iv) disconnecting external network interfaces except when explicitly needed; (v) disassembling and reassembling packet headers; and (vi) employing traffic profile analysis to detect deviations from the volume or types of traffic expected within the organization. Examples of devices enforcing strict adherence to protocol formats include, for example, deep packet inspection firewalls and XML gateways. These devices verify adherence to the protocol specification at the application layer and serve to identify vulnerabilities that cannot be detected by devices operating at the network or transport layer.

(11)   **The information system checks incoming communications to ensure that the communications are coming from an authorized source and routed to an authorized destination.**

(12)   **The information system implements host-based boundary protection mechanisms for servers, workstations, and mobile devices.**

Enhancement Supplemental Guidance: A host-based boundary protection mechanism is, for example, a host-based firewall. Host-based boundary protection mechanisms are employed on mobile devices, such as notebook/laptop computers, and other types of mobile devices where such boundary protection mechanisms are available.

(13)   **The organization isolates [*Assignment: organization defined key information security tools, mechanisms, and support components*] from other internal information system components via physically separate subnets with managed interfaces to other portions of the system.**

(14)   **The organization protects against unauthorized physical connections across the boundary protections implemented at [*Assignment: organization-defined list of managed interfaces*].**

Enhancement Supplemental Guidance: Information systems operating at different security categories may routinely share common physical and environmental controls, since the systems may share space within organizational facilities. In practice, it is possible that these separate information systems may share common equipment rooms, wiring closets, and cable distribution paths. Protection against unauthorized physical connections can be achieved, for example, by employing clearly identified and physically separated cable trays, connection frames, and patch panels for each side of managed interfaces with physical access controls enforcing limited authorized access to these items. Related control: PE-4.

(15) **The information system routes all networked, privileged accesses through a dedicated, managed interface for purposes of access control and auditing.**

Enhancement Supplemental Guidance: Related controls: AC-2, AC-3, AC-4, AU-2.

(16) **The information system prevents discovery of specific system components (or devices) composing a managed interface.**

Enhancement Supplemental Guidance: This control enhancement is intended to protect the network addresses of information system components that are part of the managed interface from discovery through common tools and techniques used to identify devices on a network. The network addresses are not available for discovery (e.g., not published or entered in the domain name system), requiring prior knowledge for access. Another obfuscation technique is to periodically change network addresses.

(17) **The organization employs automated mechanisms to enforce strict adherence to protocol format.**

Enhancement Supplemental Guidance: Automated mechanisms used to enforce protocol formats include, for example, deep packet inspection firewalls and XML gateways. These devices verify adherence to the protocol specification (e.g., IEEE) at the application layer and serve to identify significant vulnerabilities that cannot be detected by devices operating at the network or transport layer.

(18) **The information system fails securely in the event of an operational failure of a boundary protection device.**

Enhancement Supplemental Guidance: Fail secure is a condition achieved by the application of a set of information system mechanisms to ensure that in the event of an operational failure of a boundary protection device at a managed interface (e.g., router, firewall, guard, application gateway residing on a protected subnetwork commonly referred to as a demilitarized zone), the system does not enter into an unsecure state where intended security properties no longer hold. A failure of a boundary protection device cannot lead to, or cause information external to the boundary protection device to enter the device, nor can a failure permit unauthorized information release.

References: FIPS Publication 199; NIST Special Publications 800-41, 800-77.

Priority and Baseline Allocation:

P1	LOW SC-7	MOD SC-7 (1) (2) (3) (4) (5) (7)	HIGH SC-7 (1) (2) (3) (4) (5) (6) (7) (8)

SC-8   TRANSMISSION INTEGRITY

Control: The information system protects the integrity of transmitted information.

Supplemental Guidance: This control applies to communications across internal and external networks. If the organization is relying on a commercial service provider for transmission services as a commodity item rather than a fully dedicated service, it may be more difficult to obtain the necessary assurances regarding the implementation of needed security controls for transmission integrity. When it is infeasible or impractical to obtain the necessary security controls and assurances of control effectiveness through appropriate contracting vehicles, the organization either implements appropriate compensating security controls or explicitly accepts the additional risk. Related controls: AC-17, PE-4.

Control Enhancements:

(1)   **The organization employs cryptographic mechanisms to recognize changes to information during transmission unless otherwise protected by alternative physical measures.**

Enhancement Supplemental Guidance: Alternative physical protection measures include, for example, protected distribution systems. Related control: SC-13.

(2) The information system maintains the integrity of information during aggregation, packaging, and transformation in preparation for transmission.

Enhancement Supplemental Guidance: Information can be intentionally and/or maliciously modified at data aggregation or protocol transformation points, compromising the integrity of the information.

References: FIPS Publications 140-2, 197; NIST Special Publications 800-52, 800-77, 800-81, 800-113; NSTISSI No. 7003.

Priority and Baseline Allocation:

P1	**LOW** Not Selected	**MOD** SC-8 (1)	**HIGH** SC-8 (1)

SC-9   TRANSMISSION CONFIDENTIALITY

Control: The information system protects the confidentiality of transmitted information.

Supplemental Guidance: This control applies to communications across internal and external networks. If the organization is relying on a commercial service provider for transmission services as a commodity item rather than a fully dedicated service, it may be more difficult to obtain the necessary assurances regarding the implementation of needed security controls for transmission confidentiality. When it is infeasible or impractical to obtain the necessary security controls and assurances of control effectiveness through appropriate contracting vehicles, the organization either implements appropriate compensating security controls or explicitly accepts the additional risk. Related controls: AC-17, PE-4.

Control Enhancements:

(1) The organization employs cryptographic mechanisms to prevent unauthorized disclosure of information during transmission unless otherwise protected by alternative physical measures.

Enhancement Supplemental Guidance: Alternative physical protection measures include, for example, protected distribution systems. Related control: SC-13.

(2) The information system maintains the confidentiality of information during aggregation, packaging, and transformation in preparation for transmission.

Enhancement Supplemental Guidance: Information can be intentionally and/or maliciously disclosed at data aggregation or protocol transformation points, compromising the confidentiality of the information.

References: FIPS Publications 140-2, 197; NIST Special Publications 800-52, 800-77, 800-113; CNSS Policy 15; NSTISSI No. 7003.

Priority and Baseline Allocation:

P1	**LOW** Not Selected	**MOD** SC-9 (1)	**HIGH** SC-9 (1)

SC-10   NETWORK DISCONNECT

Control: The information system terminates the network connection associated with a communications session at the end of the session or after [*Assignment: organization-defined time period*] of inactivity.

Supplemental Guidance: This control applies to both internal and external networks. Terminating network connections associated with communications sessions include, for example, de-allocating associated TCP/IP address/port pairs at the operating-system level, or de-allocating networking assignments at the application level if multiple application sessions are using a single, operating system-level network connection. The time period of inactivity may, as the organization deems necessary, be a set of time periods by type of network access or for specific accesses.

Control Enhancements: None.

References: None.

Priority and Baseline Allocation:

P2	**LOW** Not Selected	**MOD** SC-10	**HIGH** SC-10

SC-11   TRUSTED PATH

Control: The information system establishes a trusted communications path between the user and the following security functions of the system: [*Assignment: organization-defined security functions to include at a minimum, information system authentication and reauthentication*].

Supplemental Guidance: A trusted path is employed for high-confidence connections between the security functions of the information system and the user (e.g., for login).

Control Enhancements: None.

References: None.

Priority and Baseline Allocation:

P0	**LOW** Not Selected	**MOD** Not Selected	**HIGH** Not Selected

SC-12   CRYPTOGRAPHIC KEY ESTABLISHMENT AND MANAGEMENT

Control: The organization establishes and manages cryptographic keys for required cryptography employed within the information system.

Supplemental Guidance: Cryptographic key management and establishment can be performed using manual procedures or automated mechanisms with supporting manual procedures. In addition to being required for the effective operation of a cryptographic mechanism, effective cryptographic key management provides protections to maintain the availability of the information in the event of the loss of cryptographic keys by users.

Control Enhancements:

(1) **The organization maintains availability of information in the event of the loss of cryptographic keys by users.**

(2) **The organization produces, controls, and distributes symmetric cryptographic keys using [*Selection: NIST-approved, NSA-approved*] key management technology and processes.**

(3) **The organization produces, controls, and distributes symmetric and asymmetric cryptographic keys using NSA-approved key management technology and processes.**

(4) **The organization produces, controls, and distributes asymmetric cryptographic keys using approved PKI Class 3 certificates or prepositioned keying material.**

(5) **The organization produces, controls, and distributes asymmetric cryptographic keys using approved PKI Class 3 or Class 4 certificates and hardware security tokens that protect the user's private key.**

References: NIST Special Publications 800-56, 800-57.

Priority and Baseline Allocation:

P1	**LOW** SC-12	**MOD** SC-12	**HIGH** SC-12 (1)

SC-13   USE OF CRYPTOGRAPHY

Control: The information system implements required cryptographic protections using cryptographic modules that comply with applicable federal laws, Executive Orders, directives, policies, regulations, standards, and guidance.

Supplemental Guidance: None.

Control Enhancements:

(1)   The organization employs, at a minimum, FIPS-validated cryptography to protect unclassified information.

(2)   The organization employs NSA-approved cryptography to protect classified information.

(3)   The organization employs, at a minimum, FIPS-validated cryptography to protect information when such information must be separated from individuals who have the necessary clearances yet lack the necessary access approvals.

(4)   The organization employs [*Selection: FIPS-validated; NSA-approved*] cryptography to implement digital signatures.

References: FIPS Publication 140-2; Web: CSRC.NIST.GOV/CRYPTVAL, WWW.CNSS.GOV.

Priority and Baseline Allocation:

P1	**LOW** SC-13	**MOD** SC-13	**HIGH** SC-13

SC-14   PUBLIC ACCESS PROTECTIONS

Control: The information system protects the integrity and availability of publicly available information and applications.

Supplemental Guidance: The purpose of this control is to ensure that organizations explicitly address the protection needs for public information and applications with such protection likely being implemented as part of other security controls.

Control Enhancements: None.

References: None.

Priority and Baseline Allocation:

P1	**LOW** SC-14	**MOD** SC-14	**HIGH** SC-14

SC-15   COLLABORATIVE COMPUTING DEVICES

Control: The information system:

a.   Prohibits remote activation of collaborative computing devices with the following exceptions: [*Assignment: organization-defined exceptions where remote activation is to be allowed*]; and

b.   Provides an explicit indication of use to users physically present at the devices.

Supplemental Guidance: Collaborative computing devices include, for example, networked white boards, cameras, and microphones. Explicit indication of use includes, for example, signals to users when collaborative computing devices are activated.

Control Enhancements:

(1)   The information system provides physical disconnect of collaborative computing devices in a manner that supports ease of use.

(2)   The information system or supporting environment blocks both inbound and outbound traffic between instant messaging clients that are independently configured by end users and external service providers.

   Enhancement Supplemental Guidance: Blocking restrictions do not include instant messaging services that are configured by an organization to perform an authorized function.

(3)   The organization disables or removes collaborative computing devices from information systems in [*Assignment: organization-defined secure work areas*].

References: None.

Priority and Baseline Allocation:

P1	**LOW** SC-15	**MOD** SC-15	**HIGH** SC-15

SC-16   TRANSMISSION OF SECURITY ATTRIBUTES

Control: The information system associates security attributes with information exchanged between information systems.

Supplemental Guidance: Security attributes may be explicitly or implicitly associated with the information contained within the information system. Related control: AC-16.

Control Enhancements:

(1)   The information system validates the integrity of security attributes exchanged between systems.

References: None.

Priority and Baseline Allocation:

P0	**LOW** Not Selected	**MOD** Not Selected	**HIGH** Not Selected

SC-17   PUBLIC KEY INFRASTRUCTURE CERTIFICATES

Control: The organization issues public key certificates under an appropriate certificate policy or obtains public key certificates under an appropriate certificate policy from an approved service provider.

Supplemental Guidance: For user certificates, each organization attains certificates from an approved, shared service provider, as required by OMB policy. For federal agencies operating a legacy public key infrastructure cross-certified with the Federal Bridge Certification Authority at medium assurance or higher, this Certification Authority will suffice. This control focuses on certificates with a visibility external to the information system and does not include certificates related to internal system operations, for example, application-specific time services.

Control Enhancements: None.

References: OMB Memorandum 05-24; NIST Special Publications 800-32, 800-63.

Priority and Baseline Allocation:

P1	**LOW** Not Selected	**MOD** SC-17	**HIGH** SC-17

SC-18   MOBILE CODE

Control: The organization:

a. Defines acceptable and unacceptable mobile code and mobile code technologies;

b. Establishes usage restrictions and implementation guidance for acceptable mobile code and mobile code technologies; and

c. Authorizes, monitors, and controls the use of mobile code within the information system.

Supplemental Guidance: Decisions regarding the employment of mobile code within organizational information systems are based on the potential for the code to cause damage to the system if used maliciously. Mobile code technologies include, for example, Java, JavaScript, ActiveX, PDF, Postscript, Shockwave movies, Flash animations, and VBScript. Usage restrictions and implementation guidance apply to both the selection and use of mobile code installed on organizational servers and mobile code downloaded and executed on individual workstations. Policy and procedures related to mobile code, address preventing the development, acquisition, or introduction of unacceptable mobile code within the information system.

Control Enhancements:

(1) **The information system implements detection and inspection mechanisms to identify unauthorized mobile code and takes corrective actions, when necessary.**

   Enhancement Supplemental Guidance: Corrective actions when unauthorized mobile code is detected include, for example, blocking, quarantine, or alerting administrator. Disallowed transfers include, for example, sending word processing files with embedded macros.

(2) **The organization ensures the acquisition, development, and/or use of mobile code to be deployed in information systems meets [*Assignment: organization-defined mobile code requirements*].**

(3) **The information system prevents the download and execution of prohibited mobile code.**

(4) **The information system prevents the automatic execution of mobile code in [*Assignment: organization-defined software applications*] and requires [*Assignment: organization-defined actions*] prior to executing the code.**

   Enhancement Supplemental Guidance: Actions required before executing mobile code, include, for example, prompting users prior to opening electronic mail attachments.

References: NIST Special Publication 800-28; DOD Instruction 8552.01.

Priority and Baseline Allocation:

P1	**LOW** Not Selected	**MOD** SC-18	**HIGH** SC-18

SC-19   VOICE OVER INTERNET PROTOCOL

Control: The organization:

a. Establishes usage restrictions and implementation guidance for Voice over Internet Protocol (VoIP) technologies based on the potential to cause damage to the information system if used maliciously; and

b. Authorizes, monitors, and controls the use of VoIP within the information system.

Supplemental Guidance: None.

Control Enhancements: None.

References: NIST Special Publication 800-58.

Priority and Baseline Allocation:

P1	LOW	Not Selected	MOD	SC-19	HIGH	SC-19

SC-20   **SECURE NAME / ADDRESS RESOLUTION SERVICE (AUTHORITATIVE SOURCE)**

Control: The information system provides additional data origin and integrity artifacts along with the authoritative data the system returns in response to name/address resolution queries.

Supplemental Guidance: This control enables remote clients to obtain origin authentication and integrity verification assurances for the host/service name to network address resolution information obtained through the service. A domain name system (DNS) server is an example of an information system that provides name/address resolution service. Digital signatures and cryptographic keys are examples of additional artifacts. DNS resource records are examples of authoritative data. Information systems that use technologies other than the DNS to map between host/service names and network addresses provide other means to assure the authenticity and integrity of response data. The DNS security controls are consistent with, and referenced from, OMB Memorandum 08-23.

Control Enhancements:

(1)   The information system, when operating as part of a distributed, hierarchical namespace, provides the means to indicate the security status of child subspaces and (if the child supports secure resolution services) enable verification of a chain of trust among parent and child domains.

Enhancement Supplemental Guidance: An example means to indicate the security status of child subspaces is through the use of delegation signer (DS) resource records in the DNS.

References: OMB Memorandum 08-23; NIST Special Publication 800-81.

Priority and Baseline Allocation:

P1	LOW	SC-20 (1)	MOD	SC-20 (1)	HIGH	SC-20 (1)

SC-21   **SECURE NAME / ADDRESS RESOLUTION SERVICE (RECURSIVE OR CACHING RESOLVER)**

Control: The information system performs data origin authentication and data integrity verification on the name/address resolution responses the system receives from authoritative sources when requested by client systems.

Supplemental Guidance: A recursive resolving or caching domain name system (DNS) server is an example of an information system that provides name/address resolution service for local clients. Authoritative DNS servers are examples of authoritative sources. Information systems that use technologies other than the DNS to map between host/service names and network addresses provide other means to enable clients to verify the authenticity and integrity of response data.

Control Enhancements:

(1)   The information system performs data origin authentication and data integrity verification on all resolution responses whether or not local clients explicitly request this service.

Enhancement Supplemental Guidance: Local clients include, for example, DNS stub resolvers.

References: NIST Special Publication 800-81.

Priority and Baseline Allocation:

| P1 | LOW Not Selected | MOD Not Selected | HIGH SC-21 |

SC-22 ARCHITECTURE AND PROVISIONING FOR NAME / ADDRESS RESOLUTION SERVICE

Control: The information systems that collectively provide name/address resolution service for an organization are fault-tolerant and implement internal/external role separation.

Supplemental Guidance: A domain name system (DNS) server is an example of an information system that provides name/address resolution service. To eliminate single points of failure and to enhance redundancy, there are typically at least two authoritative domain name system (DNS) servers, one configured as primary and the other as secondary. Additionally, the two servers are commonly located in two different network subnets and geographically separated (i.e., not located in the same physical facility). With regard to role separation, DNS servers with an internal role, only process name/address resolution requests from within the organization (i.e., internal clients). DNS servers with an external role only process name/address resolution information requests from clients external to the organization (i.e., on the external networks including the Internet). The set of clients that can access an authoritative DNS server in a particular role is specified by the organization (e.g., by address ranges, explicit lists).

Control Enhancements: None.

References: NIST Special Publication 800-81.

Priority and Baseline Allocation:

| P1 | LOW Not Selected | MOD SC-22 | HIGH SC-22 |

SC-23 SESSION AUTHENTICITY

Control: The information system provides mechanisms to protect the authenticity of communications sessions.

Supplemental Guidance: This control focuses on communications protection at the session, versus packet, level. The intent of this control is to establish grounds for confidence at each end of a communications session in the ongoing identity of the other party and in the validity of the information being transmitted. For example, this control addresses man-in-the-middle attacks including session hijacking or insertion of false information into a session. This control is only implemented where deemed necessary by the organization (e.g., sessions in service-oriented architectures providing web-based services).

Control Enhancements:

(1) The information system invalidates session identifiers upon user logout or other session termination.

(2) The information system provides a readily observable logout capability whenever authentication is used to gain access to web pages.

(3) The information system generates a unique session identifier for each session and recognizes only session identifiers that are system-generated.

(4) The information system generates unique session identifiers with [*Assignment: organization- defined randomness requirements*].

Enhancement Supplemental Guidance: Employing the concept of randomness in the generation of unique session identifiers helps to protect against brute-force attacks to determine future session identifiers.

References: NIST Special Publications 800-52, 800-77, 800-95.

Priority and Baseline Allocation:

P1	**LOW** Not Selected	**MOD** SC-23	**HIGH** SC-23

SC-24   FAIL IN KNOWN STATE

Control: The information system fails to a [*Assignment: organization-defined known-state*] for [*Assignment: organization-defined types of failures*] preserving [*Assignment: organization-defined system state information*] in failure.

Supplemental Guidance: Failure in a known state can address safety or security in accordance with the mission/business needs of the organization. Failure in a known secure state helps prevent a loss of confidentiality, integrity, or availability in the event of a failure of the information system or a component of the system. Failure in a known safe state helps prevent systems from failing to a state that may cause injury to individuals or destruction to property. Preserving information system state information facilitates system restart and return to the operational mode of the organization with less disruption of mission/business processes.

Control Enhancements: None.

References: None.

Priority and Baseline Allocation:

P1	**LOW** Not Selected	**MOD** Not Selected	**HIGH** SC-24

SC-25   THIN NODES

Control: The information system employs processing components that have minimal functionality and information storage.

Supplemental Guidance: The deployment of information system components with minimal functionality (e.g., diskless nodes and thin client technologies) reduces the need to secure every user endpoint, and may reduce the exposure of information, information systems, and services to a successful attack. Related control: SC-30.

Control Enhancements: None.

References: None.

Priority and Baseline Allocation:

P0	**LOW** Not Selected	**MOD** Not Selected	**HIGH** Not Selected

SC-26   HONEYPOTS

Control: The information system includes components specifically designed to be the target of malicious attacks for the purpose of detecting, deflecting, and analyzing such attacks.

Supplemental Guidance: None.

Control Enhancements:

(1)   The information system includes components that proactively seek to identify web-based malicious code.

Enhancement Supplemental Guidance: Devices that actively seek out web-based malicious code by posing as clients are referred to as client honeypots or honey clients.

References: None.

Priority and Baseline Allocation:

P0	**LOW** Not Selected	**MOD** Not Selected	**HIGH** Not Selected

SC-27   OPERATING SYSTEM-INDEPENDENT APPLICATIONS

Control: The information system includes: [*Assignment: organization-defined operating system-independent applications*].

Supplemental Guidance: Operating system-independent applications are applications that can run on multiple operating systems. Such applications promote portability and reconstitution on different platform architectures, increasing the availability for critical functionality within an organization while information systems with a given operating system are under attack.

Control Enhancements: None.

References: None.

Priority and Baseline Allocation:

P0	**LOW** Not Selected	**MOD** Not Selected	**HIGH** Not Selected

SC-28   PROTECTION OF INFORMATION AT REST

Control: The information system protects the confidentiality and integrity of information at rest.

Supplemental Guidance: This control is intended to address the confidentiality and integrity of information at rest in nonmobile devices and covers user information and system information. Information at rest refers to the state of information when it is located on a secondary storage device (e.g., disk drive, tape drive) within an organizational information system. Configurations and/or rule sets for firewalls, gateways, intrusion detection/prevention systems, and filtering routers and authenticator content are examples of system information likely requiring protection. Organizations may choose to employ different mechanisms to achieve confidentiality and integrity protections, as appropriate.

Control Enhancements:

(1) **The organization employs cryptographic mechanisms to prevent unauthorized disclosure and modification of information at rest unless otherwise protected by alternative physical measures.**

References: NIST Special Publications 800-56, 800-57, 800-111.

Priority and Baseline Allocation:

P1	**LOW** Not Selected	**MOD** SC-28	**HIGH** SC-28

SC-29   HETEROGENEITY

Control: The organization employs diverse information technologies in the implementation of the information system.

Supplemental Guidance: Increasing the diversity of information technologies within the information system reduces the impact of the exploitation of a specific technology. Organizations that select this control should consider that an increase in diversity may add complexity and management overhead, both of which have the potential to lead to mistakes and misconfigurations which could increase overall risk.

Control Enhancements: None.

References: None.

Priority and Baseline Allocation:

P0	**LOW** Not Selected	**MOD** Not Selected	**HIGH** Not Selected

SC-30   VIRTUALIZATION TECHNIQUES

Control: The organization employs virtualization techniques to present information system components as other types of components, or components with differing configurations.

Supplemental Guidance: Virtualization techniques provide organizations with the ability to disguise information systems, potentially reducing the likelihood of successful attacks without the cost of having multiple platforms.

Control Enhancements:

(1) **The organization employs virtualization techniques to support the deployment of a diversity of operating systems and applications that are changed [*Assignment: organization-defined frequency*].**

Enhancement Supplemental Guidance: While frequent changes to operating systems and applications pose configuration management challenges, the changes result in an increased work factor for adversaries in order to carry out successful attacks. Changing the apparent operating system or application, as opposed to the actual operating system or application, results in virtual changes that still impede attacker success while helping to reduce the configuration management effort.

(2) **The organization employs randomness in the implementation of the virtualization techniques.**

References: None.

Priority and Baseline Allocation:

P0	**LOW** Not Selected	**MOD** Not Selected	**HIGH** Not Selected

SC-31   COVERT CHANNEL ANALYSIS

Control: The organization requires that information system developers/integrators perform a covert channel analysis to identify those aspects of system communication that are potential avenues for covert storage and timing channels.

Supplemental Guidance: Information system developers/integrators are in the best position to identify potential avenues within the system that might lead to covert channels. Covert channel analysis is a meaningful activity when there is the potential for unauthorized information flows across security domains, for example, in the case of information systems containing export-controlled information and having connections to external networks (i.e., networks not controlled by the organization). Covert channel analysis is also meaningful in the case of multilevel secure (MLS) systems, multiple security level (MSL) systems, and cross domain systems.

Control Enhancements:

(1) **The organization tests a subset of the vendor-identified covert channel avenues to determine if they are exploitable.**

References: None.

Priority and Baseline Allocation:

P0	**LOW** Not Selected	**MOD** Not Selected	**HIGH** Not Selected

SC-32   INFORMATION SYSTEM PARTITIONING

Control: The organization partitions the information system into components residing in separate physical domains (or environments) as deemed necessary.

Supplemental Guidance: Information system partitioning is a part of a defense-in-depth protection strategy. An organizational assessment of risk guides the partitioning of information system components into separate physical domains (or environments). The security categorization also guides the selection of appropriate candidates for domain partitioning when system components can be associated with different system impact levels derived from the categorization. Managed interfaces restrict or prohibit network access and information flow among partitioned information system components. Related controls: AC-4, SC-7.

Control Enhancements: None.

References: FIPS Publication 199.

Priority and Baseline Allocation:

P1	**LOW** Not Selected	**MOD** SC-32	**HIGH** SC-32

SC-33   TRANSMISSION PREPARATION INTEGRITY

Control: The information system protects the integrity of information during the processes of data aggregation, packaging, and transformation in preparation for transmission.

Supplemental Guidance: Information can be subjected to unauthorized changes (e.g., malicious and/or unintentional modification) at information aggregation or protocol transformation points.

Control Enhancements: None.

References: None.

Priority and Baseline Allocation:

P0	**LOW** Not Selected	**MOD** Not Selected	**HIGH** Not Selected

SC-34   NON-MODIFIABLE EXECUTABLE PROGRAMS

Control: The information system at [*Assignment: organization-defined information system components*]:

a. Loads and executes the operating environment from hardware-enforced, read-only media; and

b. Loads and executes [*Assignment: organization-defined applications*] from hardware-enforced, read-only media.

Supplemental Guidance: In this control, the term operating environment is defined as the code upon which applications are hosted, for example, a monitor, executive, operating system, or application running directly on the hardware platform. Hardware-enforced, read-only media include, for example, CD-R/DVD-R disk drives. Use of non-modifiable storage ensures the integrity of the software program from the point of creation of the read-only image.

Control Enhancements:

(1)   **The organization employs [*Assignment: organization-defined information system components*] with no writeable storage that is persistent across component restart or power on/off.**

Enhancement Supplemental Guidance: This control enhancement: (i) eliminates the possibility of malicious code insertion via persistent, writeable storage within the designated information system component; and (ii) requires no such removable storage be employed, a requirement that may be applied directly or as a specific restriction imposed through AC-19.

(2)   **The organization protects the integrity of the information on read-only media.**

Enhancement Supplemental Guidance: This control enhancement covers protecting the integrity of information to be placed onto read-only media and controlling the media after information has been recorded onto the media. Protection measures may include, as deemed necessary by the organization, a combination of prevention and detection/response. This enhancement may be satisfied by requirements imposed by other controls such as AC-3, AC-5, CM-3, CM-5, CM-9, MP-2, MP-4, MP-5, SA-12, SC-28, SI-3, and SI-7.

References: None.

Priority and Baseline Allocation:

P0	**LOW** Not Selected	**MOD** Not Selected	**HIGH** Not Selected

___

FAMILY: SYSTEM AND INFORMATION INTEGRITY   **CLASS:** OPERATIONAL

SI-1   SYSTEM AND INFORMATION INTEGRITY POLICY AND PROCEDURES

Control: The organization develops, disseminates, and reviews/updates [*Assignment: organization-defined frequency*]:

a. A formal, documented system and information integrity policy that addresses purpose, scope, roles, responsibilities, management commitment, coordination among organizational entities, and compliance; and

b. Formal, documented procedures to facilitate the implementation of the system and information integrity policy and associated system and information integrity controls.

Supplemental Guidance: This control is intended to produce the policy and procedures that are required for the effective implementation of selected security controls and control enhancements in the system and information integrity family. The policy and procedures are consistent with applicable federal laws, Executive Orders, directives, policies, regulations, standards, and guidance. Existing organizational policies and procedures may make the need for additional specific policies and procedures unnecessary. The system and information integrity policy can be included as part of the general information security policy for the organization. System and information integrity procedures can be developed for the security program in general and for a particular information system, when required. The organizational risk management strategy is a key factor in the development of the system and information integrity policy. Related control: PM-9.

Control Enhancements: None.

References: NIST Special Publications 800-12, 800-100.

Priority and Baseline Allocation:

P1	**LOW** SI-1	**MOD** SI-1	**HIGH** SI-1

SI-2   FLAW REMEDIATION

Control: The organization:

a. Identifies, reports, and corrects information system flaws;

b. Tests software updates related to flaw remediation for effectiveness and potential side effects on organizational information systems before installation; and

c. Incorporates flaw remediation into the organizational configuration management process.

Supplemental Guidance: The organization identifies information systems containing software affected by recently announced software flaws (and potential vulnerabilities resulting from those flaws) and reports this information to designated organizational officials with information security responsibilities (e.g., senior information security officers, information system security managers, information systems security officers). The organization (including any contractor to the organization) promptly installs security-relevant software updates (e.g., patches, service packs, and hot fixes). Flaws discovered during security assessments, continuous monitoring, incident response activities, or information system error handling, are also addressed expeditiously. Organizations are encouraged to use resources such as the Common Weakness Enumeration (CWE) or Common Vulnerabilities and Exposures (CVE) databases in remediating flaws discovered in organizational information systems. By requiring that flaw remediation be incorporated into the organizational configuration management process, it is the intent of this control that required/anticipated remediation actions are tracked and verified. An example of expected flaw remediation that would be so verified is whether the procedures contained in US-

CERT guidance and Information Assurance Vulnerability Alerts have been accomplished. Related controls: CA-2, CA-7, CM-3, MA-2, IR-4, RA-5, SA-11, SI-11.

Control Enhancements:

(1) The organization centrally manages the flaw remediation process and installs software updates automatically.

Enhancement Supplemental Guidance: Due to information system integrity and availability concerns, organizations give careful consideration to the methodology used to carry out automatic updates.

(2) The organization employs automated mechanisms [*Assignment: organization-defined frequency*] to determine the state of information system components with regard to flaw remediation.

(3) The organization measures the time between flaw identification and flaw remediation, comparing with [*Assignment: organization-defined benchmarks*].

(4) The organization employs automated patch management tools to facilitate flaw remediation to [*Assignment: organization-defined information system components*].

References: NIST Special Publication 800-40.

Priority and Baseline Allocation:

P1	**LOW** SI-2	**MOD** SI-2 (2)	**HIGH** SI-2 (1) (2)

SI-3   MALICIOUS CODE PROTECTION

Control: The organization:

a. Employs malicious code protection mechanisms at information system entry and exit points and at workstations, servers, or mobile computing devices on the network to detect and eradicate malicious code:

- Transported by electronic mail, electronic mail attachments, web accesses, removable media, or other common means; or

- Inserted through the exploitation of information system vulnerabilities;

b. Updates malicious code protection mechanisms (including signature definitions) whenever new releases are available in accordance with organizational configuration management policy and procedures;

c. Configures malicious code protection mechanisms to:

- Perform periodic scans of the information system [*Assignment: organization-defined frequency*] and real-time scans of files from external sources as the files are downloaded, opened, or executed in accordance with organizational security policy; and

- [*Selection (one or more): block malicious code; quarantine malicious code; send alert to administrator;* [*Assignment: organization-defined action*]] in response to malicious code detection; and

d. Addresses the receipt of false positives during malicious code detection and eradication and the resulting potential impact on the availability of the information system.

Supplemental Guidance: Information system entry and exit points include, for example, firewalls, electronic mail servers, web servers, proxy servers, and remote-access servers. Malicious code includes, for example, viruses, worms, Trojan horses, and spyware. Malicious code can also be encoded in various formats (e.g., UUENCODE, Unicode) or contained within a compressed file. Removable media includes, for example, USB devices, diskettes, or compact disks. A variety of technologies and methods exist to limit or eliminate the effects of malicious code attacks. Pervasive configuration management and strong software integrity controls may be effective in preventing execution of unauthorized code. In addition to commercial off-the-shelf software, malicious code may also be present in custom-built software. This could include, for example, logic bombs, back doors, and other types of cyber attacks that could affect organizational missions and business functions. Traditional malicious code protection mechanisms are not built to detect such code. In these situations, organizations must rely instead on other risk mitigation measures to include, for example, secure coding practices, trusted procurement processes, configuration management and control, and monitoring practices to help ensure that software does not perform functions other than those intended. Related controls: SA-4, SA-8, SA-12, SA-13, SI-4, SI-7.

Control Enhancements:

(1)   The organization centrally manages malicious code protection mechanisms.

(2)   The information system automatically updates malicious code protection mechanisms (including signature definitions).

(3)   The information system prevents non-privileged users from circumventing malicious code protection capabilities.

(4)   The information system updates malicious code protection mechanisms only when directed by a privileged user.

(5)   The organization does not allow users to introduce removable media into the information system.

(6)   The organization tests malicious code protection mechanisms [*Assignment: organization-defined frequency*] by introducing a known benign, non-spreading test case into the information system and subsequently verifying that both detection of the test case and associated incident reporting occur, as required.

References: NIST Special Publication 800-83.

Priority and Baseline Allocation:

P1	LOW SI-3	MOD SI-3 (1) (2) (3)	HIGH SI-3 (1) (2) (3)

SI-4   INFORMATION SYSTEM MONITORING

Control: The organization:

a.   Monitors events on the information system in accordance with [*Assignment: organization-defined monitoring objectives*] and detects information system attacks;

b.   Identifies unauthorized use of the information system;

c.   Deploys monitoring devices: (i) strategically within the information system to collect organization-determined essential information; and (ii) at ad hoc locations within the system to track specific types of transactions of interest to the organization;

d.   Heightens the level of information system monitoring activity whenever there is an indication of increased risk to organizational operations and assets, individuals, other organizations, or the Nation based on law enforcement information, intelligence information, or other credible sources of information; and

e.   Obtains legal opinion with regard to information system monitoring activities in accordance with applicable federal laws, Executive Orders, directives, policies, or regulations.

Supplemental Guidance: Information system monitoring includes external and internal monitoring. External monitoring includes the observation of events occurring at the system boundary (i.e., part of perimeter defense and boundary protection). Internal monitoring includes the observation of events occurring within the system (e.g., within internal organizational networks and system components). Information system monitoring capability is achieved through a variety of tools and techniques (e.g., intrusion detection systems, intrusion prevention systems, malicious code protection software, audit record monitoring software, network monitoring software). Strategic locations for monitoring devices include, for example, at selected perimeter locations and near server farms supporting critical applications, with such devices typically being employed at the managed interfaces associated with controls SC-7 and AC-17. The Einstein network monitoring device from the Department of Homeland Security is an example of a system monitoring device. The granularity of the information collected is determined by the organization based on its monitoring objectives and the capability of the information system to support such activities. An example of a specific type of transaction of interest to the organization with regard to monitoring is Hyper Text Transfer Protocol (HTTP) traffic that bypasses organizational HTTP proxies, when use of such proxies is required. Related controls: AC-4, AC-8, AC-17, AU-2, AU-6, SI-3, SI-7.

Control Enhancements:

(1) The organization interconnects and configures individual intrusion detection tools into a systemwide intrusion detection system using common protocols.

(2) The organization employs automated tools to support near real-time analysis of events.

(3) The organization employs automated tools to integrate intrusion detection tools into access control and flow control mechanisms for rapid response to attacks by enabling reconfiguration of these mechanisms in support of attack isolation and elimination.

(4) The information system monitors inbound and outbound communications for unusual or unauthorized activities or conditions.

Enhancement Supplemental Guidance: Unusual/unauthorized activities or conditions include, for example, internal traffic that indicates the presence of malicious code within an information system or propagating among system components, the unauthorized export of information, or signaling to an external information system. Evidence of malicious code is used to identify potentially compromised information systems or information system components.

(5) The information system provides near real-time alerts when the following indications of compromise or potential compromise occur: [Assignment: organization-defined list of compromise indicators].

Enhancement Supplemental Guidance: Alerts may be generated, depending on the organization-defined list of indicators, from a variety of sources, for example, audit records or input from malicious code protection mechanisms, intrusion detection or prevention mechanisms, or boundary protection devices such as firewalls, gateways, and routers.

(6) The information system prevents non-privileged users from circumventing intrusion detection and prevention capabilities.

(7) The information system notifies [Assignment: organization-defined list of incident response personnel (identified by name and/or by role)] of suspicious events and takes [Assignment: organization-defined list of least-disruptive actions to terminate suspicious events].

Enhancement Supplemental Guidance: The least-disruptive actions may include initiating a request for human response.

(8) The organization protects information obtained from intrusion-monitoring tools from unauthorized access, modification, and deletion.

(9) The organization tests/exercises intrusion-monitoring tools [Assignment: organization-defined time-period].

Enhancement Supplemental Guidance: The frequency of testing/exercises is dependent upon the type and method of deployment of the intrusion-monitoring tools.

(10) The organization makes provisions so that encrypted traffic is visible to information system monitoring tools.

Enhancement Supplemental Guidance: The enhancement recognizes the need to balance encrypting traffic versus the need to have insight into that traffic from a monitoring perspective. For some organizations, the need to ensure the confidentiality of traffic is paramount; for others, the mission-assurance concerns are greater.

(11) The organization analyzes outbound communications traffic at the external boundary of the system (i.e., system perimeter) and, as deemed necessary, at selected interior points within the system (e.g., subnets, subsystems) to discover anomalies.

Enhancement Supplemental Guidance: Anomalies within the information system include, for example, large file transfers, long-time persistent connections, unusual protocols and ports in use, and attempted communications with suspected malicious external addresses.

(12) The organization employs automated mechanisms to alert security personnel of the following inappropriate or unusual activities with security implications: [*Assignment: organization-defined list of inappropriate or unusual activities that trigger alerts*].

(13) The organization:

(a) Analyzes communications traffic/event patterns for the information

system; (b) Develops profiles representing common traffic patterns and/or

events; and

(c) Uses the traffic/event profiles in tuning system-monitoring devices to reduce the number of false positives to [*Assignment: organization-defined measure of false positives*] and the number of false negatives to [*Assignment: organization-defined measure of false negatives*].

(14) The organization employs a wireless intrusion detection system to identify rogue wireless devices and to detect attack attempts and potential compromises/breaches to the information system.

(15) The organization employs an intrusion detection system to monitor wireless communications traffic as the traffic passes from wireless to wireline networks.

(16) The organization correlates information from monitoring tools employed throughout the information system to achieve organization-wide situational awareness.

(17) The organization correlates results from monitoring physical, cyber, and supply chain activities to achieve integrated situational awareness.

Enhancement Supplemental Guidance: Integrated situational awareness enhances the capability of the organization to more quickly detect sophisticated attacks and investigate the methods and techniques employed to carry out the attacks.

References: NIST Special Publications 800-61, 800-83, 800-92, 800-94.

Priority and Baseline Allocation:

P1	LOW Not Selected	MOD SI-4 (2) (4) (5) (6)	HIGH SI-4 (2) (4) (5) (6)

SI-5   SECURITY ALERTS, ADVISORIES, AND DIRECTIVES

Control: The organization:

a. Receives information system security alerts, advisories, and directives from designated external organizations on an ongoing basis;

b. Generates internal security alerts, advisories, and directives as deemed necessary;

c. Disseminates security alerts, advisories, and directives to [*Assignment: organization-defined list of personnel (identified by name and/or by role)*]; and

d. Implements security directives in accordance with established time frames, or notifies the issuing organization of the degree of noncompliance.

Supplemental Guidance: Security alerts and advisories are generated by the United States Computer Emergency Readiness Team (US-CERT) to maintain situational awareness across the federal government. Security directives are issued by OMB or other designated organizations with the responsibility and authority to issue such directives. Compliance to security directives is *essential* due to the critical nature of many of these directives and the potential immediate adverse affects on organizational operations and assets, individuals, other organizations, and the Nation should the directives not be implemented in a timely manner.

Control Enhancements:

(1) The organization employs automated mechanisms to make security alert and advisory information available throughout the organization as needed.

References: NIST Special Publication 800-40.

Priority and Baseline Allocation:

P1	LOW SI-5	MOD SI-5	HIGH SI-5 (1)

SI-6   SECURITY FUNCTIONALITY VERIFICATION

Control: The information system verifies the correct operation of security functions [*Selection (one or more): [Assignment: organization-defined system transitional states]; upon command by user with appropriate privilege; periodically every [Assignment: organization-defined time-period]*] and [*Selection (one or more): notifies system administrator; shuts the system down; restarts the system; [Assignment: organization-defined alternative action(s)]*] when anomalies are discovered.

Supplemental Guidance: The need to verify security functionality applies to all security functions. For those security functions that are not able to execute automated self-tests, the organization either implements compensating security controls or explicitly accepts the risk of not performing the verification as required. Information system transitional states include, for example, startup, restart, shutdown, and abort.

Control Enhancements:

(1)   The information system provides notification of failed automated security tests.

(2)   The information system provides automated support for the management of distributed security testing.

(3)   The organization reports the result of security function verification to designated organizational officials with information security responsibilities.

   Enhancement Supplemental Guidance: Organizational officials with information security responsibilities include, for example, senior information security officers, information system security managers, and information systems security officers.

References: None.

Priority and Baseline Allocation:

P1	LOW Not Selected	MOD Not Selected	HIGH SI-6

SI-7   SOFTWARE AND INFORMATION INTEGRITY

Control: The information system detects unauthorized changes to software and information.

Supplemental Guidance: The organization employs integrity verification applications on the information system to look for evidence of information tampering, errors, and omissions. The organization employs good software engineering practices with regard to commercial off-the-shelf integrity mechanisms (e.g., parity checks, cyclical redundancy checks, cryptographic hashes) and uses tools to automatically monitor the integrity of the information system and the applications it hosts.

Control Enhancements:

(1)   The organization reassesses the integrity of software and information by performing [*Assignment: organization-defined frequency*] integrity scans of the information system.

(2)   The organization employs automated tools that provide notification to designated individuals upon discovering discrepancies during integrity verification.

(3)   The organization employs centrally managed integrity verification tools.

(4)   The organization requires use of tamper-evident packaging for [*Assignment: organization-defined information system components*] during [*Selection: transportation from vendor to operational site; during operation; both*].

References: None.

Priority and Baseline Allocation:

P1	LOW Not Selected	MOD SI-7 (1)	HIGH SI-7 (1) (2)

SI-8   SPAM PROTECTION

Control: The organization:

a.   Employs spam protection mechanisms at information system entry and exit points and at workstations, servers, or mobile computing devices on the network to detect and take action on unsolicited messages transported by electronic mail, electronic mail attachments, web accesses, or other common means; and

b.   Updates spam protection mechanisms (including signature definitions) when new releases are available in accordance with organizational configuration management policy and procedures.

Supplemental Guidance: Information system entry and exit points include, for example, firewalls, electronic mail servers, web servers, proxy servers, and remote-access servers. Related controls: SC-5, SI-3.

Control Enhancements:

(1)   The organization centrally manages spam protection mechanisms.

(2)   The information system automatically updates spam protection mechanisms (including signature definitions).

References: NIST Special Publication 800-45.

Priority and Baseline Allocation:

P1	LOW Not Selected	MOD SI-8	HIGH SI-8 (1)

SI-9   INFORMATION INPUT RESTRICTIONS

Control: The organization restricts the capability to input information to the information system to authorized personnel.

Supplemental Guidance: Restrictions on organizational personnel authorized to input information to the information system may extend beyond the typical access controls employed by the system and include limitations based on specific operational/project responsibilities. Related controls: AC-5, AC-6.

Control Enhancements: None.

References: None.

Priority and Baseline Allocation:

P2	LOW Not Selected	MOD SI-9	HIGH SI-9

SI-10   INFORMATION INPUT VALIDATION

Control: The information system checks the validity of information inputs.

Supplemental Guidance: Rules for checking the valid syntax and semantics of information system inputs (e.g., character set, length, numerical range, acceptable values) are in place to verify that inputs match specified definitions for format and content. Inputs passed to interpreters are prescreened to prevent the content from being unintentionally interpreted as commands.

Control Enhancements: None.

References: None.

Priority and Baseline Allocation:

P1	**LOW** Not Selected	**MOD** SI-10	**HIGH** SI-10

SI-11   ERROR HANDLING

Control: The information system:

a.   Identifies potentially security-relevant error conditions;

b.   Generates error messages that provide information necessary for corrective actions without revealing [*Assignment: organization-defined sensitive or potentially harmful information*] in error logs and administrative messages that could be exploited by adversaries; and

c.   Reveals error messages only to authorized personnel.

Supplemental Guidance: The structure and content of error messages are carefully considered by the organization. The extent to which the information system is able to identify and handle error conditions is guided by organizational policy and operational requirements. Sensitive information includes, for example, account numbers, social security numbers, and credit card numbers.

Control Enhancements: None.

References: None.

Priority and Baseline Allocation:

P2	**LOW** Not Selected	**MOD** SI-11	**HIGH** SI-11

SI-12   INFORMATION OUTPUT HANDLING AND RETENTION

Control: The organization handles and retains both information within and output from the information system in accordance with applicable federal laws, Executive Orders, directives, policies, regulations, standards, and operational requirements.

Supplemental Guidance: The output handling and retention requirements cover the full life cycle of the information, in some cases extending beyond the disposal of the information system. The National Archives and Records Administration provides guidance on records retention. Related controls: MP-2, MP-4.

Control Enhancements: None.

References: None.

Priority and Baseline Allocation:

P2	**LOW** SI-12	**MOD** SI-12	**HIGH** SI-12

SI-13   **PREDICTABLE FAILURE PREVENTION**

Control: The organization:

a. Protects the information system from harm by considering mean time to failure for [*Assignment: organization-defined list of information system components*] in specific environments of operation; and

b. Provides substitute information system components, when needed, and a mechanism to exchange active and standby roles of the components.

Supplemental Guidance: While mean time to failure is primarily a reliability issue, this control focuses on the potential failure of specific components of the information system that provide security capability. Mean time to failure rates are defendable and based on considerations that are installation-specific, not industry-average. The transfer of responsibilities between active and standby information system components does not compromise safety, operational readiness, or security (e.g., state variables are preserved). The standby component is available at all times except where a failure recovery is in progress or for maintenance reasons. Related control: CP-2.

Control Enhancements:

(1) The organization takes the information system component out of service by transferring component responsibilities to a substitute component no later than [*Assignment: organization-defined fraction or percentage*] of mean time to failure.

(2) The organization does not allow a process to execute without supervision for more than [*Assignment: organization-defined time period*].

(3) The organization manually initiates a transfer between active and standby information system components at least once per [*Assignment: organization-defined frequency*] if the mean time to failure exceeds [*Assignment: organization-defined time period*].

(4) The organization, if an information system component failure is detected:

(a) Ensures that the standby information system component successfully and transparently assumes its role within [*Assignment: organization-defined time period*]; and

(b) [*Selection (one or more): activates [Assignment: organization-defined alarm]; automatically shuts down the information system*].

Enhancement Supplemental Guidance: Automatic or manual transfer of roles to a standby unit may occur upon detection of a component failure.

References: None.

Priority and Baseline Allocation:

P0	**LOW** Not Selected	**MOD** Not Selected	**HIGH** Not Selected

APPENDIX G

INFORMATION SECURITY PROGRAMS
ORGANIZATION-WIDE INFORMATION SECURITY PROGRAM MANAGEMENT CONTROLS

The Federal Information Security Management Act (FISMA) requires organizations to develop and implement an organization-wide information security program to address information security for the information and information systems that support the operations and assets of the organization, including those provided or managed by another organization, contractor, or other source. The information security program management (PM) controls described in this appendix complement the security controls in Appendix F and focus on the organization-wide information security requirements that are independent of any particular information system and are essential for managing information security programs. Organizations specify the individuals within the organization responsible for the development, implementation, assessment, authorization, and monitoring of the information security program management controls. Organizations document program management controls in the *information security program plan*. The organization-wide information security program plan supplements the individual security plans developed for each organizational information system. Together, the security plans for the individual information systems and the information security program cover the totality of security controls employed by the organization.

In addition to documenting the information security program management controls, the security program plan provides a vehicle for the organization, in a central repository, to document all security controls from Appendix F that have been designated as *common controls* (i.e., security controls inherited by organizational information systems). The information security program management controls and common controls contained in the information security program plan are implemented, assessed for effectiveness,[74] and authorized by a senior organizational official, with the same or similar authority and responsibility for managing risk as the authorization officials for information systems.[75] Plans of action and milestones are developed and maintained for the program management and common controls that are deemed through assessment to be less than effective. Information security program management and common controls are also subject to the same continuous monitoring requirements as security controls employed in individual organizational information systems.

Cautionary Note

Organizations are required to implement security program management controls to provide a foundation for the organization's information security program. The successful implementation of security controls for organizational information systems depends on the successful implementation of the organization's program management controls.

---

[74] Assessment procedures for program management controls and common controls can be found in NIST Special Publication 800-53A.

[75] In situations where common controls are inherited from external environments, organizations should consult the guidance provided in Section 3.4.

PM-1   INFORMATION SECURITY PROGRAM PLAN

Control: The organization:

a. Develops and disseminates an organization-wide information security program plan that:

   - Provides an overview of the requirements for the security program and a description of the security program management controls and common controls in place or planned for meeting those requirements;

   - Provides sufficient information about the program management controls and common controls (including specification of parameters for any *assignment* and *selection* operations either explicitly or by reference) to enable an implementation that is unambiguously compliant with the intent of the plan and a determination of the risk to be incurred if the plan is implemented as intended;

   - Includes roles, responsibilities, management commitment, coordination among organizational entities, and compliance;

   - Is approved by a senior official with responsibility and accountability for the risk being incurred to organizational operations (including mission, functions, image, and reputation), organizational assets, individuals, other organizations, and the Nation;

b. Reviews the organization-wide information security program plan [*Assignment: organization-defined frequency*]; and

c. Revises the plan to address organizational changes and problems identified during plan implementation or security control assessments.

Supplemental Guidance: The information security program plan can be represented in a single document or compilation of documents at the discretion of the organization. The plan documents the organization-wide program management controls and organization-defined common controls. The security plans for individual information systems and the organization-wide information security program plan together, provide complete coverage for all security controls employed within the organization. Common controls are documented in an appendix to the organization's information security program plan unless the controls are included in a separate security plan for an information system (e.g., security controls employed as part of an intrusion detection system providing organization-wide boundary protection inherited by one or more organizational information systems). The organization-wide information security program plan will indicate which separate security plans contain descriptions of common controls.

Organizations have the flexibility to describe common controls in a single document or in multiple documents. In the case of multiple documents, the documents describing common controls are included as attachments to the information security program plan. If the information security program plan contains multiple documents, the organization specifies in each document the organizational official or officials responsible for the development, implementation, assessment, authorization, and monitoring of the respective common controls. For example, the organization may require that the Facilities Management Office develop, implement, assess, authorize, and continuously monitor common physical and environmental protection controls from the PE family when such controls are not associated with a particular information system but instead, support multiple information systems. Related control: PM-8.

Control Enhancements: None.

References: None.

PM-2   SENIOR INFORMATION SECURITY OFFICER

Control: The organization appoints a senior information security officer with the mission and resources to coordinate, develop, implement, and maintain an organization-wide information security program.

Supplemental Guidance: The security officer described in this control is an organizational official. For a federal agency (as defined in applicable federal laws, Executive Orders, directives, policies, or regulations) this official is the Senior Agency Information Security Officer. Organizations may also refer to this organizational official as the Senior Information Security Officer or Chief Information Security Officer.

Control Enhancements: None.

References: None.

PM-3   INFORMATION SECURITY RESOURCES

Control: The organization:

a.   Ensures that all capital planning and investment requests include the resources needed to implement the information security program and documents all exceptions to this requirement;

b.   Employs a business case/Exhibit 300/Exhibit 53 to record the resources required; and c.

Ensures that information security resources are available for expenditure as planned.

Supplemental Guidance: Organizations may designate and empower an Investment Review Board (or similar group) to manage and provide oversight for the information security-related aspects of the capital planning and investment control process. Related controls: PM-4, SA-2.

Control Enhancements: None.

References: NIST Special Publication 800-65.

PM-4   PLAN OF ACTION AND MILESTONES PROCESS

Control: The organization implements a process for ensuring that plans of action and milestones for the security program and the associated organizational information systems are maintained and document the remedial information security actions to mitigate risk to organizational operations and assets, individuals, other organizations, and the Nation.

Supplemental Guidance: The plan of action and milestones is a key document in the information security program and is subject to federal reporting requirements established by OMB. The plan of action and milestones updates are based on the findings from security control assessments, security impact analyses, and continuous monitoring activities. OMB FISMA reporting guidance contains instructions regarding organizational plans of action and milestones. Related control: CA-5.

Control Enhancements: None.

References: OMB Memorandum 02-01; NIST Special Publication 800-37.

PM-5   INFORMATION SYSTEM INVENTORY

Control: The organization develops and maintains an inventory of its information systems.

Supplemental Guidance: This control addresses the inventory requirements in FISMA. OMB provides guidance on developing information systems inventories and associated reporting requirements.

Control Enhancements: None.

References: None.

PM-6   INFORMATION SECURITY MEASURES OF PERFORMANCE

Control: The organization develops, monitors, and reports on the results of information security measures of performance.

Supplemental Guidance: Measures of performance are outcome-based metrics used by an organization to measure the effectiveness or efficiency of the information security program and the security controls employed in support of the program.

Control Enhancements: None.

References: NIST Special Publication 800-55.

PM-7   ENTERPRISE ARCHITECTURE

Control: The organization develops an enterprise architecture with consideration for information security and the resulting risk to organizational operations, organizational assets, individuals, other organizations, and the Nation.

Supplemental Guidance: The enterprise architecture developed by the organization is aligned with the Federal Enterprise Architecture. The integration of information security requirements and associated security controls into the organization's enterprise architecture helps to ensure that security considerations are addressed by organizations early in the system development life cycle and are directly and explicitly related to the organization's mission/business processes. This also embeds into the enterprise architecture, an integral security architecture consistent with organizational risk management and information security strategies. Security requirements and control integration are most effectively accomplished through the application of the Risk Management Framework and supporting security standards and guidelines. The Federal Segment Architecture Methodology provides guidance on integrating information security requirements and security controls into enterprise architectures. Related controls: PL-2, PM-11, RA-2.

Control Enhancements: None.

References: NIST Special Publication 800-39; Web: WWW.FSAM.GOV.

PM-8   CRITICAL INFRASTRUCTURE PLAN

Control: The organization addresses information security issues in the development, documentation, and updating of a critical infrastructure and key resources protection plan.

Supplemental Guidance: The requirement and guidance for defining critical infrastructure and key resources and for preparing an associated critical infrastructure protection plan are found in applicable federal laws, Executive Orders, directives, policies, regulations, standards, and guidance. Related controls: PM-1, PM-9, PM-11, RA-3.

Control Enhancements: None.

References: HSPD 7.

PM-9   RISK MANAGEMENT STRATEGY

Control: The organization:

a. Develops a comprehensive strategy to manage risk to organizational operations and assets, individuals, other organizations, and the Nation associated with the operation and use of information systems; and

b. Implements that strategy consistently across the organization.

Supplemental Guidance: An organization-wide risk management strategy includes, for example, an unambiguous expression of the risk tolerance for the organization, acceptable risk assessment methodologies, risk mitigation strategies, a process for consistently evaluating risk across the organization with respect to the organization's risk tolerance, and approaches for monitoring risk over time. The use of a risk executive function can facilitate consistent, organization-wide application of the risk management strategy. The organization-wide risk management strategy can be informed by risk-related inputs from other sources both internal and external to the organization to ensure the strategy is both broad-based and comprehensive. Related control: RA-3.

Control Enhancements: None.

References: NIST Special Publications 800-30, 800-39.

PM-10   SECURITY AUTHORIZATION PROCESS

Control: The organization:

a. Manages (i.e., documents, tracks, and reports) the security state of organizational information systems through security authorization processes;

b. Designates individuals to fulfill specific roles and responsibilities within the organizational risk management process; and

c. Fully integrates the security authorization processes into an organization-wide risk management program.

Supplemental Guidance: The security authorization process for information systems requires the implementation of the Risk Management Framework and the employment of associated security standards and guidelines. Specific roles within the risk management process include a designated authorizing official for each organizational information system. Related control: CA-6.

Control Enhancements: None.

References: NIST Special Publications 800-37, 800-39.

PM-11   MISSION/BUSINESS PROCESS DEFINITION

Control: The organization:

a. Defines mission/business processes with consideration for information security and the resulting risk to organizational operations, organizational assets, individuals, other organizations, and the Nation; and

b. Determines information protection needs arising from the defined mission/business processes and revises the processes as necessary, until an achievable set of protection needs is obtained.

Supplemental Guidance: Information protection needs are technology-independent, required capabilities to counter threats to organizations, individuals, or the Nation through the compromise of information (i.e., loss of confidentiality, integrity, or availability). Information protection needs are derived from the mission/business needs defined by the organization, the mission/business processes selected to meet the stated needs, and the organizational risk management strategy. Information protection needs determine the required security controls for the organization and the associated information systems supporting the mission/business processes. Inherent in defining an organization's information protection needs is an understanding of the level of adverse impact that could result if a compromise of information occurs. The security categorization process is used to make such potential impact determinations. Mission/business process definitions and associated information protection requirements are documented by the organization in accordance with organizational policy and procedure. Related controls: PM-7, PM-8, RA-2.

Control Enhancements: None.

References: FIPS Publication 199; NIST Special Publication 800-60.

APPENDIX H

INTERNATIONAL INFORMATION SECURITY STANDARDS

SECURITY CONTROL MAPPINGS FOR ISO/IEC 27001

The mapping tables in this appendix provide organizations with a *general* indication of security control coverage with respect to ISO/IEC 27001, *Information technology–Security techniques–Information security management systems–Requirements.*[76] ISO/IEC 27001 applies to all types of organizations (e.g., commercial, government) and specifies requirements for establishing, implementing, operating, monitoring, reviewing, maintaining, and improving a documented information security management system (ISMS) within the context of the organization's overall business risks. While the risk management approach established by NIST originally focused on managing risk from information systems (as required by FISMA and described in NIST Special Publication 800-39), the approach is being expanded to include risk management at the organizational level. A forthcoming version of NIST Special Publication 800-39 will incorporate ISO/IEC 27001 to manage organizational information security risk through the establishment of an ISMS. Since NIST's mission includes the adoption of international and national standards where appropriate, NIST intends to pursue convergence to reduce the burden on organizations that must conform to both sets of standards. The convergence initiative will be carried out in three phases. Phase I, the subject of this appendix, provides a two-way mapping between the security controls in NIST Special Publication 800-53 and the controls in ISO/IEC 27001 (Annex A). Phase II will provide a two-way mapping between the organization-level risk management concepts in NIST Special Publication 800-39 (forthcoming version) and general requirements in ISO/IEC 27001. Phase III will use the results from Phase I and II to fully integrate ISO/IEC 27001 into NIST's risk management approach such that an organization that complies with NIST standards and guidelines can also comply with ISO/IEC 27001 (subject to appropriate assessment requirements for ISO/IEC 27001 certification).

Table H-1 provides a forward mapping from the security controls in NIST Special Publication 800-53 to the controls in ISO/IEC 27001 (Annex A). The mappings are created by using the primary security topic identified in each of the Special Publication 800-53 security controls and associated control enhancements (if any) and searching for a similar security topic in ISO/IEC 27001 (Annex A). Security controls with similar functional meaning are included in the mapping table. For example, Special Publication 800-53 contingency planning and ISO/IEC 27001 (Annex A) business continuity were deemed to have similar, but not the same, functionality. In some cases, similar topics are addressed in the security control sets but provide a different context, perspective, or scope. For example, Special Publication 800-53 addresses information flow control broadly in terms of approved authorizations for controlling access between source and destination objects, whereas ISO/IEC 27001 (Annex A) addresses the information flow more narrowly as it applies to interconnected network domains. Table H-2 provides a reverse mapping from the security controls in ISO/IEC 27001 (Annex A) to the security controls in Special Publication 800-53.[77]

---

[76] ISO/IEC 27001 was published in October 2005 by the International Organization for Standardization (ISO) and the International Electrotechnical Commission (IEC).

[77] The use of the term *XX-1 controls* in mapping Table H-2 refers to the set of security controls represented by the first control in each family in NIST Special Publication 800-53, where *XX* is a placeholder for the two-letter family identifier. These security controls primarily focus on policies and procedures for each topic area addressed by the respective security control family.

Organizations are encouraged to use the mapping tables as a starting point for conducting further analyses and interpretation of the extent of compliance with ISO/IEC 27001 from compliance with the NIST security standards and guidelines and visa versa. Organizations that use the security controls in Special Publication 800-53 as an extension to the security controls in Annex A in their ISO/IEC 27001 implementations will have a higher probability of complying with NIST security standards and guidelines than those organizations that use only Annex A.

TABLE H-1: MAPPING NIST SP 800-53 TO ISO/IEC 27001 (ANNEX A)

NIST SP 800-53 CONTROLS		ISO/IEC 27001 (Annex A) CONTROLS
AC-1	Access Control Policy and Procedures	A5.1.1, A5.1.2, A.6.1.1, A.6.1.3, A.8.1.1, A10.1.1, A.10.8.1, A.11.1.1, A.11.2.1, A11.2.2, A11.4.1, A.11.7.1, A.11.7.2, A.15.1.1, A.15.2.1
AC-2	Account Management	A.8.3.3, A.11.2.1, A.11.2.2, A.11.2.4, A15.2.1
AC-3	Access Enforcement	A.10.8.1 A.11.4.4, A.11.4.6, A.11.5.4, A.11.6.1, A.12.4.2
AC-4	Information Flow Enforcement	A.10.6.1, A.10.8.1, A.11.4.5, A.11.4.7, A.11.7.2, A.12.4.2, A.12.5.4
AC-5	Separation of Duties	A.6.1.3, A.8.1.1, A.10.1.3, A.11.1.1, A.11.4.1
AC-6	Least Privilege	A.6.1.3, A.8.1.1, A.11.1.1, A.11.2.2, A.11.4.1, A.11.4.4, A.11.4.6, A.11.5.4, A.11.6.1, A.12.4.3
AC-7	Unsuccessful Login Attempts	A.11.5.1
AC-8	System Use Notification	A.6.2.2, A.8.1.1, A.11.5.1, A.15.1.5
AC-9	Previous Logon (Access) Notification	A.11.5.1
AC-10	Concurrent Session Control	A.11.5.1
AC-11	Session Lock	A.11.3.2, A.11.3.3, A.11.5.5
AC-12	**Withdrawn**	---
AC-13	**Withdrawn**	---
AC-14	Permitted Actions without Identification or Authentication	A.11.6.1
AC-15	**Withdrawn**	---
AC-16	Security Attributes	A.7.2.2
AC-17	Remote Access	A.10.6.1, A.10.8.1, A.11.1.1, A.11.4.1, A.11.4.2, A.11.4.4, A.11.4.6, A.11.4.7, A.11.7.1, A.11.7.2
AC-18	Wireless Access	A.10.6.1, A.10.8.1, A.11.1.1, A.11.4.1, A.11.4.2, A.11.4.4, A.11.4.6, A.11.4.7, A.11.7.1, A.11.7.2
AC-19	Access Control for Mobile Devices	A.10.4.1, A.11.1.1, A.11.4.3, A.11.7.1
AC-20	Use of External Information Systems	A.7.1.3, A.8.1.1, A.8.1.3, A.10.6.1, A.10.8.1, A.11.4.1, A.11.4.2
AC-21	User-Based Collaboration and Information Sharing	A.11.2.1, A.11.2.2
AC-22	Publicly Accessible Content	None
AT-1	Security Awareness and Training Policy and Procedures	A.5.1.1, A.5.1.2, A.6.1.1, A.6.1.3, A.8.1.1, A.10.1.1, A.15.1.1, A.15.2.1
AT-2	Security Awareness	A.6.2.2, A.8.1.1, A.8.2.2, A.9.1.5, A.10.4.1
AT-3	Security Training	A.8.1.1, A.8.2.2, A.9.1.5
AT-4	Security Training Records	None
AT-5	Contacts with Security Groups and Associations	A.6.1.7
AU-1	Audit and Accountability Policy and Procedures	A.5.1.1, A.5.1.2, A.6.1.1, A.6.1.3, A.8.1.1, A.10.1.1, A.10.10.2, A.15.1.1, A.15.2.1, A.15.3.1
AU-2	Auditable Events	A.10.10.1, A.10.10.4, A.10.10.5, A.15.3.1
AU-3	Content of Audit Records	A.10.10.1
AU-4	Audit Storage Capacity	A.10.10.1, A.10.3.1
AU-5	Response to Audit Processing Failures	A.10.3.1, A.10.10.1
AU-6	Audit Review, Analysis, and Reporting	A.10.10.2, A.10.10.5, A.13.1.1, A.15.1.5
AU-7	Audit Reduction and Report Generation	A.10.10.2
AU-8	Time Stamps	A.10.10.1, A.10.10.6
AU-9	Protection of Audit Information	A.10.10.3, A.13.2.3, A.15.1.3, A.15.3.2
AU-10	Non-repudiation	A.10.9.1, A.12.2.3
AU-11	Audit Record Retention	A.10.10.1, A.10.10.2, A.15.1.3

NIST SP 800-53 CONTROLS		ISO/IEC 27001 (Annex A) CONTROLS
AU-12	Audit Generation	A.10.10.1, A.10.10.4, A.10.10.5
AU-13	Monitoring for Information Disclosure	None
AU-14	Session Audit	None
CA-1	Security Assessment and Authorization Policies and Procedures	A.5.1.1, A.5.1.2, A.6.1.1, A.6.1.3 A.6.1.4, A.8.1.1, A.10.1.1, A.15.1.1, A.15.2.1
CA-2	Security Assessments	A.6.1.8, A.10.3.2, A.15.2.1, A.15.2.2
CA-3	Information System Connections	A.6.2.1, A.6.2.3, A.10.6.1, A.10.8.1, A.10.8.2, A.10.8.5, A.11.4.2
CA-4	**Withdrawn**	---
CA-5	Plan of Action and Milestones	None
CA-6	Security Authorization	A.6.1.4, A.10.3.2
CA-7	Continuous Monitoring	A.6.1.8, A.15.2.1, A.15.2.2
CM-1	Configuration Management Policy and Procedures	A.5.1.1, A.5.1.2, A.6.1.1, A.6.1.3, A.8.1.1, A.10.1.1, A.10.1.2, A.12.4.1, A.12.5.1, A.15.1.1, A.15.2.1
CM-2	Baseline Configuration	A.12.4.1, A.10.1.4
CM-3	Configuration Change Control	A.10.1.1, A.10.1.2, A.10.3.2, A.12.4.1, A.12.5.1, A.12.5.2, A.12.5.3
CM-4	Security Impact Analysis	A.10.1.2, A.10.3.2, A.12.4.1, A.12.5.2, A.12.5.3
CM-5	Access Restrictions for Change	A.10.1.2, A.11.1.1, A.11.6.1, A.12.4.1, A.12.4.3, A.12.5.3
CM-6	Configuration Settings	None
CM-7	Least Functionality	None
CM-8	Information System Component Inventory	A.7.1.1, A.7.1.2
CM-9	Configuration Management Plan	A.6.1.3, A.7.1.1, A.7.1.2, A.8.1.1, A.10.1.1, A.10.1.2, A.10.3.2, A.12.4.1, A.12.4.3, A.12.5.1, A.12.5.2, A.12.5.3
CP-1	Contingency Planning Policy and Procedures	A.5.1.1, A.5.1.2, A.6.1.1, A.6.1.3, A.8.1.1, A.9.1.4, A.10.1.1, A.10.1.2, A.14.1.1, A.14.1.3, A.15.1.1, A.15.2.1
CP-2	Contingency Plan	A.6.1.2, A.9.1.4, A.10.3.1, A.14.1.1, A.14.1.2, A.14.1.3, A.14.1.4, A.14.1.5
CP-3	Contingency Training	A.8.2.2, A.9.1.4, A.14.1.3
CP-4	Contingency Plan Testing and Exercises	A.6.1.2, A.9.1.4, A.14.1.1, A.14.1.3, A.14.1.4, A.14.1.5
CP-5	**Withdrawn**	---
CP-6	Alternate Storage Site	A.9.1.4, A.14.1.3
CP-7	Alternate Processing Site	A.9.1.4, A.14.1.3
CP-8	Telecommunications Services	A.9.1.4, A.10.6.1, A.14.1.3
CP-9	Information System Backup	A.9.1.4, A.10.5.1, A.14.1.3, A.15.1.3
CP-10	Information System Recovery and Reconstitution	A.9.1.4, A.14.1.3
IA-1	Identification and Authentication Policy and Procedures	A.5.1.1, A.5.1.2, A.6.1.1, A.6.1.3, A.8.1.1, A.10.1.1, A.11.2.1, A.15.1.1, A.15.2.1
IA-2	Identification and Authentication (Organizational Users)	A.11.3.2, A.11.5.1, A.11.5.2, A.11.5.3
IA-3	Device Identification and Authentication	A.11.4.3
IA-4	Identifier Management	A.11.5.2
IA-5	Authenticator Management	A.11.2.1, A.11.2.3, A.11.3.1, A.11.5.2, A.11.5.3
IA-6	Authenticator Feedback	A.11.5.1
IA-7	Cryptographic Module Authentication	A.12.3.1, A.15.1.1, A.15.1.6, A.15.2.1
IA-8	Identification and Authentication (Non-Organizational Users)	A.10.9.1, A.11.4.2, A.11.5.1, A.11.5.2
IR-1	Incident Response Policy and Procedures	A.5.1.1, A.5.1.2, A.6.1.1, A.6.1.3, A.8.1.1, A.10.1.1, A.13.1.1, A.13.2.1, A.15.1.1, A.15.2.1
IR-2	Incident Response Training	A.8.2.2
IR-3	Incident Response Testing and Exercises	None
IR-4	Incident Handling	A.6.1.2, A.13.2.2, A.13.2.3
IR-5	Incident Monitoring	None
IR-6	Incident Reporting	A.6.1.6, A.13.1.1
IR-7	Incident Response Assistance	None
IR-8	Incident Response Plan	None
MA-1	System Maintenance Policy and Procedures	A.5.1.1, A.5.1.2, A.6.1.1, A.6.1.3, A.8.1.1, A.9.2.4, A.10.1.1, A.15.1.1, A.15.2.1
MA-2	Controlled Maintenance	A.9.2.4

NIST SP 800-53 CONTROLS		ISO/IEC 27001 (Annex A) CONTROLS
MA-3	Maintenance Tools	A.9.2.4, A.11.4.4
MA-4	Non-Local Maintenance	A.9.2.4, A.11.4.4
MA-5	Maintenance Personnel	A.9.2.4, A.12.4.3
MA-6	Timely Maintenance	A.9.2.4
MP-1	Media Protection Policy and Procedures	A.5.1.1, A.5.1.2, A.6.1.1, A.6.1.3, A.8.1.1, A.10.1.1, A.10.7.1, A.10.7.2, A.10.7.3, A.11.1.1, A.15.1.1, A.15.1.3, A.15.2.1
MP-2	Media Access	A.7.2.2, A.10.7.1, A.10.7.3
MP-3	Media Marking	A.7.2.2, A.10.7.1, A.10.7.3
MP-4	Media Storage	A.10.7.1, A.10.7.3, A.10.7.4, A.15.1.3
MP-5	Media Transport	A.9.2.5, A.9.2.7, A.10.7.1, A.10.7.3, A.10.8.3
MP-6	Media Sanitization	A.9.2.6, A.10.7.1, A.10.7.2, A.10.7.3
PE-1	Physical and Environmental Protection Policy and Procedures	A.5.1.1, A.5.1.2, A.6.1.1, A.6.1.3, A.8.1.1, A.9.1.4, A.9.2.1, A.9.2.2, A.10.1.1, A.11.1.1, A.11.2.1, A.11.2.2, A.15.1.1, A.15.2.1
PE-2	Physical Access Authorizations	A.9.1.5, A.11.2.1, A.11.2.2, A.11.2.4
PE-3	Physical Access Control	A.9.1.1, A.9.1.2, A.9.1.3, A.9.1.5, A.9.1.6, A.11.3.2, A.11.4.4
PE-4	Access Control for Transmission Medium	A.9.1.3, A.9.1.5, A.9.2.3
PE-5	Access Control for Output Devices	A.9.1.2, A.9.1.3, A.10.6.1, A.11.3.2
PE-6	Monitoring Physical Access	A.9.1.2, A.9.1.5, A.10.10.2
PE-7	Visitor Control	A.9.1.2, A.9.1.5, A.9.1.6
PE-8	Access Records	A.9.1.5, A.10.10.2, A.15.2.1
PE-9	Power Equipment and Power Cabling	A.9.1.4, A.9.2.2, A.9.2.3
PE-10	Emergency Shutoff	A.9.1.4
PE-11	Emergency Power	A.9.1.4, A.9.2.2
PE-12	Emergency Lighting	A.9.2.2
PE-13	Fire Protection	A.9.1.4
PE-14	Temperature and Humidity Controls	A.9.2.2
PE-15	Water Damage Protection	A.9.1.4
PE-16	Delivery and Removal	A.9.1.6, A.9.2.7, A.10.7.1
PE-17	Alternate Work Site	A.9.2.5, A.11.7.2
PE-18	Location of Information System Components	A.9.2.1, A.11.3.2
PE-19	Information Leakage	A.12.5.4
PL-1	Security Planning Policy and Procedures	A.5.1.1, A.5.1.2, A.6.1.1, A.6.1.2, A.6.1.3, A.8.1.1, A.10.1.1, A.15.1.1, A.15.2.1
PL-2	System Security Plan	None
PL-3	**Withdrawn**	---
PL-4	Rules of Behavior	A.6.1.5, A.6.2.2, A.7.1.3. A.8.1.1, A.8.1.3, A.8.2.1, A.9.1.5, A.10.8.1, A.11.7.1, A.11.7.2, A.12.4.1, A.13.1.2, A.15.1.5
PL-5	Privacy Impact Assessment	A.15.1.4
PL-6	Security-Related Activity Planning	A.6.1.2, A.15.3.1
PS-1	Personnel Security Policy and Procedures	A.5.1.1, A.5.1.2, A.6.1.1, A.6.1.3, A.8.1.1, A.10.1.1, A.15.1.1, A.15.2.1
PS-2	Position Categorization	A.8.1.1
PS-3	Personnel Screening	A.8.1.2
PS-4	Personnel Termination	A.8.3.1, A.8.3.2, A.8.3.3
PS-5	Personnel Transfer	A.8.3.1, A.8.3.2, A.8.3.3
PS-6	Access Agreements	A.6.1.5, A.8.1.1, A.8.1.3, A.8.2.1, A.9.1.5, A.10.8.1, A.11.7.1, A.11.7.2, A.15.1.5
PS-7	Third-Party Personnel Security	A.6.2.3, A.8.1.1, A.8.2.1, A.8.1.3
PS-8	Personnel Sanctions	A.8.2.3, A.15.1.5
RA-1	Risk Assessment Policy and Procedures	A.5.1.1, A.5.1.2, A.6.1.1, A.6.1.3, A.8.1.1, A.10.1.1, A.14.1.2, A.15.1.1, A.15.2.1
RA-2	Security Categorization	A.7.2.1, A.14.1.2
RA-3	Risk Assessment	A.6.2.1, A.10.2.3, A.12.6.1, A.14.1.2
RA-4	**Withdrawn**	---
RA-5	Vulnerability Scanning	A.12.6.1, A.15.2.2
SA-1	System and Services Acquisition Policy and Procedures	A.5.1.1, A.5.1.2, A.6.1.1, A.6.1.3, A.6.2.1, A.8.1.1, A.10.1.1, A.12.1.1, A.12.5.5, A.15.1.1, A.15.2.1
SA-2	Allocation of Resources	A.6.1.2, A.10.3.1

NIST SP 800-53 CONTROLS		ISO/IEC 27001 (Annex A) CONTROLS
SA-3	Life Cycle Support	A.12.1.1
SA-4	Acquisitions	A.12.1.1, A.12.5.5
SA-5	Information System Documentation	A.10.7.4, A.15.1.3
SA-6	Software Usage Restrictions	A.12.4.1, A.12.5.5, A.15.1.2
SA-7	User-Installed Software	A.12.4.1, A.12.5.5, A.15.1.5
SA-8	Security Engineering Principles	A.10.4.1, A.10.4.2, A.11.4.5, A.12.5.5
SA-9	External Information System Services	A.6.1.5, A.6.2.1, A.6.2.3, A.8.1.1, A.8.2.1, A.10.2.1, A.10.2.2, A.10.2.3, A.10.6.2, A.10.8.2, A.12.5.5
SA-10	Developer Configuration Management	A.12.4.3, A.12.5.1, A.12.5.5
SA-11	Developer Security Testing	A.10.3.2, A.12.5.5
SA-12	Supply Chain Protections	A.12.5.5
SA-13	Trustworthiness	A.12.5.5
SA-14	Critical Information System Components	None
SC-1	System and Communications Protection Policy and Procedures	A.5.1.1, A.5.1.2, A.6.1.1, A.6.1.3, A.8.1.1, A.10.1.1, A.15.1.1, A.15.2.1
SC-2	Application Partitioning	A.10.4.1, A.10.4.2
SC-3	Security Function Isolation	A.10.4.1, A.10.4.2, A.10.9.1, A.10.9.2
SC-4	Information In Shared Resources	None
SC-5	Denial of Service Protection	A.10.3.1
SC-6	Resource Priority	None
SC-7	Boundary Protection	A.6.2.1, A.10.4.1, A.10.4.2, A.10.6.1, A.10.8.1, A.10.9.1, A.10.9.2, A.10.10.2, A.11.4.5, A.11.4.6
SC-8	Transmission Integrity	A.10.4.2, A.10.6.1, A.10.6.2, A.10.9.1, A.10.9.2, A.12.2.3, A.12.3.1
SC-9	Transmission Confidentiality	A.10.6.1, A.10.6.2, A.10.9.1, A.10.9.2, A.12.3.1
SC-10	Network Disconnect	A.10.6.1, A.11.3.2, A.11.5.1, A.11.5.5
SC-11	Trusted Path	None
SC-12	Cryptographic Key Establishment and Management	A.12.3.2
SC-13	Use of Cryptography	A.12.3.1, A.15.1.6
SC-14	Public Access Protections	A.10.4.1, A.10.4.2, A.10.9.1, A.10.9.2, A.10.9.3
SC-15	Collaborative Computing Devices	None
SC-16	Transmission of Security Attributes	A.7.2.2, A.10.8.1
SC-17	Public Key Infrastructure Certificates	A.12.3.2
SC-18	Mobile Code	A.10.4.2
SC-19	Voice Over Internet Protocol	A.10.6.1
SC-20	Secure Name /Address Resolution Service (Authoritative Source)	A.10.6.1
SC-21	Secure Name /Address Resolution Service (Recursive or Caching Resolver)	A.10.6.1
SC-22	Architecture and Provisioning for Name/Address Resolution Service	A.10.6.1
SC-23	Session Authenticity	A.10.6.1
SC-24	Fail in Known State	None
SC-25	Thin Nodes	None
SC-26	Honeypots	None
SC-27	Operating System-Independent Applications	None
SC-28	Protection of Information at Rest	None
SC-29	Heterogeneity	None
SC-30	Virtualization Techniques	None
SC-31	Covert Channel Analysis	None
SC-32	Information System Partitioning	None
SC-33	Transmission Preparation Integrity	None
SC-34	Non-Modifiable Executable Programs	None
SI-1	System and Information Integrity Policy and Procedures	A.5.1.1, A.5.1.2, A.6.1.1, A.6.1.3, A.8.1.1, A.10.1.1, A.15.1.1, A.15.2.1
SI-2	Flaw Remediation	A.10.10.5, A.12.5.2, A.12.6.1, A.13.1.2
SI-3	Malicious Code Protection	A.10.4.1
SI-4	Information System Monitoring	A.10.10.2, A.13.1.1, A.13.1.2

NIST SP 800-53 CONTROLS		ISO/IEC 27001 (Annex A) CONTROLS
SI-5	Security Alerts, Advisories, and Directives	A.6.1.6, A.12.6.1, A.13.1.1, A.13.1.2
SI-6	Security Functionality Verification	None
SI-7	Software and Information Integrity	A.10.4.1, A.12.2.2, A.12.2.3
SI-8	Spam Protection	None
SI-9	Information Input Restrictions	A.10.8.1, A.11.1.1, A.11.2.2, A.12.2.2
SI-10	Information Input Validation	A.12.2.1, A.12.2.2
SI-11	Error Handling	None
SI-12	Information Output Handling and Retention	A.10.7.3, A.15.1.3, A.15.1.4, A.15.2.1
SI-13	Predictable Failure Prevention	None
PM-1	Information Security Program Plan	A.5.1.1, A.5.1.2, A.6.1.1, A.6.1.3 A.8.1.1, A.15.1.1, A.15.2.1
PM-2	Senior Information Security Officer	A.6.1.1, A.6.1.2, A.6.1.3
PM-3	Information Security Resources	None
PM-4	Plan of Action and Milestones Process	None
PM-5	Information System Inventory	A.7.1.1, A.7.1.2
PM-6	Information Security Measures of Performance	None
PM-7	Enterprise Architecture	None
PM-8	Critical Infrastructure Plan	None
PM-9	Risk Management Strategy	A.6.2.1, A.14.1.2
PM-10	Security Authorization Process	A.6.1.4
PM-11	Mission/Business Process Definition	None

TABLE H-2: MAPPING ISO/IEC 27001 (ANNEX A) TO NIST SP 800-53

ISO/IEC 27001 (Annex A) CONTROLS	NIST SP 800-53 CONTROLS
A.5 Security Policy	
A.5.1 Information security policy	
A.5.1.1 Information security policy document	XX-1 controls
A.5.1.2 Review of the information security policy	XX-1 controls
A.6 Organization of information security	
A.6.1 Internal	
A.6.1.1 Management commitment to information security	XX-1 controls, PM-2; SP 800-39, SP 800-37
A.6.1.2 Information security coordination	CP-2, CP-4, IR-4, PL-1, PL-6, PM-2, SA-2; SP 800-39, SP 800-37
A.6.1.3 Allocation of information security responsibilities	XX-1 controls, AC-5, AC-6, CM-9. PM-2; SP 800-39, SP 800-37
A.6.1.4 Authorization process for information processing facilities	CA-1, CA-6, PM-10; SP 800-37
A.6.1.5 Confidentiality agreements	PL-4, PS-6, SA-9
A.6.1.6 Contact with authorities	Multiple controls with contact reference (e.g., IR-6, SI-5); SP 800-39; SP 800-37
A.6.1.7 Contact with special interest groups	AT-5
A.6.1.8 Independent review of information security	CA-2, CA-7; SP 800-39, SP 800-37
A.6.2 External Parties	
A.6.2.1 Identification of risks related to external parties	CA-3, PM-9, RA-3, SA-1, SA-9, SC-7
A.6.2.2 Addressing security when dealing with customers	AC-8 , AT-2, PL-4
A.6.2.3 Addressing security in third party agreements	CA-3, PS-7, SA-9
A.7 Asset Management	
A.7.1 Responsibility for assets	
A.7.1.1 Inventory of assets	CM-8, CM-9, PM-5
A.7.1.2 Ownership of assets	CM-8, CM-9, PM-5
A.7.1.3 Acceptable use of assets	AC-20, PL-4
A.7.2 Information Classification	
A.7.2.1 Classification Guidelines	RA-2
A.7.2.2 Information labeling and handling	AC-16, MP-2, MP-3, SC-16
A.8 Human Resources Security	
A.8.1 Prior to Employment	
A.8.1.1 Roles and Responsibilities	XX-1 controls, AC-5, AC-6, AC-8, AC-20, AT-2, AT-3, CM-9, PL-4, PS-2, PS-6, PS-7, SA-9
A.8.1.2 Screening	PS-3
A.8.1.3 Terms and conditions of employment	AC-20, PL-4, PS-6, PS-7
A.8.2 During employment	
A.8.2.1 Management responsibilities	PL-4, PS-6, PS-7, SA-9
A.8.2.2 Awareness, education, and training	AT-2, AT-3, IR-2
A.8.2.3 Disciplinary process	PS-8
A.8.3 Termination or change of employment	
A.8.3.1 Termination responsibilities	PS-4, PS-5
A.8.3.2 Return of assets	PS-4, PS-5
A.8.3.3 Removal of access rights	AC-2, PS-4, PS-5
A.9 Physical and environmental security	
A.9.1 Secure areas	
A.9.1.1 Physical security perimeter	PE-3
A.9.1.2 Physical entry controls	PE-3, PE-5, PE-6, PE-7
A.9.1.3 Securing offices, rooms, facilities	PE-3, PE-4, PE-5
A.9.1.4 Protecting against external and environmental threats	CP Family; PE-1, PE-9, PE-10, PE-11, PE-13, PE-15
A.9.1.5 Working in secure areas	AT-2, AT-3 , PL-4, PS-6, PE-2, PE-3, PE-4, PE-6, PE-7, PE-8
A.9.1.6 Public access, delivery and loading areas	PE-3 , PE-7, PE-16
A.9.2 Equipment security	
A.9.2.1 Equipment siting and protection	PE-1, PE-18
A.9.2.2 Supporting utilities	PE-1, PE-9, PE-11, PE-12, PE-14
A.9.2.3 Cabling security	PE-4, PE-9
A.9.2.4 Equipment maintenance	MA Family

ISO/IEC 27001 (Annex A) CONTROLS	NIST SP 800-53 CONTROLS
A.9.2.5 Security of equipment off-premises	MP-5, PE-17
A.9.2.6 Secure disposal or reuse of equipment	MP-6
A.9.2.7 Removal of property	MP-5, PE-16
A.10 Communications and operations management	
A.10.1 Operational procedures and responsibilities	
A.10.1.1 Documented operating procedures	XX-1 controls, CM-9
A.10.1.2 Change management	CM-1, CM-3, CM-4, CM-5, CM-9
A.10.1.3 Segregation of duties	AC-5
A.10.1.4 Separation of development, test and operational facilities	CM-2
A.10.2 Third-party service delivery management	
A.10.2.1 Service delivery	SA-9
A.10.2.2 Monitoring and review of third-party services	SA-9
A.10.2.3 Managing changes to third-party services	RA-3, SA-9
A.10.3 System planning and acceptance	
A.10.3.1 Capacity management	AU-4, AU-5, CP-2, SA-2, SC-5
A.10.3.2 System acceptance	CA-2, CA-6, CM-3, CM-4, CM-9, SA-11
A.10.4 Protection against malicious and mobile code	
A.10.4.1 Controls against malicious code	AC-19, AT-2, SA-8, SC-2, SC-3, SC-7, SC-14, SI-3, SI-7
A.10.4.2 Controls against mobile code	SA-8, SC-2, SC-3, SC-7, SC-14, SC-8, SC-18
A.10.5 Backup	
A.10.5.1 Information backup	CP-9
A.10.6 Network security management	
A.10.6.1 Network controls	AC-4, AC-17, AC-18, AC-20, CA-3, CP-8, PE-5, SC-7, SC-8, SC-9, SC-10, SC-19, SC-20, SC-21, SC-22, SC-23
A.10.6.2 Security of network services	SA-9, SC-8, SC-9
A.10.7 Media handling	
A.10.7.1 Management of removable media	MP Family, PE-16
A.10.7.2 Disposal of media	MP-6
A.10.7.3 Information handling procedures	MP Family, SI-12
A.10.7.4 Security of system documentation	MP-4, SA-5
A.10.8 Exchange of information	
A.10.8.1 Information exchange policies and procedures	AC-1, AC-3, AC-4, AC-17, AC-18, AC-20, CA-3, PL-4, PS-6, SC-7, SC-16, SI-9
A.10.8.2 Exchange agreements	CA-3, SA-9
A.10.8.3 Physical media in transit	MP-5
A.10.8.4 Electronic messaging	Multiple controls; electronic messaging not addressed separately in SP 800-53
A.10.8.5 Business information systems	CA-1, CA-3
A.10.9 Electronic commerce services	
A.10.9.1 Electronic commerce	AU-10, IA-8, SC-7, SC-8, SC-9, SC-3, SC-14
A.10.9.2 Online transactions	SC-3, SC-7, SC-8, SC-9, SC-14
A.10.9.3 Publicly available information	SC-14
A.10.10 Monitoring	
A.10.10.1 Audit logging	AU-1, AU-2, AU-3, AU-4, AU-5, AU-8, AU-11, AU-12
A.10.10.2 Monitoring system use	AU-1, AU-6, AU-7, PE-6, PE-8, SC-7, SI-4
A.10.10.3 Protection of log information	AU-9
A.10.10.4 Administrator and operator logs	AU-2, AU-12
A.10.10.5 Fault logging	AU-2, AU-6, AU-12, SI-2
A.10.10.6 Clock synchronization	AU-8
A.11 Access Control	
A.11.1 Business requirement for access control	
A.11.1.1 Access control policy	AC-1, AC-5, AC-6, AC-17, AC-18, AC-19, CM-5, MP-1, SI-9
A.11.2 User access management	
A.11.2.1 User registration	AC-1, AC-2, AC-21, IA-5, PE-1, PE-2
A.11.2.2 Privilege management	AC-1, AC-2, AC-6, AC-21, PE-1, PE-2, SI-9
A.11.2.3 User password management	IA-5

ISO/IEC 27001 (Annex A) CONTROLS	NIST SP 800-53 CONTROLS
A.11.2.4 Review of user access rights	AC-2, PE-2
A 11.3 User responsibilities	
A.11.3.1 Password use	IA-2, IA-5
A.11.3.2 Unattended user equipment	AC-11, IA-2, PE-3, PE-5, PE-18, SC-10
A.11.3.3 Clear desk and clear screen policy	AC-11
A.11.4 Network access control	
A.11.4.1 Policy on use of network services	AC-1, AC-5, AC-6, AC-17, AC-18, AC-20
A.11.4.2 User authentication for external connections	AC-17, AC-18, AC-20, CA-3, IA-2, IA-8
A.11.4.3 Equipment identification in networks	AC-19, IA-3
A.11.4.4 Remote diagnostic and configuration port protection	AC-3, AC-6, AC-17, AC-18, PE-3, MA-3, MA-4
A.11.4.5 Segregation in networks	AC-4, SA-8, SC-7
A.11.4.6 Network connection control	AC-3, AC-6, AC-17, AC-18, SC-7
A.11.4.7 Network routing control	AC-4, AC-17, AC-18
A 11.5 Operating system access control	
A.11.5.1 Secure log-on procedures	AC-7, AC-8, AC-9, AC-10, IA-2, IA-6, IA-8, SC-10
A.11.5.2 User identification and authentication	IA-2, IA-4, IA-5, IA-8
A.11.5.3 Password management system	IA-2, IA-5
A.11.5.4 Use of system utilities	AC-3, AC-6
A.11.5.5 Session time-out	AC-11, SC-10
A.11.5.6 Limitation of connection time	None
A.11.6 Application and information access control	
A.11.6.1 Information access restriction	AC-3, AC-6, AC-14, CM-5
A.11.6.2 Sensitive system isolation	None; SP 800-39
A.11.7 Mobile computing and teleworking	
A.11.7.1 Mobile computing and communications	AC-1, AC-17, AC-18, AC-19, PL-4, PS-6
A.11.7.2 Teleworking	AC-1, AC-4, AC-17, AC-18, PE-17, PL-4, PS-6
A.12 Information systems acquisition, development and maintenance	
A.12.1 Security requirements of information systems	
A.12.1.1 Security requirements analysis and specification	SA-1, SA-3, SA-4
A.12.2 Correct processing in applications	
A.12.2.1 Input data validation	SI-10
A.12.2.2 Control of internal processing	SI-7, SI-9, SI-10
A.12.2.3 Message integrity	AU-10, SC-8, SI-7
A.12.2.4 Output data validation	None
A.12.3 Cryptographic controls	
A.12.3.1 Policy on the use of cryptographic controls	Multiple controls address cryptography (e.g., IA-7, SC-8, SC-9, SC-12, SC-13)
A.12.3.2 Key management	SC-12, SC-17
A.12.4 Security of system files	
A.12.4.1 Control of operational software	CM-1, CM-2, CM-3, CM-4, CM-5, CM-9, PL-4, SA-6, SA-7
A.12.4.2 Protection of system test data	Multiple controls; protection of test data not addressed separately in SP 800-53 (e.g., AC-3, AC-4)
A.12.4.3 Access control to program source code	AC-3, AC-6, CM-5, CM-9, MA-5, SA-10
A.12.5 Security in development and support processes	
A.12.5.1 Change control procedures	CM-1, CM-3, CM-9, SA-10
A.12.5.2 Technical review of applications after operating system changes	CM-3, CM-4, CM-9, SI-2
A.12.5.3 Restrictions on changes to software packages	CM-3, CM-4, CM-5, CM-9
A.12.5.4 Information leakage	AC-4, PE-19
A.12.5.5 Outsourced software development	SA-1, SA-4, SA-6, SA-7, SA-8, SA-9, SA-11, SA-12, SA-13
A.12.6 Technical Vulnerability Management	
A.12.6.1 Control of technical vulnerabilities	RA-3, RA-5, SI-2, SI-5
A.13 Information security incident management	
A.13.1 Reporting information security events and weaknesses	
A.13.1.1 Reporting information security events	AU-6, IR-1, IR-6, SI-4, SI-5

ISO/IEC 27001 (Annex A) CONTROLS	NIST SP 800-53 CONTROLS
A.13.1.2 Reporting security weaknesses	PL-4, SI-2, SI-4, SI-5
A.13.2 Management of information security incidents and improvements	
A.13.2.1 Responsibilities and procedures	IR-1
A.13.2.2 Learning from information security incidents	IR-4
A.13.2.3 Collection of evidence	AU-9, IR-4
A.14 Business continuity management	
A.14.1 Information security aspects of business continuity management	
A.14.1.1 Including information security in the business continuity management process	CP-1, CP-2, CP-4
A.14.1.2 Business continuity and risk assessment	CP-2, PM-9, RA Family
A.14.1.3 Developing and implementing continuity plans including information security	CP Family
A.14.1.4 Business continuity planning framework	CP-2, CP-4
A.14.1.5 Testing, maintaining and reassessing business continuity plans	CP-2, CP-4
A.15 Compliance	
A.15.1 Compliance with legal requirements	
A.15.1.1 Identification of applicable legislation	XX-1 controls, IA-7
A.15.1.2 Intellectual property rights (IPR)	SA-6
A.15.1.3 Protection of organizational records	AU-9, AU-11, CP-9, MP-1, MP-4, SA-5, SI-12
A.15.1.4 Data protection and privacy of personal information	PL-5; SI-12
A.15.1.5 Prevention of misuse of information processing facilities	AC-8, AU-6, PL-4, PS-6, PS-8, SA-7
A.15.1.6 Regulation of cryptographic controls	IA-7, SC-13
A.15.2 Compliance with security policies and standards, and technical compliance	
A.15.2.1 Compliance with security policies and standards	XX-1 controls, AC-2, CA-2, CA-7, IA-7, PE-8, SI-12
A.15.2.2 Technical compliance checking	CA-2, CA-7, RA-5
A.15.3 Information systems audit considerations	
A.15.3.1 Information systems audit controls	AU-1, AU-2, PL-6
A.15.3.2 Protection of information systems audit tools	AU-9

APPENDIX I

INDUSTRIAL CONTROL SYSTEMS
SECURITY CONTROLS, ENHANCEMENTS, AND SUPPLEMENTAL GUIDANCE

Industrial control systems (ICS)[78] are information systems that differ significantly from traditional administrative, mission support, and scientific data processing information systems. ICS typically have many unique characteristics—including a need for real-time response and extremely high availability, predictability, and reliability. These types of specialized systems are pervasive throughout the critical infrastructure, often being required to meet several and often conflicting safety, operational, performance, reliability, and security requirements such as: (i) minimizing risk to the health and safety of the public; (ii) preventing serious damage to the environment; (iii) preventing serious production stoppages or slowdowns that result in negative impact to the Nation's economy and ability to carry out critical functions; (iv) protecting the critical infrastructure from cyber attacks and common human error; and (v) safeguarding against the compromise of proprietary information.[79]

Previously, ICS had little resemblance to traditional information systems in that they were isolated systems running proprietary software and control protocols. However, as these systems have been increasingly integrated more closely into mainstream organizational information systems to promote connectivity, efficiency, and remote access capabilities, portions of these ICS have started to resemble the more traditional information systems. Increasingly, ICS use the same commercially available hardware and software components as are used in the organization's traditional information systems. While the change in ICS architecture supports new information system capabilities, it also provides significantly less isolation from the outside world for these systems, introducing many of the same vulnerabilities that exist in current networked information systems. The result is an even greater need to secure ICS.

FIPS 200, supported by NIST Special Publication 800-53, requires that federal agencies (and organizations subordinate to those agencies) implement minimum security controls for their organizational information systems based on the FIPS 199 security categorization of those systems. This includes implementing the baseline security controls described in this document in ICS that are operated by or on behalf of federal agencies. Section 3.3, *Tailoring the Initial Baseline*, allows organizations[80] to modify or adjust recommended security control baselines when certain conditions exist that require that flexibility. NIST recommends that ICS owners take advantage of the ability to tailor the initial baselines applying the ICS-specific guidance in this appendix. This appendix also contains additions to the initial security control baselines that have been determined to be generally required for ICS.

---

[78] An ICS is an information system used to control industrial processes such as manufacturing, product handling, production, and distribution. Industrial control systems include supervisory control and data acquisition (SCADA) systems, distributed control systems (DCS), and programmable logic controllers (PLC). ICS are typically found in the electric, water, oil and gas, chemical, pharmaceutical, pulp and paper, food and beverage, and discrete manufacturing (automotive, aerospace, and durable goods) industries as well as in air and rail transportation control systems.

[79] See Executive Order 13231 on Critical Infrastructure Protection, October 16, 2001.

[80] NIST Special Publication 800-53 employs the term *organization* to refer to the owner or operator of an information system. In this Appendix, organization may refer to the owner or operator of an ICS.

NIST has worked cooperatively with ICS communities in the public and private sectors to develop specific guidance on the application of the security controls in this document to ICS. That guidance, contained in this Appendix, includes ICS-specific:

- Tailoring guidance;

- Supplements to the security control baselines; and

- Supplemental guidance.

ICS Tailoring Guidance

Tailoring guidance for ICS can include scoping guidance and the application of compensating security controls. Due to the unique characteristics of ICS, these systems may require a greater use of compensating security controls than is the case for general-purpose information systems.

Implementation Tip

In situations where the ICS cannot support, or the organization determines it is not advisable to implement particular security controls or control enhancements in an ICS (e.g., performance, safety, or reliability are adversely impacted), the organization provides a complete and convincing rationale for how the selected compensating controls provide an equivalent security capability or level of protection for the ICS and why the related baseline security controls could not be employed.

In accordance with the Technology-related Considerations of the Scoping Guidance in Section 3.3, if automated mechanisms are not readily available, cost-effective, or technically feasible in the ICS, compensating security controls, implemented through nonautomated mechanisms or procedures are employed.

Compensating controls are not exceptions or waivers to the baseline controls; rather, they are alternative safeguards and countermeasures employed within the ICS that accomplish the intent of the original security controls that could not be effectively employed. Organizational decisions on the use of compensating controls are documented in the security plan for the ICS.

The security controls and control enhancements listed in Table I-1 are likely candidates for tailoring with the applicability of scoping guidance indicated for each control/enhancement. In Table I-1, the citation of a control without enhancements (e.g., AC-17) refers only to the base control without any enhancements, while reference to an enhancement by a parenthetical number following the control identification (e.g., AC-17(1)) refers only to the specific control enhancement.

TABLE I-1: SECURITY CONTROL CANDIDATES FOR TAILORING

CONTROL NUMBER	CONTROL NAME	TAILORING OPTIONS	
		SCOPING GUIDANCE	COMPENSATING CONTROLS
AC-2	Account Management	NO	YES
AC-5	Separation of Duties	NO	YES
AC-6	Least Privilege	NO	YES
AC-7	Unsuccessful Login Attempts	NO	YES
AC-8	System Use Notification	NO	YES
AC-10	Concurrent Session Control	NO	YES
AC-11	Session Lock	NO	YES
AC-17	Remote Access	NO	YES
AC-17 (2)	Remote Access	NO	YES
AC-18 (1)	Wireless Access	NO	YES
AC-19	Access Control for Mobile Devices	NO	YES
AU-2	Auditable Events	NO	YES
AU-5	Response to Audit Processing Failure	YES	YES
AU-7	Audit Reduction and Report Generation	YES	YES
AU-12	Audit Generation	NO	YES
AU-12 (1)	Audit Generation	NO	YES
CA-2	Security Assessments	NO	YES
CP-4	Contingency Plan Testing and Exercises	NO	YES
CP-4 (1)	Contingency Plan Testing and Exercises	NO	YES
CP-4 (2)	Contingency Plan Testing and Exercises	NO	YES
CP-4 (4)	Contingency Plan Testing and Exercises	NO	YES
CP-7	Alternate Processing Site	NO	YES
IA-2	User Identification and Authentication (Organizational Users)	NO	YES
IA-3	Device Identification and Authentication	NO	YES
MA-4 (3)	Non-Local Maintenance	YES	YES
MP-5 (4)	Media Transport	YES	YES
PE-6 (2)	Monitoring Physical Access	YES	YES
RA-5	Vulnerability Scanning	NO	YES
SC-2	Application Partitioning	YES	YES
SC-3	Security Function Isolation	NO	YES
SC-7 (6)	Boundary Protection	YES	NO
SC-7 (8)	Boundary Protection	YES	YES
SC-10	Network Disconnect	NO	YES
SI-2 (1)	Flaw Remediation	YES	YES
SI-3 (1)	Malicious Code Protection	YES	YES
SI-8 (1)	Spam Protection	YES	YES

ICS Supplements to the Security Control Baselines

The following table lists the recommended ICS supplements (highlighted in **bold** text) to the security control baselines in Appendix D.

TABLE I-2: ICS SUPPLEMENTS TO SECURITY CONTROL BASELINES

CNTL NO.	CONTROL NAME	CONTROL BASELINES		
		LOW	MOD	HIGH
Access Control				
AC-3	Access Enforcement	AC-3	AC-3 **(2)**	AC-3 **(2)**
Physical and Environmental Protection				
PE-9	Power Equipment and Power Cabling	Not Selected	PE-9 **(1)**	PE-9 **(1)**
PE-11	Emergency Power	**PE-11**	PE-11 **(1)**	PE-11 (1) **(2)**
System and Communications Protection				
SC-24	Fail in Known State	Not Selected	**SC-24**	SC-24
System and Information Integrity				
SI-13	Predictable Failure Prevention	Not Selected	Not Selected	**SI-13**

In addition to the security controls added for ICS in the table above, the security control supplement process described in Section 3.4 is still applicable to ICS. Organizations are required to conduct a risk assessment taking into account the tailoring and supplementing performed in arriving at the agreed-upon set of security controls for the ICS and the risk to the organization's operations and assets, individuals, other organizations, and the Nation being incurred by operation of the ICS with the intended controls. The organization decides whether that risk is acceptable, and if not, supplements the control set with additional controls until an acceptable level of risk is obtained.

ICS Supplemental Guidance

ICS Supplemental Guidance provides organizations with additional information on the application of the security controls and control enhancements in Appendix F to ICS and the environments in which these specialized systems operate. The Supplemental Guidance also provides information as to why a particular security control or control enhancement may not be applicable in some ICS environments and may be a candidate for tailoring (i.e., the application of scoping guidance and/or compensating controls). ICS Supplemental Guidance does not replace the original Supplemental Guidance in Appendix F.

ACCESS CONTROL

AC-2   ACCOUNT MANAGEMENT

ICS Supplemental Guidance: In situations where physical access to the ICS (e.g., workstations, hardware components, field devices) predefines account privileges or where the ICS (e.g., certain remote terminal units, meters, relays) cannot support account management, the organization employs appropriate compensating controls (e.g., providing increased physical security, personnel security, intrusion detection, auditing measures) in accordance with the general tailoring guidance.

Control Enhancement: (1)

ICS Enhancement Supplemental Guidance: In situations where the ICS (e.g., field devices) cannot support the use of automated mechanisms for the management of information system accounts, the organization employs nonautomated mechanisms or procedures as compensating controls in accordance with the general tailoring guidance.

AC-3   ACCESS ENFORCEMENT

ICS Supplemental Guidance: The organization ensures that access enforcement mechanisms do not adversely impact the operational performance of the ICS.

References: NIST Special Publication 800-82.

AC-5   SEPARATION OF DUTIES

ICS Supplemental Guidance: In situations where the ICS cannot support the differentiation of roles, the organization employs appropriate compensating controls (e.g., providing increased personnel security and auditing) in accordance with the general tailoring guidance. The organization carefully considers the appropriateness of a single individual performing multiple critical roles.

AC-6   LEAST PRIVILEGE

ICS Supplemental Guidance: In situations where the ICS cannot support differentiation of privileges, the organization employs appropriate compensating controls (e.g., providing increased personnel security and auditing) in accordance with the general tailoring guidance. The organization carefully considers the appropriateness of a single individual having multiple critical privileges.

AC-7   UNSUCCESSFUL LOGIN ATTEMPTS

ICS Supplemental Guidance: In situations where the ICS cannot support account/node locking or delayed login attempts, or the ICS cannot perform account/node locking or delayed logins due to significant adverse impact on performance, safety, or reliability, the organization employs appropriate compensating controls (e.g., logging or recording all unsuccessful login attempts and alerting ICS security personnel though alarms or other means when the number of organization-defined consecutive invalid access attempts is exceeded) in accordance with the general tailoring guidance.

AC-8   SYSTEM USE NOTIFICATION

ICS Supplemental Guidance: In situations where the ICS cannot support system use notification, the organization employs appropriate compensating controls (e.g., posting physical notices in ICS facilities) in accordance with the general tailoring guidance.

AC-10   CONCURRENT SESSION CONTROL

ICS Supplemental Guidance: In situations where the ICS cannot support concurrent session control, the organization employs appropriate compensating controls (e.g., providing increased auditing measures) in accordance with the general tailoring guidance.

AC-11   SESSION LOCK

ICS Supplemental Guidance: The ICS employs session lock to prevent access to specified workstations/nodes. The ICS activates session lock mechanisms automatically after an organization-defined time period for designated workstations/nodes on the ICS. In some cases, session lock for ICS operator workstations/nodes is not advised (e.g., when immediate operator responses are required in emergency situations). Session lock is not a substitute for logging out of the ICS. In situations where the ICS cannot support session lock, the organization employs appropriate compensating controls (e.g., providing increased physical security, personnel security, and auditing measures) in accordance with the general tailoring guidance.

References: NIST Special Publication 800-82.

AC-17   REMOTE ACCESS

ICS Supplemental Guidance: In situations where the ICS cannot implement any or all of the components of this control, the organization employs other mechanisms or procedures as compensating controls in accordance with the general tailoring guidance.

Control Enhancement: (1)

ICS Enhancement Supplemental Guidance: In situations where the ICS cannot support the use of automated mechanisms for monitoring and control of remote access methods, the organization employs nonautomated mechanisms or procedures as compensating controls (e.g., following manual authentication [see IA-2 in this appendix], dial-in remote access may be enabled for a specified period of time or a call may be placed from the ICS site to the authenticated remote entity) in accordance with the general tailoring guidance.

Control Enhancement: (2)

ICS Enhancement Supplemental Guidance: ICS security objectives typically follow the priority of availability, integrity and confidentiality, in that order. The use of cryptography is determined after careful consideration of the security needs and the potential ramifications on system performance. For example, the organization considers whether latency induced from the use of cryptography would adversely impact the operational performance of the ICS. The organization explores all possible cryptographic mechanism (e.g., encryption, digital signature, hash function). Each mechanism has a different delay impact. In situations where the ICS cannot support the use of cryptographic mechanisms to protect the confidentiality and integrity of remote sessions, or the components cannot use cryptographic mechanisms due to significant adverse impact on safety, performance, or reliability, the organization employs appropriate compensating controls (e.g., providing increased auditing for remote sessions or limiting remote access privileges to key personnel) in accordance with the general tailoring guidance.

References: NIST Special Publication 800-82.

AC-18   WIRELESS ACCESS

ICS Supplemental Guidance: In situations where the ICS cannot implement any or all of the components of this control, the organization employs other mechanisms or procedures as compensating controls in accordance with the general tailoring guidance.

Control Enhancement: (1)

ICS Enhancement Supplemental Guidance: ICS security objectives typically follow the priority of availability, integrity, and confidentiality, in that order. The use of cryptography is determined after careful consideration of the security needs and the potential ramifications on system performance. For example, the organization considers whether latency induced from the use of cryptography would adversely impact the operational performance of the ICS. The organization explores all possible cryptographic mechanism (e.g., encryption, digital signature, hash function). Each mechanism has a different delay impact. In situations where the ICS cannot support the use of cryptographic mechanisms to protect the confidentiality and integrity of wireless access, or the components cannot use cryptographic mechanisms due to significant adverse impact on safety, performance, or reliability, the organization employs appropriate compensating controls (e.g., providing increased auditing for wireless access or limiting wireless access privileges to key personnel) in accordance with the general tailoring guidance.

References: NIST Special Publication 800-82.

AC-19   ACCESS CONTROL FOR MOBILE DEVICES

ICS Supplemental Guidance: In situations where the ICS cannot implement any or all of the components of this control, the organization employs other mechanisms or procedures as compensating controls in accordance with the general tailoring guidance.

AC-22   PUBLICLY ACCESSIBLE CONTENT

ICS Supplemental Guidance: Generally, public access to ICS information is not permitted.

AWARENESS AND TRAINING

AT-2   SECURITY AWARENESS

ICS Supplemental Guidance: Security awareness training includes initial and periodic review of ICS-specific policies, standard operating procedures, security trends, and vulnerabilities. The ICS security awareness program is consistent with the requirements of the security awareness and training policy established by the organization.

AT-3   SECURITY TRAINING

ICS Supplemental Guidance: Security training includes initial and periodic review of ICS-specific policies, standard operating procedures, security trends, and vulnerabilities. The ICS security training program is consistent with the requirements of the security awareness and training policy established by the organization.

AUDITING AND ACCOUNTABILITY

AU-2   AUDITABLE EVENTS

ICS Supplemental Guidance: Most ICS auditing occurs at the application level.

AU-5   RESPONSE TO AUDIT PROCESSING FAILURES

ICS Supplemental Guidance: In general, audit record processing is not performed on the ICS, but on a separate information system. In situations where the ICS cannot support auditing, including response to audit failures, the organization employs compensating controls (e.g., providing an auditing capability on a separate information system) in accordance with the general tailoring guidance.

AU-7   AUDIT REDUCTION AND REPORT GENERATION

ICS Supplemental Guidance: In general, audit reduction and report generation is not performed on the ICS, but on a separate information system. In situations where the ICS cannot support auditing including audit reduction and report generation, the organization employs compensating controls (e.g., providing an auditing capability on a separate information system) in accordance with the general tailoring guidance.

AU-12   AUDIT GENERATION

ICS Supplemental Guidance: In situations where the ICS cannot support the use of automated mechanisms to generate audit records, the organization employs nonautomated mechanisms or procedures as compensating controls in accordance with the general tailoring guidance.

Control Enhancement: (1)

ICS Enhancement Supplemental Guidance: In situations where the ICS cannot support the use of automated mechanisms to generate audit records, the organization employs nonautomated mechanisms or procedures as compensating controls in accordance with the general tailoring guidance.

SECURITY ASSESSMENT AND AUTHORIZATION

CA-2   SECURITY ASSESSMENTS

ICS Supplemental Guidance: Assessments are performed and documented by qualified assessors (i.e., experienced in assessing ICS) authorized by the organization. The organization ensures that assessments do not interfere with ICS functions. The individual/group conducting the assessment fully understands the organizational information security policies and procedures, the ICS security policies and procedures, and the specific health, safety, and environmental risks associated with a particular facility and/or process. A production ICS may need to be taken off-line, or replicated to the extent feasible, before an assessment can be conducted. If an ICS must be taken off-line to conduct an assessment, the assessment is scheduled to occur during planned ICS outages whenever possible. In situations where the organization cannot, for operational reasons, conduct a live assessment of a production ICS, the organization employs compensating controls (e.g., providing a replicated system to conduct the assessment) in accordance with the general tailoring guidance.

CA-7   CONTINUOUS MONITORING

ICS Supplemental Guidance: Assessments are performed and documented by qualified assessors (i.e., experienced in assessing ICS) authorized by the organization. The organization ensures that assessments do not interfere with ICS functions. The individual/group conducting the assessment fully understands the organizational information security policies and procedures, the ICS security policies and procedures, and the specific health, safety, and environmental risks associated with a particular facility and/or process. Ongoing assessments of ICS may not be feasible. See CA-2 ICS Supplemental Guidance in this appendix.

CONFIGURATION MANAGEMENT

CM-3   CONFIGURATION CHANGE CONTROL

Control Enhancement: (1)

ICS Enhancement Supplemental Guidance: In situations where the ICS cannot support the use of automated mechanisms to implement configuration change control, the organization employs nonautomated mechanisms or procedures as compensating controls in accordance with the general tailoring guidance.

CM-4   SECURITY IMPACT ANALYSIS

ICS Supplemental Guidance: The organization considers ICS safety and security interdependencies.

CM-5   ACCESS RESTRICTIONS FOR CHANGE

Control Enhancement: (1)

ICS Enhancement Supplemental Guidance: In situations where the ICS cannot support the use of automated mechanisms to enforce access restrictions and support auditing of enforcement actions, the organization employs nonautomated mechanisms or procedures as compensating controls in accordance with the general tailoring guidance.

Control Enhancement: (3)

ICS Enhancement Supplemental Guidance: In situations where the ICS cannot prevent the installation of software programs that are not signed with an organizationally-recognized and approved certificate, the organization employs alternative mechanisms or procedures as compensating controls (e.g., auditing of software installation) in accordance with the general tailoring guidance.

CM-6   CONFIGURATION SETTINGS

Control Enhancement: (1)

ICS Enhancement Supplemental Guidance: In situations where the ICS cannot support the use of automated mechanisms to centrally manage, apply, and verify configuration settings, the organization employs nonautomated mechanisms or procedures as compensating controls in accordance with the general tailoring guidance.

CM-7   LEAST FUNCTIONALITY

Control Enhancement: (2)

ICS Enhancement Supplemental Guidance: In situations where the ICS cannot employ automated mechanisms to prevent program execution, the organization employs compensating controls (e.g., external automated mechanisms, procedures) in accordance with the general tailoring guidance.

CONTINGENCY PLANNING

CP-2   CONTINGENCY PLAN

ICS Supplemental Guidance: The organization defines contingency plans for categories of disruptions or failures. In the event of a loss of processing within the ICS or communication with operational facilities, the ICS executes predetermined procedures (e.g., alert the operator of the failure and then do nothing, alert the operator and then safely shut down the industrial process, alert the operator and then maintain the last operational setting prior to failure). Consideration is given to restoring system state variables as part of restoration (e.g., valves are restored to their original settings prior to the disruption).

References: NIST Special Publication 800-82.

CP-4   CONTINGENCY PLAN TESTING AND EXERCISES

ICS Supplemental Guidance: In situations where the organization cannot test or exercise the contingency plan on production ICS due to significant adverse impact on performance, safety, or reliability, the organization employs appropriate compensating controls (e.g., using scheduled and unscheduled system maintenance activities including responding to ICS component and system failures, as an opportunity to test or exercise the contingency plan) in accordance with the general tailoring guidance.

CP-10   INFORMATION SYSTEM RECOVERY AND RECONSTITUTION

ICS Supplemental Guidance: Reconstitution of the ICS includes restoration of system state variables (e.g., valves are restored to their appropriate settings as part of the reconstitution).

IDENTIFICATION AND AUTHENTICATION

IA-2   USER IDENTIFICATION AND AUTHENTICATION (ORGANIZATIONAL USERS)

ICS Supplemental Guidance: Where users function as a single group (e.g., control room operators), user identification and authentication may be role-based, group-based, or device-based. For certain ICS, the capability for immediate operator interaction is critical. Local emergency actions for ICS are not hampered by identification or authentication requirements. Access to these systems may be restricted by appropriate physical security controls. In situations where the ICS cannot support user identification and authentication, or the organization determines it is not advisable to perform user identification and authentication due to significant adverse impact on performance, safety, or reliability, the organization employs appropriate compensating controls (e.g., providing increased physical security, personnel security, and auditing measures) in accordance with the general tailoring guidance. For example, manual voice authentication of remote personnel and local, manual actions may be required in order to establish a remote access. See AC-17 ICS Supplemental Guidance in this appendix. Local user access to ICS components is enabled only when necessary, approved, and authenticated.

Control Enhancements: (1) (2) (3)

ICS Enhancement Supplemental Guidance: In situations where the ICS cannot support multifactor authentication, the organization employs compensating controls in accordance with the general tailoring guidance (e.g., implementing physical security measures).

IA-3   DEVICE IDENTIFICATION AND AUTHENTICATION

ICS Supplemental Guidance: In situations where the ICS cannot support device identification and authentication (e.g., serial devices), the organization employs compensating controls (e.g., implementing physical security measures) in accordance with the general tailoring guidance.

IA-4   IDENTIFIER MANAGEMENT

ICS Supplemental Guidance: Where users function as a single group (e.g., control room operators), user identification may be role-based, group-based, or device-based.

References: NIST Special Publication 800-82.

IA-5   AUTHENTICATOR MANAGEMENT

References: NIST Special Publication 800-82.

IA-7   CRYPTOGRAPHIC MODULE AUTHENTICATION

ICS Supplemental Guidance: The use of cryptography is determined after careful consideration of the security needs and the potential ramifications on system performance. For example, the organization considers whether latency induced from the use of cryptography would adversely impact the operational performance of the ICS.

INCIDENT RESPONSE

IR-6   INCIDENT REPORTING

ICS Supplemental Guidance: The United States Computer Emergency Readiness Team (US-CERT) maintains the ICS Security Center at http://www.uscert.gov/control_systems.

References: NIST Special Publication 800-82.

MAINTENANCE

MA-4   NON-LOCAL MAINTENANCE

Control Enhancement: (3)

ICS Enhancement Supplemental Guidance: In crisis or emergency situations, the organization may need immediate access to non-local maintenance and diagnostic services in order to restore essential ICS operations or services. In situations where the organization may not have access to non-local maintenance or diagnostic service at the required level of security, the organization employs appropriate compensating controls (e.g., limiting the extent of the maintenance and diagnostic services to the minimum essential activities, carefully monitoring and auditing the non-local maintenance and diagnostic activities) in accordance with the general tailoring guidance.

MEDIA PROTECTION

MP-5   MEDIA TRANSPORT

Control Enhancement: (4)

ICS Enhancement Supplemental Guidance: In situations where the ICS cannot support cryptographic mechanisms, the organization employs compensating controls in accordance with the general tailoring guidance (e.g., implementing physical security measures).

PHYSICAL AND ENVIRONMENTAL PROTECTION

PE-3   PHYSICAL ACCESS CONTROL

ICS Supplemental Guidance: The organization considers ICS safety and security interdependencies. The organization considers access requirements in emergency situations. During an emergency-related event, the organization may restrict access to ICS facilities and assets to authorized individuals only. ICS are often constructed of devices that either do not have or cannot use comprehensive access control capabilities due to time-restrictive safety constraints. Physical access controls and defense-in-depth measures are used by the organization when necessary and possible to supplement ICS security when electronic mechanisms are unable to fulfill the security requirements of the organization's security plan.

References: NIST Special Publication 800-82.

PLANNING

PL-2   SYSTEM SECURITY PLAN

References: NIST Special Publication 800-82.

RISK ASSESSMENT

RA-2   SECURITY CATEGORIZATION

References: NIST Special Publication 800-82.

RA-3   RISK ASSESSMENT

References: NIST Special Publication 800-82.

RA-5   VULNERABILITY SCANNING

ICS Supplemental Guidance: Vulnerability scanning and penetration testing are used with care on ICS networks to ensure that ICS functions are not adversely impacted by the scanning process. Production ICS may need to be taken off-line, or replicated to the extent feasible, before scanning can be conducted. If ICS are taken off-line for scanning, scans are scheduled to occur during planned ICS outages whenever possible. If vulnerability scanning tools are used on non-ICS networks, extra care is taken to ensure that they do not scan the ICS network. In situations where the organization cannot, for operational reasons, conduct vulnerability scanning on a production ICS, the organization employs compensating controls (e.g., providing a replicated system to conduct scanning) in accordance with the general tailoring guidance.

References: NIST Special Publication 800-82.

SYSTEM AND SERVICES ACQUISITION

SA-4   ACQUISITIONS

ICS Supplemental Guidance: The SCADA/Control Systems Procurement Project provides example cyber security procurement language for ICS.

References: Web: WWW.MSISAC.ORG/SCADA.

SA-8   SECURITY ENGINEERING PRINCIPLES

References: NIST Special Publication 800-82.

SYSTEM AND COMMUNICATIONS PROTECTION

SC-2   APPLICATION PARTITIONING

ICS Supplemental Guidance: In situations where the ICS cannot separate user functionality from information system management functionality, the organization employs compensating controls (e.g., providing increased auditing measures) in accordance with the general tailoring guidance.

SC-3   SECURITY FUNCTION ISOLATION

ICS Supplemental Guidance: In situations where the ICS cannot support security function isolation, the organization employs compensating controls (e.g., providing increased auditing measures, limiting network connectivity) in accordance with the general tailoring guidance.

SC-7   BOUNDARY PROTECTION

Control Enhancements: (1) (2)

ICS Enhancement Supplemental Guidance: Generally, public access to ICS information is not permitted.

Control Enhancement: (6)

ICS Enhancement Supplemental Guidance: The organization selects an appropriate failure mode (e.g., fail closed, fail open).

SC-8   TRANSMISSION INTEGRITY

Control Enhancement: (1)

ICS Enhancement Supplemental Guidance: The use of cryptography is determined after careful consideration of the security needs and the potential ramifications on system performance. For example, the organization considers whether latency induced from the use of cryptography would adversely impact the operational performance of the ICS. The organization explores all possible cryptographic integrity mechanisms (e.g., digital signature, hash function). Each mechanism has a different delay impact.

SC-9   TRANSMISSION CONFIDENTIALITY

Control Enhancement: (1)

ICS Enhancement Supplemental Guidance: ICS security objectives typically follow the priority of availability, integrity and confidentiality, in that order. The use of cryptography is determined after careful consideration of the security needs and the potential ramifications on system performance. For example, the organization considers whether latency induced from the use of cryptography would adversely impact the operational performance of the ICS.

SC-10   NETWORK DISCONNECT

ICS Supplemental Guidance: In situations where the ICS cannot terminate a network connection at the end of a session or after an organization-defined time period of inactivity, or the ICS cannot terminate a network connection due to significant adverse impact on performance, safety, or reliability, the organization employs appropriate compensating controls (e.g., providing increased auditing measures or limiting remote access privileges to key personnel) in accordance with the general tailoring guidance.

SC-12   CRYPTOGRAPHIC KEY ESTABLISHMENT AND MANAGEMENT

ICS Supplemental Guidance: The use of cryptography, including key management, is determined after careful consideration of the security needs and the potential ramifications on system performance. For example, the organization considers whether latency induced from the use of cryptography would adversely impact the operational performance of the ICS. The use of cryptographic key management in ICS is intended to support internal nonpublic use.

SC-13   USE OF CRYPTOGRAPHY

ICS Supplemental Guidance: The use of cryptography is determined after careful consideration of the security needs and the potential ramifications on system performance. For example, the organization considers whether latency induced from the use of cryptography would adversely impact the operational performance of the ICS.

SC-14   PUBLIC ACCESS PROTECTIONS

ICS Supplemental Guidance: Generally, public access to ICS is not permitted.

SC-15   COLLABORATIVE COMPUTING DEVICES

ICS Supplemental Guidance: Generally, collaborative computing mechanisms are not permitted on ICS.

SC-19   VOICE OVER INTERNET PROTOCOL

ICS Supplemental Guidance: The use of VoIP technologies is determined after careful consideration and after verification that it does not adversely impact the operational performance of the ICS.

SC-20   SECURE NAME / ADDRESS RESOLUTION SERVICE (AUTHORITATIVE SOURCE)

ICS Supplemental Guidance: The use of secure name/address resolution services is determined after careful consideration and after verification that it does not adversely impact the operational performance of the ICS.

SC-21   SECURE NAME / ADDRESS RESOLUTION SERVICE (RECURSIVE OR CACHING RESOLVER)

ICS Supplemental Guidance: The use of secure name/address resolution services is determined after careful consideration and after verification that it does not adversely impact the operational performance of the ICS.

SC-22   ARCHITECTURE AND PROVISIONING FOR NAME / ADDRESS RESOLUTION SERVICE

ICS Supplemental Guidance: The use of secure name/address resolution services is determined after careful consideration and after verification that it does not adversely impact the operational performance of the ICS.

SC-23   SESSION AUTHENTICITY

ICS Supplemental Guidance: In situations where the ICS cannot protect the authenticity of communications sessions, the organization employs compensating controls (e.g., auditing measures) in accordance with the general tailoring guidance.

SYSTEM AND INFORMATION INTEGRITY

SI-2   FLAW REMEDIATION

Control Enhancement: (1)

ICS Enhancement Supplemental Guidance: In situations where the organization cannot centrally manage flaw remediation and automatic updates, the organization employs nonautomated mechanisms or procedures as compensating controls in accordance with the general tailoring guidance.

Control Enhancement: (2)

ICS Enhancement Supplemental Guidance: In situations where the ICS cannot support the use of automated mechanisms to conduct and report on the status of flaw remediation, the organization employs nonautomated mechanisms or procedures as compensating controls in accordance with the general tailoring guidance.

References: NIST Special Publication 800-82.

SI-3   MALICIOUS CODE PROTECTION

ICS Supplemental Guidance: The use of malicious code protection is determined after careful consideration and after verification that it does not adversely impact the operational performance of the ICS.

Control Enhancement: (1)

ICS Enhancement Supplemental Guidance: In situations where the organization cannot centrally manage malicious code protection mechanisms, the organization employs appropriate compensating controls in accordance with the general tailoring guidance.

Control Enhancement: (2)

ICS Enhancement Supplemental Guidance: In situations where the ICS cannot support the use of automated mechanisms to update malicious code protection mechanisms, the organization employs nonautomated mechanisms or procedures as compensating controls in accordance with the general tailoring guidance.

References: NIST Special Publication 800-82.

SI-4   INFORMATION SYSTEM MONITORING

ICS Supplemental Guidance: The organization ensures that the use of monitoring tools and techniques does not adversely impact the operational performance of the ICS.

Control Enhancement: (2)

ICS Enhancement Supplemental Guidance: In situations where the ICS cannot support the use of automated tools to support near-real-time analysis of events, the organization employs nonautomated mechanisms or procedures as compensating controls in accordance with the general tailoring guidance.

Control Enhancement: (6)

ICS Enhancement Supplemental Guidance: In situations where the ICS cannot prevent non-privileged users from circumventing intrusion detection and prevention capabilities, the organization employs appropriate compensating controls (e.g., enhanced auditing) in accordance with the general tailoring guidance.

SI-6   SECURITY FUNCTIONALITY VERIFICATION

ICS Supplemental Guidance: Generally, it is not recommended to shut down and restart the ICS upon the identification of an anomaly.

SI-7   SOFTWARE AND INFORMATION INTEGRITY

ICS Supplemental Guidance: The organization ensures that the use of integrity verification applications does not adversely impact the operational performance of the ICS.

Control Enhancements: (1)

ICS Enhancement Supplemental Guidance: The organization ensures that the use of integrity verification applications does not adversely impact the operational performance of the ICS.

Control Enhancement: (2)

ICS Enhancement Supplemental Guidance: In situations where the organization cannot employ automated tools that provide notification of integrity discrepancies, the organization employs nonautomated mechanisms or procedures as compensating controls in accordance with the general tailoring guidance.

SI-8   SPAM PROTECTION

ICS Supplemental Guidance: The organization removes unused and unnecessary functions and services (e.g., electronic mail, Internet access). Due to differing operational characteristics between ICS and general purpose information systems, ICS do not generally employ spam protection mechanisms. Unusual traffic flow (e.g., during crisis situations), may be misinterpreted and detected as spam, which can cause issues with the ICS and possible system failure.

Control Enhancement: (1)

ICS Enhancement Supplemental Guidance: In situations where the organization cannot centrally manage spam protection mechanisms, the organization employs local mechanisms or procedures as compensating controls in accordance with the general tailoring guidance.

www.ingramcontent.com/pod-product-compliance
Lightning Source LLC
Chambersburg PA
CBHW080403060326

40689CB00019B/4121